S0-AWI-405

Parallel Flights:

A Father-Daughter Memoir

by

Marilyn McCord

For Dorothy, my singing buddy love — Marilyn

© 2002 by Marilyn McCord. All rights reserved.

No part of this book may be reproduced, stored in a retrieval system, or transmitted by any means, electronic, mechanical, photocopying, recording, or otherwise, without written permission from the author.

ISBN: 1-4033-7595-X (e-book)
ISBN: 1-4033-7596-8 (Paperback)
ISBN: 1-4033-7597-6 (Dust Jacket)

Library of Congress Control Number: 2002094583

This book is printed on acid free paper.

Printed in the United States of America
Bloomington, IN

1stBooks – rev. 01/07/03

For reprints, permissions, photos or other information, please contact the author:

Marilyn McCord
1625 County Road 500
Bayfield, CO 81122
970.884.2220
mccord@gobrainstorm.net

Acknowledgments

The most significant person enabling these stories was of course and without a doubt my father, Hal H. McCord. The pack rat who saved stuff such as old photos, letters, clippings, a stray B-25, and his military 201 file also saved memories and details. I'm grateful to have had all of the above as resources. (Except he didn't get to keep the B-25.) Hal's late third wife, Noni, prompted him for stories and details during the time we were recording the war stories in 1996, obviously enjoying every word and eager to see the project come to fruition. She only lived to see early drafts of the individual WWII stories. Dad was so good to let me exhaust him with questions and requests for more details. Even details which were painful to remember.

Mollie Roberts, now living in Alaska, was one of two women comprising Secretaries-at-Law in Durango, Colorado. She did the transcription of the tapes in early 1997 when I finally gave up on doing it myself. She put everything into a text document for me. From that, I broke the transcript into the individual stories and worked with them one by one. I remember sitting with Dad in St. John's Hospital in Springfield, Missouri, while his beloved Noni was undergoing back surgery. I tried to distract him from worry and at the same time correct my early drafts, especially for names and places in the transcript.

Linda Glasgow and Cheryl Collins at the Riley County Historical Society provided data on my family and early Manhattan, Kansas, events, newspaper articles and yearbooks from their archives. Kyle Dillinger, my son, located and tramped around the Pleasant Valley Cemetery at Zeandale and helped uncover Worrel family information.

Much of the McCord family history information comes from the hard work of Eleanor McCord Whitney, who lived in Manhattan until her death in 1996. Her research—a loving gift to her cousins—provided enough stories and details to convince me to add a family history section.

The McCord Clan, a family association of those interested in McCord family research and genealogy, has been gathering the work of many researchers. Sources for the Manhattan McCords include the Henry J. McCord family bible, census records, Pioneers of the Bluestem Prairie,[1] local newspapers, and information from various family members, especially Eleanor Whitney and Richard Gan "Dick" Young. James McCord is currently the Clan president/chief, Howard McCord the convener and secretary, and my brother Donald H. McCord the chaplain. Members are loosely tied together via e-mail. For more information see the McCord Clan website at http://mccord.home.mindspring.com.

Family members came through with significant help. Cousins Phyllis Irwin and Dick Young, and my sister Janice McCord Winchell all contributed wonderful photos in addition to those in my father's albums. All four of my siblings contributed family memories as did some of the extended family—Pat Towner in addition to Phyllis and

---

[1] Compiled and published by the Riley County (Kansas) Genealogical Society in 1976.

Dick. Marcia McCord sent me a copy of the "Henry Jackson McCord 1864 Civil War Diary" and provided some background on ancestors and family history. Dick Young added favorite entries from the additional diary years in his possession.[2] Marc McCord expanded on details of guns that Dad used to have in his collection. Orlando-days family friend Phil Steinmetz added remembrances of hunting and fishing with Hal.

Don Anderson, my friend and companion, gave support both emotional and practical—looking up and discussing aircraft details, reading every page to find typos, identifying confusions, driving to Kansas and Missouri, cooking meals, caring for the house and Nelson Nelson, our Labrador—while I worked on the manuscript. My brother-in-law Bill Winchell and my son Eric Dillinger both provided additional research on aircraft and located various Internet sites.

Two dear friends were particularly influential. Charlotte Roe, who is an artist, poet, and musician, encouraged my putting more heart into the writing. I used to think paintings came from some sort of photographic image in your mind that you simply recorded on canvas. I now understand what she means when she says "Won't it be interesting to see what the hands come up with!" Details emerge as surprises; some you like and others you paint over.

Ruth Loyd, a dear friend from my days at Texas Instruments and now my quilting buddy, read the war years stories, made notes, and kept asking, "But what was going on with the rest of the family?" As

---

[2] Dick Young published the Civil War Diaries in 2002 under the title Glory! Glory! Glory!.

in quilting, the secret to beauty in the piecing is contrast. She was interested in the effects of war on the wives and families left behind. When I decided to include that aspect, Agnes Chartier, a friend of my mother's for 70 years, helped provide some of Mother's perspective beyond things my siblings and I remembered from childhood.

Without Robin Higham and Angela Dawdy at Sunflower University Press in Manhattan this project would likely not have ever really come together. They provided the broad patterns. I needed their suggestions for overall form as the coordinating impetus for the bits and pieces of stories that I had. Robin and Angela also identified additional resources and supplied much needed encouragement.

Ruth Cross, Durango, Colorado, became my superb in-house editor when she and her husband Bart graciously took us into their home during our 18-day evacuation as wildfire threatened our home and community. Bart also arranged for necessary computer equipment so that I could continue working on this book. I left home with only my CPU. My heartfelt thanks go to both of them.

This book is a story, not a data repository. I am responsible for any errors, which are certainly inadvertent. With so many names, places, dates, etc., it was impossible to research everything and still get this book to the publisher in a timely fashion.

* * * * *

Notes for reading: "I" refers to many different people and may present some confusion. Is the "I" referring to me, my father or someone else? When my father is narrating the story, his quotes are shown in *italics*. I have tried to identify all storytellers specifically who are neither my father nor I. An unidentified, unitalicized "I" refers to me as the narrator. The World War II context information in Part Five is not in first person, and will, I think, be obvious.

There are three appendices that condense additional information:

Appendix 1 is a **Chronology** of my father's life;

Appendix 2 is a **Partial Descendancy Chart** for the McCord family from Henry Jackson McCord;

Appendix 3 contains my **Notes on Aircraft** mentioned in the memoir.

Introduction

Hal McCord, in the middle of Deep Creek near Manhattan, Kansas, circa 1914.

This is the story of my father, Hal H. McCord.[3] It is also my story and the story of my family. Six generations of our family have lived in the Manhattan, Kansas, area and have been shaped by Midwest landscapes and sunsets, Midwest values and events, Midwest people and pioneer history. Some people think of Kansas and picture tornadoes with Dorothy and Toto from the Wizard of Oz; Kansas

---

[3] The middle "H." is not an abbreviation; it represents his father's three names, all of which began with the letter H.

capitalizes on those images and advertises itself as "The Land of Ahs…"

Writing Dad's biography in parallel with my own partial autobiography has occasioned both "ahs" and awe. I have had to take several steps backward to view the similarities in our journeys from various perspectives. We have, in many ways, experienced parallel flights, wingtip to wingtip, but a generation apart.

Dad's life could also be told in rivers. From rural Riley County's Wildcat Creek and Deep Creek to the Big Blue near Manhattan, the Kaw (or Kansas River), the San Antonio River in the city of the same name, the Potomac in our nation's capital, the mouth of the Amazon in Brazil, the Ganges in India, the Yangtze in China, the Nile in Africa, the Seine in France and finally to the Pomme de Terre in the Ozarks of Missouri …

Two themes have played constant tag in the corners of my consciousness during this writing: flying and quilting. They will forever be interrelated to me. The bird's eye view lets you see the big picture, the mosaic. The mistakes just sort of fuzz out. Otherwise, you can get lost in the individual features of a landscape or in the imperfect joins and irregularities of a quilt. Only the aerial view reveals the overall patterns in either activity, with the whole spread out below you.

In seeking to re-create the story of my father's life, I discovered my own life history has shifted. How I know myself takes yet another tumble in my personal kaleidoscope and my life becomes a richer, still more brilliant design. From this perspective of age and experience, the individual valleys and peaks of my life's landscape lose much of their impressiveness. The broad patterns emerging from my six decades come to have a bit more sense to them.

This is an Air Transport Command (ATC) photo taken 12 April 1944 in Yunnan Province, China, along the Yangtze River, Western Loop, just above the big bend. Note agriculture along banks. Altitude 15,000 feet. This was among several such photos in my father's files.

"The aerial view … strips the facades from our constructions, and by raising us above the constraints of the treeline and the highway it imposes a brutal honesty on our perceptions. It lets us see ourselves in context, as creatures struggling through life on the face of a planet, not separate from nature, but its most expressive agents. It lets us see that our struggles form patterns on the land, that these patterns repeat to an extent which before we had not known, and that there is a sense to them."[4]

Examining My Stash

Recently I decided to become a quilter. The fabrics, colors, geometry, textures and patterns fascinate me. Quilters, I have learned, collect fabric the same way anyone else collects anything. You don't have to ever use the fabrics actually—it is perfectly acceptable to just collect them if that is your pleasure. This collection is called your stash. It is not unlike the pilot's ground school of bits and pieces of information regarded as essential for learning to fly. You can collect the trivia of flying without ever actually flying.

Writing this book occasioned the examination of my stash of experiences with my father. The notes are there, penciled in the back inside covers of a book I completed during an airline trip to Atlanta,

[4] William Langewiesche, "Inside the Sky," page 4. Published by Random House, ISBN 0-679-42983-2, ©1998. Langewiesche is a pilot, the son of a pilot, and writes for the Atlantic Monthly.

<u>Flight of Passage</u>, by Rinker Buck,[5] a touching memoir of two teenage brothers flying a Piper Cub coast to coast in 1966. I studied my own scribblings in some amazement. Both the size of the stash and the number of pieces of Dad's life replayed in my own life astonished me.

I could not have predicted as a child the influence my father would have on me. After all, from ages 11 to 19 I never saw him. Not even once. My brother has sometimes remarked about all the football and basketball games, plays, concerts, performances, tennis matches—all the times when Dad wasn't there. Even in the years before that period, Dad's presence had been minimal.

My father was ordered to active duty in Omaha only three weeks before my birth in 1940. He was busy with military wartime responsibilities in Texas when I was a toddler. He spent 20 months, a significant part of my most formative years, overseas. Even after he returned to the States, his jobs often kept him away from home. It would have been easy to assume he didn't care. Easy, but wrong.

My notes gave me pause.

Why is it I have had a life-long love affair with flying? Someone recently asked me, "Do you <u>like</u> to fly?" "I love flying," I answered, "it's <u>airports</u> I don't like." When I went to the Smithsonian in 1990, the place I most wanted to see was the Air and Space Museum, especially the astronaut exhibits. At the age of 55 I finally earned my

---

[5] Published by Hyperion, paperback ISBN 0-7868-8315-4, ©1997.

private pilot's license, scoring 100 percent on the written exam and doing a passable job on the check-ride. It was a goal I had longed for forever, it seems, and one I had previously written off as just not plausible in this lifetime.

From ninth grade on, it was clear that I would major in mathematics. Why? Mother wanted me to take Home Economics, something "useful." Although I now try to avoid competitive situations, then it meant little to me to compete and win in a woman's world. What society valued—and paid for—was those who found their way to the top in traditionally male pursuits. How did I come to dismiss my mother's gentle persuasiveness on behalf of traditionally nurturing, feminine vocations? I would play wife and mother roles anyway, I reasoned, and so I set my sights on a career in math.

Yet my aspirations still were limited. "Women could be teachers, nurses or secretaries" was the landscape of tradition. What about women pilots, astronauts, engineers and physicians? I say that now. Then, I became a teacher. What if I had had my father around during my growing-up years? Might I have had the mentoring to encourage me into engineering? Even trying for the astronaut program? I would have signed up in a heartbeat. Would my father's varied experiences have expanded my images of what was possible? Would he have enabled me to see an aerial view of life? I believe my father's love of flying would have been an even more intense influence had I grown up with him present.

How is it I have such a deep love and appreciation for the land, for its beauty, for birds and animals, for wilderness? Visual scenes of childhood picnics are among my most treasured early remembrances of my father. I now live, by definite choice, at the edge of the largest wilderness area in Colorado—the Weminuche Wilderness—at an elevation of 8000 feet.

I can walk into the forest at will, generally needing to snowshoe in the winter. It is beautiful. Shy red columbine shelter under the white furs; delicate fuchsia-and-yellow lady slipper orchids creep out in season. Chanterelle mushrooms pop up when there has been enough rain.

Magnificent bald eagles sometimes circle overhead. A medium-sized cinnamon-colored black bear has ambled up my driveway. I once came suddenly upon a fawn in the spots, hidden beneath a fallen log and told to stay put by mama. Wild turkeys scrounged my yard the past couple of winters for seeds dropped by greedy nuthatches at our feeder. Eager hummingbirds drink from the feeder still swaying in my hand before I can finish hanging it.

Within 30 minutes I can hike to a rock outcropping with a fantastic view that overlooks the entire Vallecito Valley. Not only that, but our home is directly under the United Express air route between Durango and Denver. Though I don't set my watch by their less than regular schedule, I do take note of their patterns and often have the pleasure of flying directly over my own home and the majestic San Juan Mountains which surround it.

How is it that swimming and diving were the only sports at which I once excelled? That's easier to answer. I grew up a block from the city pool in Manhattan and somehow my mother always managed season pool passes for the three of us children every summer. I showed a definite lack of athletic ability except for swimming; I could pass all of the requirements for senior lifesaving before I was 12 and old enough to receive the junior lifesaving certificate. Two semesters of physical education were required when I attended K-State, and thankfully those courses were not a part of my GPA. The tennis balls always went right through the holes in <u>my</u> racquet.

Curiously, I ended up playing my father's oboe. My older brother, Don, played clarinet before me and stayed with it. I, on the other hand, got a late start on an instrument and after my first year feared I was not going to be good enough on clarinet to pass auditions for the combined eighth and ninth grade orchestra at Manhattan Junior High School.

"What if I switched to oboe?" I suggested to our conductor. "Fine, but where would you get an oboe?" "Oh, I have one at home…" Boy was he excited, and he set me up right away to take lessons from Clyde Jussila, who played viola with the K-State string quartet, and also played oboe and bassoon among other instruments.

I continued with the oboe through college at Kansas State and played in the orchestra under Luther Leavengood. I did not know at the time that Dr. Leavengood had sent music to my dad in Casablanca during the war. Dad and I enjoy much of the same music; we both are particularly fond of waltzes and what we call "gypsy" music—compositions such as the Hungarian Rhapsody and the Slavic Dances. Oboe music.

Why did I end up with Dad's old slide rule? A slide rule was an essential for the engineering physics course undergraduates took in those years, and it pleased me greatly that Mother had never disposed of the fine old slide rule with Dad's name hand-lettered distinctively on it. Somehow it gave me a sense of rootedness in my mathematical pursuits, an assurance that I was indeed in the right place. Continuity. I was not just out there in mathematical space alone—there was some family history supporting my decision.

How is it I love to travel? To see new and exotic places? My brother and my sister have both lived in Europe and speak excellent German. Why did I end up in Taipei, Taiwan for three years and in rural India for nearly another year? Why those countries?[6]

The quilt pieced together from my own years and the quilt of my father's years have so many parallels in their patterns. They both contain numerous pieces of the same sizes, shapes and colors. How rich a stash it is.

Piecing the Blocks

Yet, I know that I am primarily a product of my mother and her convictions on raising children. She had many opinions on that

---

[6] I spent six years, 1972-78, as full-time staff of the Ecumenical Institute and its sister organization, the Institute of Cultural Affairs. Both were nonprofits, and my husband and I did community development and demonstration village work, teaching three years at the American School in Taipei to bring in money for staff self-support. All three of our children were with us in Taipei; our daughter attended fourth grade in India. Because there was no appropriate school situation for our seventh and eighth grade sons, they participated in a Student House for staff children in Chicago that year.

subject that was her life's work both personally and professionally. Parenting, when done well, is absolutely the toughest job I know of. Mother did it well, often sacrificing her own desires to be attentive to her children because caring for them <u>was</u> her highest desire. It was she who was always there when I was a child. It was Mother who encouraged, who listened, who made suggestions. It was her humor that brought us laughter. It was Mother who instilled basic values and a strong sense of responsibility. In 1980, she was the Volunteer of the Year for Manhattan Hospice, and her work with that organization was one of her great joys and many credits.

My political views mirror my mother much more than they resonate with my father's views. I am, in many ways, fairly liberal and social-action oriented. Basically a pacifist. A registered Democrat though not ever a straight-party woman. Dad, on the other hand, is what I would call a conservative Republican and totally supportive of the military. We often simply agree to disagree when it comes to politics. Once, exasperated with my positions but clear they were strongly held and I was entitled to them, he good-naturedly yet resignedly said, *I'd sooner try to change the stripes on a tiger.* We are both staunch environmentalists.

In no way would I want to minimize my mother's task nor the excellence with which she performed it unfailingly. Nevertheless, this project has been an adventure of its own in getting to know, as an adult, this father who life and conditions beyond my control denied me the pleasure of knowing when I was a child. I am most grateful for <u>both</u> my mother and my father.

Adding Contrast, Then Putting the Layers Together

Nothing is ever all black or all white; life is varying shades of gray. Always. With many layers. My father was, and is, very human. Not larger than life. A man who made the best he could out of the circumstances life dealt him. A man who gave himself passionately to his task within those circumstances. A people person. Understanding the worth of ordinary people, paying attention to people. A penchant for details from his engineering training and love of mathematics, he remembers names, details about people, about places. Even at age 90 only a little of that memory has faded. Given the diversity of our politics, I have been impressed with how in tune our overall objectives often are; we just may see quite different paths for achieving them.

Dad lived in remarkable times. He shouldered huge responsibilities for his relatively young age—so did a lot of young men then—and without complaint or apology. No ifs or buts. Duty. He took often-dire surroundings and provided light and laughter for those around him. I have seen him crack up with laughter to the point his eyes would tear up and he could hardly continue speaking.

Likewise, I have seen his eyes bleary with sorrow, his voice so choked with emotion that he could not voice the waiting words. My father is a very emotional man. He is also a consummate worrier about those he loves. Even in my 60s, I will always be his *little girl*. And he is generous. Not afraid to risk. These qualities provide an endearing vulnerability.

The military brought out some of the best of this man and he in turn brought out the best in many who served under him. Honor, accountability, caring. Humble pride in accomplishment. Acknowledging losses, focusing on gains. Virtues my mother taught me, ones I tried to instill in my own children. And now, they in their children.

It is a tragedy that I did not know my father sooner. War has many casualties beyond the count of the dead and wounded, and wounds take on many different disguises. What a joy to listen now to the childhood stories I missed. It's never too late; even after the death of a parent it is possible to recover something of your heritage and come to know your ancestors. In so doing, you come to better know yourself. My grandfather, who died before I was born, was always an unknown quantity to me. It seemed there was an unwritten rule not to ask questions about him. A suicide has many different sufferings surrounding it, and my perceived unacceptability of asking questions was just one facet. It has been a delight to read and hear about him, how universally well liked he seemed to be and how genuine and caring a man all the stories about him depict.

Dancing with the Skeletons

Contrast is what gives a quilt life and vibrancy. As in life, the black spaces provide appreciation for the colors. The deeper sorrow carves out your cup, the more joy it can hold. This is my life-long paraphrase of a passage from <u>The Prophet</u>, by Kahlil Gibran.[7] One aspect of writing this biography has been a decision to acknowledge all the varying family relationships.

Perfect families don't exist; every family has skeletons in their closets. To ignore them or pretend they don't exist seems dishonest, to flaunt them unnecessarily smacks of sensationalism. D. H. Lawrence ends his poem *Elemental* with the lines "I am sick of lovable people, somehow they are a lie." This is the only family I have, and I love every person in it.

To embrace the skeletons means to bring them out of the closet and dance with them. Love them as they are, with their failings and imperfections. My intent is to honor each individual for his or her unique gifts to the larger family and to tell the stories as truthfully as possible, yet in a way that no one feels any new or added pain above the old pains inherent in the humbling knowledge of our family as being incredibly human. "To err is human, to forgive divine." We erred. Where we forgave, the healing was evident. And divinely unifying. Forgiving <u>ourselves</u> is always the hardest step and the only possible starting point.

A few years ago, I attended a Halloween costume party as a witch. For the most part no one knew who I was. There's a wonderfully freeing aspect in that, and I did things I might not otherwise have done. I decided to be a witch with an attitude—an assertive witch. One group of partygoers had, at one end of their table, a dummy, their

---

[7] ©1923 by Kahlil Gibran, published by Alfred A. Knopf, New York.

xxiii

designated driver. I asked the dummy to dance. He had a foot-long 2-by-4 for his hips and I could hold him up by that board, place one of his hands on my shoulder and hold his other hand. I reported back to his colleagues, "He follows like a dream but I wish he were a bit lighter on his feet."

My image of dancing with the family skeletons is that it would be like dancing with that dummy; a bit heavy yet freeing. When you take the skeletons out of the closet, they lose their power. They no longer own you but become a pawn to your lead. Life is not dictated by events but by what you do with those events.

What transpired, or didn't transpire, between my parents was painful for both of them. For us, their children. For both grandmothers. For others. Friends don't know how to divide their loyalties. They ache on your behalf.

War does things to people. After spending months in stressful and demanding situations, the return to ordinary life must seem a bit trivial by comparison. My father received—and deserved—high praise for the job he did during those war years. This appeared to be the opposite of what he experienced when he returned home. In particular, he could never seem to measure up in his mother-in-law's eyes.

Parents want the best for their children, which is good, but the juxtaposition of evaluations must have been devastating. Attention to the family suffered; attention to work suffered. In Dad's own words, *I don't know what happened... I don't know how it happened... I don't know how I let it happen. The war cost me this family...*

There were only two things I think my mother never was fully able to forgive. One was my father's abandonment of her and their children. Initially, that was the farthest thing from my father's mind. Later, it must have become for him, in his eyes, a matter of survival.

The second unforgivable act was the usurping of her home church in Norton, Kansas, by the fundamentalist element of her church. Instead of dancing with those realities, she became brittle and harsh in all references to them. Otherwise, she approached sainthood.

Families are fragile. Families are sometimes stubborn and hardheaded. But there is also a great power simply in being family. I have been amazed at the strength and beauty I have found. I have uncovered truths about my own family I never knew, found photos I didn't know existed, and discovered wonderful distant cousins I had never before met.

The Quilting

Quilting is the stitching you add when the piecing is complete; it holds the layers together. It is what makes a quilt beautiful, especially in an otherwise plain quilt. The embellishments on top of everything else. Generally the more quilting you do, the more attractive the quilt becomes. There are many decisions to make: hand or machine quilting? What overall finished look do you want? Which design choices will enhance the beauty of the pieces?

It is the same with writing the pieces of a life. You create the patterns, revealing the beauty, the love, the contrasts. You decide how to weave them together and what meaning you assign to various events. You are the creator of the finished product. This is also true with your own life. History is a repetition of pieces and patterns. History is there to recreate in the adornments, the new stories you tell of the meaning of those given events.

Why should anyone else care about this man, these stories, this quilt-narrative?

I enjoyed hearing my father's war stories so much that I recorded them in 1996. Initially, that was all I planned to do. That would have been like creating some key pieces—the showpieces for the quilt—but never assembling them into a whole. A more comprehensive biography has grown from those recordings.

Similar treatment should be accorded my mother's life experiences. She was less controversial and just as rich in spinning a story with both insight and humor. Yet, it is this story that is mine to tell. For all of the reasons listed earlier and just because. There is no way to tell it without including some of my mother's story, some of mine, some of my siblings'. My father's life affected us all. This work is a legacy to my family. And, I hope, an inspiration for all families. Sinners all, we can bridge our separations. Divisions dissolve when we can accept reunion with ourselves, with others and with the very foundations of life. And all we have to do, all we can do, is simply accept the acceptance that life itself extends to us. These thoughts from a sermon by Paul Tillich, "You Are Accepted,"[8] have been an important part of my own life's journey.

Appreciating the Patterns

This photo is another ATC agricultural detail taken 17 April 1944, in Yunnan Province, eight miles north of Kunming, China, from an altitude of 9000 feet.

Again, it's like being up in a small plane. High enough to get beyond individual features of the landscape below yet not so high you miss the broad designs revealed. The harmonious and intricate weaving of the events of my life emerging below. A somewhat crazy patchwork quilt, glittering in the sunset of my middle age. I experience a certain pity for those airline passengers who insist on

---

[8] A chapter from The Shaking of the Foundations, by Paul Tillich, © 1955, published by Charles Scribner's Sons, New York. Now out of print.

pulling down the cabin shades to be distracted by some movie. You draw nothing from the aerial view unless you embrace it.

I am a believer in the value of patterns. Mathematics, after all, is nothing but patterns. The ratio of the distance around a circle to the distance across the middle is constant. For <u>every</u> circle. We call that ratio pi; $c = \Pi d$. Mathematics only formalizes those constant patterns. Stability in the midst of seeming chaos. And even chaos theory has its patterns.

I am tearing down the protective façades I constructed over my childhood, over my own many and painful mistakes. I looked deeply at the treasures revealed in the midst of the lifetime of accumulation, took those pieces and began constructing. I had no idea what the finished product would look like, only that a lot of love would be stitched in. The broad patterns emerged, and I like them very much. There should be a signature block in one corner for each family member to add his or her signature.

A decade ago, my daughter Lara Dillinger toured Kansas as the youngest of seven women in a production of the play "Quilters." As various quilts were removed from a trunk, each was symbolic. Each told a story of pioneer life. Some stories were joyous, others heart-rending. They represented the pieces of the lives of those women who lived in homesteads on the American prairies and frontiers. Lives of loneliness, starvation, despair, achievement, celebration.

The quilt pieced from my father's life is sometimes familiar, yet it is uniquely his. The patterns relate his rich experiences, tell his story. I know just by looking at it that I am my father's daughter. I am proud to place this quilt, this story, into our family's trunk of collected mementos.

Part 1: McCord Family History

Henry Jackson McCord

This version of the McCord family history beginning in 1827 opens with Henry Jackson McCord. Henry's Civil War service and fantastic diary account[9] of those war years solidify a family interest in the military.

Additionally, Henry's move to Riley County and the Manhattan area grounds this branch of the family in what is to become the hometown for many of his descendants, including me. Henry, at least second generation American born, is from the branch of the family known as the "R" McCords, for Robert, the cabinetmaker.

The McCord family ancestors before Henry came to the United States from the west coast of Scotland via Ireland. Henry's grandfather Robert had 17 children by two wives. William and Barbara (Jackson) McCord were Henry's parents. Henry was the fifth of 12 children: four girls, then four boys, three more girls and the last, another boy. My father said he understood that the family then *adopted two more to fill the table.*

Henry Jackson McCord, Hal's grandfather, was a man of conviction, a man of adventure, a man of passion—quite a remarkable fellow. Born in Sandusky County, Ohio, on January 12, 1827, he

---

[9] Phyllis Ann Irwin, a great-granddaughter, transcribed the original diary in 1983. My younger sister, Marcia McCord, another great-granddaughter, transcribed from Phyllis' copy in February 1997 and put it into electronic form. Dick Young, a great-grandson of Henry, has the original diary and recently published it.

grew up on his parents' farm. He had plenty of experience in the usual farm chores—seeding, harvesting and haying. After completing his schooling, he tested out several occupations. First, he taught school for three months but didn't like it. He made cider, contracting for two months, then spending the winter "recuperating." He chopped wood and worked on the railroad and went on a peddling excursion. He worked some at home and hunted. Nothing seemed to suit him.

He was living at home helping his father when he decided to try his luck in the newly opened California gold fields. But there was a hitch. He didn't have the $200 needed for passage so he continued working through the spring, summer and fall. Finally, on November 12, 1849, he was ready to begin his big adventure.

From Sandusky he took the Queen City boat to Buffalo; Bennet's Temperance House provided him lodging there. Next he took the railroad to Albany, stopping at the Phoenix Hotel. Then he took passage to New York and stayed at the Planters Hotel for a week while he made arrangements for the ocean voyage around Cape Horn. Finally, sailing from NY harbor on the brig Orleans in December of 1849, he arrived in San Francisco nine months later, September 1850. His daily journal of the voyage in the sailing ship was another priceless heritage left to his descendants.

The gold fields proved to be more lucrative for merchants than for most of the miners. My great-grandfather, who arrived in California late for the rush, was unsuccessful in realizing any financial gains from this adventure. So, in 1853, Henry returned to Ohio, bought a team of horses and resumed farming with one of his brothers, John D.

McCord. In August, 1855, Henry and John bought a 116-acre tract and a 58-acre tract from their father for $6,000. Henry once said that his father always took a jug of whiskey to the field. "When the time came that all his sons turned it down, there would be no more whiskey!"

The Civil War Years

In 1862, Henry enrolled as a captain in the 111th Ohio Volunteer Infantry at Sandusky. He kept a daily journal of his four years in the Civil War. Marcia McCord says her favorite passages from that diary are "those describing the soldiers playing baseball while waiting for their assignment, Henry's discussions of qualities of leadership, and his descriptions of the merits of the local young ladies during his travels through our country."

Though a bullet destroyed the journal pages from 1862 and '63 journals, what remains from 1864 and '65 is a remarkable record. Henry wrote that the bullet that hit the 1862 diary "made a mouse's nest of my memorasilliness book."[10] His service to the end of the war is also well documented both by the Soldiers and Sailors Benevolent Society and G. S. A. military records. "He bore a gallant part in the engagements of his regiment," was promoted to major, and was mustered out in 1865 at Cleveland, Ohio.

---

[10] Eleanor Whitney's daughters were able to reconstruct parts of that 1862 diary.

Dec. 2, 1864 Civil War 111th Regiment officers—Henry Jackson McCord is seated second from right in the right-hand picture.

Here are a few excerpts from Henry Jackson McCord's Civil War diary, retaining his own unique spellings and style:

"Dec. 1, 1864: Fought and won a glorious battle [at Franklin, Tennessee] yesterday. Fought until midnight and then drew of and crossed the river—marched all night until noon today. Went into position at Nashville. Regret very much having to leave our dead and wounded in the hands of the rebels.

"Dec. 2, 1864: Officers of the 111th Regt. went to the Cambeland Gallery and had our Photographs taken in a group.

"January 29, 1865: Was ordered out after night to a posit. where 5 of the 13th Ky Guys were captured day before yesterday—got there about 11 past 10—put out sentinals—firing more or less through with night—heard one fellow cry out that he was wounded. I got a ball hole through my over coat sleeve—wish they would be a little careful—if they keep on with this foolishness they will hit me.

"May 17, 1865: After getting battery in position so as to shell their fort our forces soon drove them from their works. This should have been done in the first place, the Rebs suffered much greater loss than we did, taking the whole thing together. I never wish to witness another battle field even if it is strewn with the dead and wounded of the enemy. Johnson is making a precipitate retreat leaving his dead and wounded and every manner of thing that an army carries with it. Oh, such sights!"

HJM Marries Rachel Elizabeth Howell

When Henry returned from the Civil War, he was with his folks on their newly acquired land grant, awarded from the U.S. Government for William's part in the War of 1812. Then Henry went to Iowa, where he married Rachel Howell in 1869. Rachel was the third daughter of Stephen Howell and Mary Cox.

The History of Blackhawk Co., IA (1915) states, "It is said that Stephen Howell, of Indiana, was the first white man to settle in the (Fox) township, locating in the southeastern part. His son, James, was the first white child born in the township. ... The first breaking ... was done by Henry Gray, Stephen Howell and Peter Cox who used their three yokes of oxen to do the work. The first house was built by Stephen Howell in '49."

Moving to Riley County, Kansas

Henry and Rachel moved farther west and established a homestead and timber claim in Riley County in 1878, eight miles northwest of Manhattan, Kansas.[11] The 320 acres were in Wildcat Township, Section 28. During the first winter the young couple and their three children lived with the Hiram Kearns family, 11 people in a two-room house. The crowd must have saved on heating costs.

The house Henry and Rachel built was on top of a hill with sweeping vistas to the south and west. It was fully exposed to the potential ravages of winds and the occasional Kansas tornado spiraling in. To prevent the house from blowing away, my father relates that *Henry filled the voids between the stud framing with stones. Although a tornado did blow through south of them, sounding like a "swarm of angry bees" in my father's words, their house suffered no damage.*

I remember my father wanted to get a cutting of the white lilacs—still at the homestead just southeast of the house—to transplant to his Missouri home. He also talked of gooseberries near by and gooseberry pies baked by his mother.

---

[11] If you drive out on Marlatt Avenue in Manhattan and go west past the Top o' The World hill, the road turns to the north. The home site is on the west side of the road.

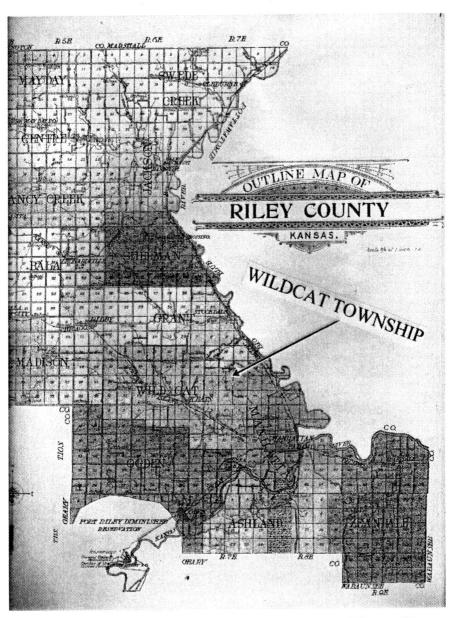

**Map of Riley County—Manhattan is 120 miles due west of Kansas City;
Wildcat Township just below and right of center, near Keats.**

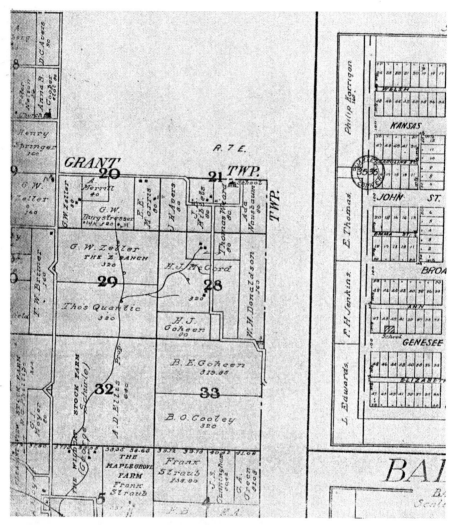

Wildcat Township detail showing H. J. McCord homestead at upper right in Section 28.

Will, Fred and Mayme

Henry and Rachel had six children. The oldest three, born in Iowa, were Will, Fred and Mayme, whose real name was Mary.

As a young man, Will, the oldest of the six children, farmed, worked on a surveying party and worked for the railroad at McCook,

Nebraska and Iola, Kansas. When war was declared with Spain in 1898, he left his railroad job in Iola and enlisted in the 20th Kansas Volunteer Infantry. He was sent to the Philippines, where many soldiers died of disease.

Will was once so near death he wrote a note asking that his affairs be settled and his family told "what has become of me." On the strength of the telegram sent to Henry and Rachel, the <u>Manhattan Nationalist</u> printed the story of his death. About a week later, the newspaper had to print a retraction. Will recovered and returned home to live almost another 50 years.

On September 21, 1901, he married Ellen Jane Haynes in Pottawatomie County, where she had been reared. They made their home in Manhattan, the corner of Third and Humboldt Streets. Will was one of the first rural mail carriers in Manhattan when Congress established the Rural Free Delivery service. He began the route on McDowell Creek and carried Route 4, now under Tuttle Creek Lake, for more than 30 years. My childhood memories include Dad's Uncle Will dying in a fire at his 600 Bluemont home in Manhattan in 1947. He suffocated when he slipped down between the bed and the wall in a vain attempt to avoid the smoke.

Fred, the second son, drowned at age 18. The <u>Manhattan Nationalist</u> of July 29, 1892, told the story:

"A SAD DROWNING. Late Tuesday evening the startling news of the drowning of Fred McCord, the sixteen-year-old son [age wrong] of Henry McCord of Sedalia, reached

9

Manhattan. It seems he had taken a team and gone to the south of Pfeil Creek in the Blue River, with companions, for a swim. Fred was not an expert swimmer, and getting some distance from shore he went beyond his depth and soon went down.

"One of his companions went immediately to his rescue and succeeded in getting him part way to the shore, but gave out. Fred said, 'I'm gone, save yourself.' Neighbors were aroused and a party formed and a search made in the river until a late hour that night, but with no success. Wednesday morning the search was renewed and about 8 o'clock the body was found about ten feet from where it was last seen. The deceased was buried Wednesday afternoon in our cemetery."

The McCords were not the only family to lose a son to the vagaries of the Big Blue River.[12]

The third child born was Dad's Aunt Mayme, grandmother of the Irwin cousins. From the <u>Manhattan Nationalist,</u> April 16, 1896:

"At noon today Miss Mamie McCord and William Irwin were united in marriage at the home of the bride's parents, near Riley. Miss McCord is one of Riley County's successful school teachers and taught the school at Highland this past

---

[12] I could go on my soapbox here. I am a firm believer that every child should be taught to swim. During the years when I lived on a farm in Northwest Kansas and my own children were young, I gathered up all the neighborhood children and took a carload in for swimming lessons in the summers. When we lived in Taipei in the middle 1970s, one of our colleagues was an elderly Chinese gentleman. Peter Hu had been a company commander in China and told of the time his company, pursued by the Japanese, came to a river. Those who could swim survived; the non-swimmers perished.

year. Mr. Irwin lives in this city and is in the employ of C. A. Haulenbeck. The wedding was a quiet one, only the immediate relatives of the contracting parties being present. Mr. and Mrs. Irwin will go to housekeeping at once in their house on the corner of Second and Pierre streets."

Another story about William Irwin appeared in the <u>Manhattan Nationalist</u> dated July 24, 1913:

"FATHER SAVES SON. When Stove Exploded William Irwin Forgot About Himself. WRAPPED LAD IN BLANKET. Irwin was severely burned about the arms and hands—tried to pour gasoline on generator.

"When William Irwin, living near the Rock Island cut, a short distance southwest of Manhattan, wrapped his 7-year-old son[13] up in a blanket early this morning to keep the lad from being burned to death, he forgot about himself and was seriously burned. The boy escaped with a few slight burns and owes his life to his father.

"The trouble came when Mr. Irwin started to light the gasoline stove. The gasoline failed to generate, so Irwin attempted to start it by the cup routine, that is, he filled a cup full of gasoline and there was an explosion the instant he

---

[13] That son was also named William. He was born in 1905, retired from the Postal Service and later became director of a boys' camp in NY.

applied the match. Burning oil was thrown all over Irwin and his son, who was standing near watching the proceedings.

"Irwin grabbed a blanket and wrapped it around the lad and the flames were quickly smothered, but while he was doing it Irwin was severely burned about the arms and hands. The physician who was called says Irwin's right and left arm were burned the most. The physician also says that the boy would have been burned to death had it not been for the prompt work on the part of the father.

"Irwin is an employee of the Correll Manufacturing Company."

McCord homestead photo, circa 1900. From left: George, Henry, Will, Rachel, Hal (on his burro) and Carrie McCord

Highland School, Riley County, Kansas, circa 1895. Back Row, Left to Right:Anna Dodge, Mame McCord (teacher), Jo Dodge, Etta Neusbaum, Carrie McCord, Jack (lop-eared burro, the McCord children's transportation for the 1 1/4 miles to school), George McCord, Harry Listuge, Will Dodge, Hal McCord, Albert Twible, Tom Dodge. Front Row: Willie Drake, Myrtle Grover, Pearl Grover, Vernon Neusbaum, Winnifred Neusbaum, Ada Dodge, Dan Dodge. "Sister Mame grasps the pointer with which she ruled the natives. The wee ring of hair on my forehead was known as a beau-catcher. CMR |Carrie McCord Roper|"

George, Carrie and Hal

The youngest three children, born in Riley County, were George, Carrie and my father's father, Hal, born August 18, 1884. The story goes that Rachel knew this would be her last child, so she heaped all the names she liked on this son, including her own maiden name. He was Henry Howell Hiram McCord, known to all as Hal.

George married Olive Mae "Ollie" Worrel in 1902. Oma Alvaretta Worrel, a first cousin of Ollie's, would later become Hal's bride. The Worrels were from Zeandale, Kansas, [14] just east of Manhattan. Again, from the Nationalist:

> "Mr. and Mrs. [George] McCord will be at home on the Vance farm about 3 miles up the Blue. These young people are well known and belong to two of the oldest and most substantial families in Riley County."

George had a pony act in vaudeville at the McCord homestead for a while but didn't want to work on the farm. He later went to work for Dan Casement as an overseer on the ranch. George had a tremendous way with animals and even trained polo ponies. I remember riding a horse at the Casement Ranch as a child but that good bottomland area has been under the waters of Tuttle Creek Reservoir since 1962.

My father remembered that George had a Mexican horse groom who helped brush and curry the horses. One time a skunk or civet cat came near. The groom said, "I smell skunk."

George said, "No, civet cat."

"No, skunk!"

"I say civet cat."

"Well, all the same smell," remarked the groom with a grin.

From the December 3, 1903, Manhattan Nationalist:

---

[14] Richard Worrel moved with his two sons, Robert and William, to the Zeandale Township after the death of his wife, Jane. The date on the original homestead papers is Dec. 6, 1870. Robert Worrel was my dad's maternal great-grandfather.

"The marriage of William B. Roper [known as simply "B"] and Miss Carrie McCord occurred Thanksgiving Day at the home of the bride's parents, Mr. and Mrs. H. J. McCord of Sedalia. The ceremony, which was performed by Rev. J. T. Copley, was witnessed by only the relatives. The bride is widely and favorably known in this vicinity. The groom, who is the son of Mr. and Mrs. Richard Roper of Keats, is a young man of excellent character. He is employed in P. C. Hostrop's barbershop. Mr. and Mrs. Roper will live at the home of A. H. McCutchan on Poyntz Ave. They have many friends who wish them an abundance of happiness."

Dad said that "B", who was from Keats, sent all the Roper kids— and there were eight of them—to college on what he made at his barbershop. By 1912 B's partner-owned barbershop ran ads in the Daily Nationalist that read:

W. B. Roper—V. P. Morris

You are "next!"

If you go to the Manhattan Barber Shop

402 Poyntz Ave.

Nice line of cigars

Razors honed

A few years later Carrie and B were featured in another newspaper story. From the August 18, 1910, Manhattan Nationalist:

"CELLAR WALL CAVED IN ON HIM. B. Roper, a barber employed at the Manhattan barbershop, is thanking his wife today for his life. Last night she rescued him from their cellar after a wall had caved in upon him. In two minutes time after he escaped from his perilous position the cellar was full of water.

"Roper lives on Vattier Street and like nearly every other resident on that street, he had trouble last night with water in his cellar. When the water was about two feet deep in his cellar, Roper decided he had better go down and take out some of the fruit or place it higher at least. He hadn't been there more than a few minutes when a wall, which had been loosened by the water, caved in upon him. He was about half buried but luckily he was able to keep his head up out of the water. He struggled and floundered to free himself, but failing, he called to his wife for help.

"As the cellar was filling fast with water the only help which Mrs. Roper had time to secure was herself and she fell desperately to work digging away at the dirt and rocks which pinned her husband down. Within two minutes from the time that Roper was free and out of the cellar, it was full of water.

"Mr. Roper has not been able to get downtown today. He is suffering from a wrenched knee and some other bruises. But they are consolations when he thinks about the fate which he barely escaped."

Hal, Sr. and Oma Worrel were married at one minute after midnight on January 1, 1911, at 612 Leavenworth in Manhattan. This was a two-story rooming house owned by Oma's mother, Mrs. Carolyn Viola "Carrie" Hull Worrel, and it had telephones all over the house. The man who sold them the house worked for the telephone company. The January 2, 1911, <u>Manhattan Nationalist</u> reported on the wedding:

"The bride is a very attractive and charming young lady, well known in Manhattan where she has lived for the past eleven years. McCord has been for three years employed in W. S. Elliot's clothing store and is a young man of excellent qualities, and is liked and admired by all who know him. Mr. and Mrs. McCord have gone to housekeeping at 601 Thurston."

McCord family portrait, circa 1903. Standing, L to R: Mary "Mayme", Hal, George and Carrie. Seated: Henry, Rachel and Will.

Sedalia Items

The McCords were considered one of the mainstays of the old Sedalia community northeast of Keats. Several years after Dad's grandparents Henry and Rachel settled near Manhattan, they helped build a Presbyterian Church north of their homestead. Henry cut the stone for it. Rachel was a midwife in the Sedalia community and attended numerous births, including the birth of Riley County historian, Winifred Slagg. Little bits of community gossip found their way to the Sedalia Items columns in the local newspapers and give some insight into the daily lives of the McCords.

Daily Republic, March 12, 1889:

"FROM SEDALIA—The L. M. I. Society met with Mrs. Howe. Roll call was answered with quotations from Scott. Music by Anna Cooper assisted by Mrs. Freeman of Grandview and Mrs. Howe. Subjects under discussion were 'Professions for Women' and 'The Relation of the Parents to the School.' There were no papers upon these topics, but the talk was general and was joined in by all. Mrs. Howe then read a biography of Mrs. Alden (author of Pansy Books), which was very interesting. R. E. [Rachel Elizabeth] McCord then read 'No Sect in Heaven.'

"It was decided to hold our first anniversary on the 15th of March at Sedalia school house. We hope to have a full attendance and all come prepared to give a brief review of what we have been doing. The election of officers then followed: President, R. E. McCord; Vice-president, Anna Cooper; Secretary, Mrs. Howe. … Adjourned to meet in four weeks with Mrs. McCord."

Daily Republic, May 13, 1890:

"The younger portion of the Sedaliaites had a picnic Monday at Rocky Ford, in honor of Fred McCord's sixteenth birthday."

Manhattan Nationalist, Sept. 27, 1895:

19

"Stanfield Puett and McCord are making hay together. They are covering the whole country with stacks.

"The Sedalia ladies met on Wednesday, Sept. 18, at the school house and organized a society for the purpose of helping on the church work with Mrs. Cooper for President, Mrs. Dodge, Treas. and Mrs. McCord, Secretary, with membership of twelve for a starter.

Manhattan Nationalist, Dec. 31, 1897:

"Mrs. C. M. Howe entertained on Christmas Day the families of Mr. O. Dodge, Capt. H. J. McCord, H. F. Cooper, and O. White. Miss Margaret Minis was also an honored guest. Turkey and its accompaniments was the juiciest, the tenderest and the daintiest that one could desire. After dinner the young folks spent an hour with their skates on Wildcat Creek. The old folks had a comfortable visit as is the manner of their kind.

Manhattan Nationalist, Jan. 21, 1898:

"W. B. McCord has gone to Iola, Kansas to visit his sister, Mrs. W. H. Irwin. He expects to remain for some time.

"Mrs. H. J. McCord gave a dinner party last Wednesday in honor of her husband's birthday. Mr. McCord has just passed the seventy-first milestone on life's journey. His friends gave him hearty congratulation on the physical and mental rigor that he still enjoys and wish him many happy returns of his birthday.

Manhattan Nationalist, Feb. 25, 1898:

"Capt. H. J. McCord lost a cow last week. It was killed by another cow in the herd who pushed it down and then hooked it till it died. George immediately drove the herd to Will Dodge's who dehorned them.

Manhattan Nationalist, Mar. 20, 1898:

"Carrie McCord is home from college this week on account of illness.

Manhattan Nationalist, Nov. 18, 1898:

"George McCord led a very interesting C. E. meeting last evening. The topic, Christian Recreation, was one in which all were interested and it was discussed with zeal and animation. The song service was especially enjoyed.

Manhattan Nationalist, July 27, 1898:

"George McCord returned home Saturday from western harvest fields, well pleased with his venture.

Manhattan Nationalist, Jan. 20, 1899:

"George McCord went to Manhattan Monday to attend college.

Nationalist, Aug. 11, 1899:

"The laying of the corner stone of the new church on Monday afternoon was largely attended. The ceremony was very impressive.

Nationalist, Sept. 1, 1899:

"George McCord has a new top buggy.

Nationalist, Nov. 3, 1899:

"WELCOME HOME. KANSAS WELCOMES THE HOMECOMING OF THE HEROES OF THE PHILIPPINES. MANHATTAN WELCOMES FOX, McCORD, ADAMS AND FRANK. ... Cheers for the living and tears for the dead."

The article gives a short sketch of the four Riley County boys who were returning. Will "was educated in the district school except one year at KSAC. [Kansas State Agricultural College] ... He joined the K.N.G. in the second year of its organization and it was there that he received his military training. He was always very enthusiastic in anything pertaining to military display and was member of Co. I., K.N.G., up to time of the enlistment in the Twentieth Kansas."
Nationalist, Jan. 12, 1900:

"The Sedalia Presbyterian Church was dedicated the Sabbath of January 7. The day proved to be perfect with bright sunshine and balmy air. ... Dr. Gragg [of Emporia College] preached an impressive sermon after which an offering of $200 was taken which enabled the Doctor to present the house to God as an unblemished offering. ... A bountiful dinner was served to over 100 guests and a happy and social hour was enjoyed.
Nationalist, May 7, 1904:

"The large herd of cattle that have been wintered in the neighborhood are being driven to White City this week. Hal McCord, Ned Howe and James Hibbets have gone to help drive them. Capt. and Mrs. H. J. McCord went to Manhattan to see and hear President [Theodore] Roosevelt."

Watching Politics

In a letter Henry wrote to his son Will, then en route to the Philippines from Hawaii during the Spanish-American War, he talks about a trip that he and Rachel had taken.

"At Home, November 18, 1898

"… Only spent two days with Will [Irwin] and Mayme as we felt that we must be home to vote—took four days to go and four and a half to return—got to our place about noon. I hitched the mules to the buggy and drove over to Keats and voted. We carried by 22 majority. The county ticket was elected by from 350 to 660 majority. Coldeshrad's majority in the Dist. is considerably over 2400. We have elected the whole state ticket from governor down. The whole delegation to congress except one and it is said that the vote of the Soldier boys may change that. Roosevelt the Leader of 'The Rough Riders' is elected governor of New York State, McKinley has been handsomely sustained. Both branches of Congress will be in perfect accord with the Pres. Hip! Hurrah! Glory enough for one day!

"I saw Sargeant Gray of your company while we were in Iola. He spoke very favorably of you. Said you would get along all right. That you was temperate in all things and knew how to take care of yourself. We enjoyed our visit very much—would like to have stayed longer but couldn't think of losing our votes.

"Mama will give you all the news. I am tired and sleepy so good night."

Hunters and Nature Lovers

The McCord men were hunters. There reportedly was plenty of game near the homestead, and they did their own butchering. When Dad's Uncle Will was still a boy, he killed what Dad said was a white Canadian lynx near the homestead in Manhattan. Rather rare and larger than an ordinary bobcat, the animal was carried home on his back. Will subsequently had the animal stuffed and gave it to KSAC for their natural history museum.

From the Manhattan Nationalist, January 22, 1892:

"Fred McCord killed a large Washington eagle one day last week; it measured seven feet two inches from tip to tip. He will present it to KSAC."

Another Manhattan Nationalist item reported on April 16, 1896, that "George McCord captured 12 young wolves last week."

Dad also told me about his father, Hal, Sr, having a burro named Jack that he used to hunt for coyote dens. *The $1 scalp bounty on* *coyotes provided enough for Dad* (Hal, Sr.) *to buy his spring clothes each year. When they came to a fence, he would pull up the lower strand of fence wire and Jack would roll under. He loved that burro.*

In addition to being hunters, the family all seemed to have a great fondness for their surroundings and the beauty of Kansas. From the <u>Manhattan Nationalist</u>, October 13, 1897:

"Mr. Fred Howe and sister Miss Nora and Mr. George McCord and sister Miss Carrie have just returned from a camping expedition to Topeka. The fine roads and beautiful autumn days made the trip a pleasure long to be remembered."

Carrie was a teacher, a remarkable woman with boundless energy and diverse interests. Dick Young, her grandson, said "she entertained her grandchildren with stories, willow whistles, turtle pancakes and many other creatures of her imagination. She loved the outdoors— prairies, beaches and mountains. Her family was her greatest love and interest."

Henry Jackson McCord with grandchildren, July 4, 1908. Upper row, L to R:
Pauline Roper, Rachel Roper, Rick Roper, Ruth McCord. Lower row: Landon
McCord, Irene McCord and Ray McCord.

Death of a Patriarch

Henry's occupation, though quite varied, was generally listed as
farmer. He lived more than 90 years, and at his death in 1917, the
<u>Manhattan Nationalist</u> included in his obituary: "Mr. McCord was a
man that tried to be honest with all men and ever thoughtful in his
family for the little comforts of home, wife and children."

He was buried in Sunset Cemetery in Manhattan. Rachel had died
previously in 1905 at the age of 54; she is also buried at Sunset.

Again, from the <u>Nationalist</u>: "Mrs. McCord was a faithful member of the Presbyterian Church and was universally respected and beloved." Hal, Sr., 21 at the time of his mother's death, was then living at the old home place.

Hal, Sr. and Oma

Hal, Sr. and Oma were simple, good folk. After initially working for Elliot's Clothing at 312 Poyntz Avenue, Hal later had his own clothing store at 108 South Fourth. It prospered prior to the depression. McCord Clothing bought ads for both the Manhattan High <u>Blue M</u> and K-State <u>Royal Purple</u> yearbooks during the years my father was in school and advertised Hart, Shaffner & Marx clothes, Stetson hats and Arrow shirts. My dad said of his father, *Father was a good judge of cloth and felt hats. We learned early that a cheap garment was not a good investment if the quality was poor.*

Hal, Sr. was one of six members of the school board and was elected for his first three-year term in 1927. There is a special tribute page with photos in the 1930 <u>Blue M</u>, honoring the board's work. "Their duty consists of carrying on the business of the schools—letting contracts, supervising the repair and upkeep of the buildings, purchasing supplies, employing and discharging teachers, principals and the superintendent."

My dad says, *One of the things that Dad always regretted was that he only got to go through the 4th grade. He later was the teacher at the Highland Grade School northeast of the home place, a one-*

room school. His experience made up for his lack of formal schooling.
(Note: My father's statement that his father only got through the fourth grade seems inconsistent with the family emphasis on education, especially given that most of the children did attend at least some college classes.)

My grandmother, Oma, was rare in her time as she attended Kansas State College for two years, 1909 and 1910.[15] When I looked through her 1909 and 1910 <u>Royal Purple</u>, the school yearbooks, only the graduating seniors were in named pictures so I was not sure I recognized her in any of the group photos. Besides, it was legendary in our family about how much she hated to have her picture taken and thought photos of her were never good.

There were, however, named photos of the Grand Champion Steer and the Reserve Grand Champion Steer from the December '09 International Livestock Show in Chicago, both raised and shown by K-Staters. I was surprised to find in a special section at the end of the seniors, a single black graduate, one Harley M. Hunter, who planned to teach agriculture at Tuskegee Institute. Apparently even the photos were segregated then.

The 1909 RP billed the seniors that year as "the last of the 'noughties'." That yearbook was dedicated to Michael Francis Ahearn, esteemed coach of athletics. One of the pages had several paragraphs extolling "The Moral Advantages of College Athletics."

---

[15] Both grandmothers were rare. My Grandmother Hedge also attended two years of college—one at Drake, the second at Washburn in Topeka, KS. I never had a choice about college—I was just expected to go. And to graduate, and with honors.

There were more literary societies (seven) than there were Greeks (three fraternities in '09, one more in '10 plus two sororities).

The 1910 R. P. was dedicated to the K-State President, Henry Jackson Waters. There are extensive paragraphs of each faculty member, one being Mrs. Mary P. Van Zile ... "the woman keeping up the reputation of KSAC for sending out the best housewives in the world." The yearbook contained lots of stories of activities, a history of each class and cartoons. Seniors warranted a paragraph and a poem. There was a clear emphasis on the military.

Dad said that Oma had dated Milton Eisenhower some during her years in school. Milton, younger brother of Dwight Eisenhower, grew up in Abilene, Kansas, and earned a journalism degree from K-State. In 1943, he became the ninth president of K-State, the only alumnus to serve in that capacity. I remember sometimes walking to elementary school at Eugene Field with his daughter, Ruth. When I was an undergraduate at Kansas State, I had language and history classes in [Milton] Eisenhower Hall, built in 1950. My dad later worked at KSAC for Milton Eisenhower after his years overseas in WWII.

Grandmother McCord once told me that in her college home economics class, then called domestic science, she was supposed to make bread without putting her hands into the mixture. But she confessed that she put her bowl down behind her desk, got down on her knees, stuck both fists in, and out of sight of the teacher "kneaded the dough properly."

She was an excellent cook. Her coffee was something special. She would put a whole egg into her percolator, shell and all. It coagulated the coffee grounds, took the bitterness out and made mild, flavorful coffee. Thanksgiving dinners were always memorable at 1504 Houston. My sister Janice and I would generally try to steal black olives ahead of the official sitting down. It was then a challenge as to where to park the evidence of the crime—olives in those days always came unpitted.

Dinners would often be followed by card games. Hearts initially and later when we grandchildren were older, bridge. My family was a competitive, card-playing bunch. Sometimes the rivalry was so intense that I would cry when I ended up with the Queen of Spades and less than 13 accompanying hearts. If I did break down under the pressure, I got teased for it; a good incentive to try to remain cool.

The McCords Easter 1947 photo at Oma's home, 1504 Houston. Back row: Carrie Worrel, Baby Melissa, Oma, Hal, Ivalee, Michael, Max, Ann; Front row: Janice, Marilyn, Don, Max, Jr. and Mary Peg.

Grandmother McCord also taught me how to play a good game of cribbage. She never coddled anyone, and if I didn't see all of my points, she would peg them for herself. Even then excellence was encouraged and expected. These folks were perfectionists.

For years Oma kept chickens, milked a cow and put in a garden annually. Her windowsills were full of African violets, purple, pink and white. She had a knack for knowing exactly what plants liked, and they always thrived for her. My sister Janice and I missed out on that gene. My sister has said, "Not many folks can actually kill a Mother-in-law's tongue plant, but I can."

As the oldest granddaughter, I later inherited the Bavarian china Oma bought in the 1920s with her milk and egg money. I also now wear a ring she wore as a girl, a dainty onyx circle surrounding a tiny diamond. It was the perfect size without any adjustments.

Grandmother was an outstanding seamstress, and the granddaughters all benefited from these talents. As little girls, we cousins all had wonderful formal gowns made of fairytale fabrics like taffeta and organdy in wondrous pastel floral prints. We were so elegant! I remember other special matching dresses my sister and I had—one pair made with yards and yards of dotted Swiss trimmed with white eyelet lace.

Three McCord cousins: Mary Peg, Marilyn and Janice at Oma's, circa 1946.

Janice, dog Skipper and Marilyn, circa 1948.

Oma was a very stylish lady. Always fashionable, immaculate and tasteful in both dress and manner. There were a couple of milliners in Manhattan who made hats for Oma. One of my mother's dearest friends, Agnes Chartier, remembers Oma's beautiful hats and where Oma and Hal sat in church.

Because Oma was so short, barely over five feet, she usually wore shoes with platform soles. This shortened the back of her calves over time, and eventually it was painful for her to stand in bare feet.

And I remember mousetraps on the furniture, so her two little Pekinese dogs, Singli and Ching, would stay off that plush upholstery. In her later years, I remember her hair being almost blue. She hated yellowed gray.

33

Dad once remarked that Oma's mother, Carrie Hull Worrel, was *a classy lassie* so apparently it ran in the family. With both his mom and his grandmother as role models, no wonder Dad likes to be surrounded by good-looking women, including his grown daughters. I always pay attention to the clothes I pack when I go to visit because I know he notices and cares. He feels I do him honor by dressing attractively.

I have sometimes wondered if Oma disliked having her picture taken because her mother was so attractive and photogenic. Carrie Hull was born in Kentucky. Her folks had a distillery but *they never touched a drop* according to Dad. Carrie married Leif Worrel,[16] also of Zeandale.

Leif was an expert tinsmith and among other jobs he worked on the 1928 restoration of the First Kansas Territorial Capitol at Ft. Riley. I don't know much about Leif except that *he drank too much, which caused some embarrassment to the family.* When I was a child, he lived for a time in Oma's basement, almost invisibly, and died in 1951. He is buried in Pleasant Valley Cemetery south of Zeandale, Kansas.

Tragedy and Loss

Depression days brought tragedy. Hal, Sr. was doing a lot of bartering at the clothing store he owned. Perhaps he would take a pig

---

[16] Some genealogy listings call him Levi Worrel but he was called "Leif." In fact, my father never remembers hearing him called anything but Leif. He was born in 1864 in Kentucky.

as payment for new school clothes and past bills, helping neighbors make it. It was a devastating time for many, and Dad's parents were no exception.

One Friday my grandfather took the store's weekly income to the bank, where it was gladly accepted. But the bank would not open come Monday morning. Hal, Sr. felt betrayed by the banker, a man in his eight-couple bridge group and someone he considered a close friend. He couldn't understand why his friend would deposit the money knowing the bank's situation.

By 1935, Hal had lost the clothing business he had owned for eight years. By early 1937, he was clerk of the district court and had just been elected to a second term in that office, due to begin the following Monday. But debts from the store had continued to pile up and bankruptcy seemed to be inevitable. They were behind around $10,000 on accounts receivable (by Dad's estimates), and there was little hope of ever collecting. Hal, Sr. considered bankruptcy a cardinal sin and apparently could not face the humiliation of such a failure.

After work on the evening of January 5, 1937, he had a highball with his friend Del Close and said good-bye. He spent the evening cleaning up the store's accounting books, then burned them all. No records of the debts would remain. There had been too many years of frustrating economic and emotional setbacks.

On January 6, 1937, Hal, Sr. finally went back to the land near where he was born. He drove the car out to the Highland School, where he had taught, piped the exhaust into the car and ended his life. I never had the privilege of knowing him except through these stories.

The Jan. 7, 1937 <u>Manhattan Daily Nationalist</u> announced the tragedy. It told of special delivery letters Hal had written to the sheriff, the undertaker and his pastor, posted the afternoon of his death. A letter to his wife, Oma, was found on the body.

The letter to the sheriff was an apology for throwing the tragedy upon him at the close of his term in office and asking him to tell the deputy clerk that he had enjoyed working in the office with her. The letter to the undertaker, his bridge club buddy Jim Ryan, gave instructions on funeral plans and desired pallbearers. The letter to Rev. J. David Arnold asked his forgiveness. His friends rushed to the abandoned schoolhouse with an ambulance following them as soon as they received the letters, but they arrived too late.

The <u>Manhattan Mercury</u> of Jan. 8, 1937 reported:

"The Christian church was filled this afternoon with friends and associates of Hal H. McCord. ... The Rev. J. David Arnold, pastor, in paying tribute to McCord, said he had been given the highest office in the church and said that of the 'six best men I ever knew he would be high up in the list.' Referring to the tragic death, the pastor said that 'in a moment of lost equilibrium he did that which seemed to him good'."

Talking about my grandfather seemed to be taboo when I was young. Sort of an unwritten code of ethics, I was just not to ask questions. Probably partly from the scandal that ensued, partly from the sheer pain of remembering. But I never got to know anything about my grandfather as he was always surrounded by an aura of mystery.

And there were so many good and positive things to know about this man. How I wish the family had talked about him. I can see from this vantage point how much added distress his actions caused the family. I know from personal experience that it is easy to slide into a depression so deep that death seems a better solution than life. But how much easier it would have been for the family to deal with everything as a whole family rather than as a fractured, partial, grieving one.

After my grandfather died, my grandmother's life changed drastically. She contacted my dad, then at Ft. Leavenworth, to come home as soon as possible. He got a vehicle and a driver from the motor pool and left immediately. Life insurance provided no benefits under the circumstances.

No more golfing and bridge club parties. Oma sold her piano and many other possessions. She was forced to go to work. Her middle bedroom was let out and she took in a roomer, usually a college student.

Instead of socializing with her friends, she was now sewing for them. She did alterations for Stevenson's Ladies Department at 317-319 Poyntz Avenue, a far cry from her previous life. Her cubbyhole workroom was on the third floor. I remember trooping through ladies fashions to go see her and saying hello to the glamorous clerks who worked there, then climbing the steep back stairway obviously not meant for public use.

Happily for me, remnants from her alteration work provided many creative and joyous hours making an extensive wardrobe for my doll. Bits of straw trimmed from a hat, taffeta from a gown, net and lace, jewel-like buttons. My personal treasures as a child. My doll clothes collection, displayed at Manhattan's annual Pet & Hobby Show at the pavilion in the City Park each summer, consistently won blue ribbons. I also drew my own paper dolls. I was going to be a dress designer when I grew up.

Familiar Family Stories

There are a couple of family stories my siblings and I know so well that we can finish them once anybody starts one. My family spent a holiday at Uncle Max's, who that year lived just across the street and a house west from Oma on Houston. All of us were downstairs after the big noon meal except for Janice, my younger sister, and Mary Peg, my cousin.

When the kids are too quiet the adults worry. Someone called upstairs, "What are you two doing up there?" The response came back, "Playing beauty parlor." It seemed innocuous enough, but when the two little girls came downstairs Janice's bangs looked like someone had sawed them off with a razor for a too-short, jagged look. Mother took her to a barber the next day, but basically there was nothing to do except let her hair grow back.

Another family favorite happened at Oma's. Brother Don and Cousin Max, Jr. were playing in the basement, doing whatever elementary-school-age boys might be doing during a holiday time. Cousin Mike, probably about four then, could hear them from upstairs through the floor furnace vent and hollered down to ask, "Hey, what are you doing down there?" They responded and said, "Come on down." So Mike did just that. He took the wooden grate off the floor opening and went down!

It took a bit of maneuvering on the basement end to extract him from the furnace duct, but he emerged in fine shape. It had seemed perfectly logical to him. After all, that's where the older boys obviously were.

Once Mary Peg somehow contracted ringworm on her head. As part of the treatment, she had to have her head shaved. I remember her wearing turbans and hats, an especially lovely hat that Easter.

There is a very dear letter that she sent several years later from Ft. Sam Houston to my father then in Washington D.C. The letter is written on stationery that has a little cartoon at the top with a man at the Bonds & Stamps Window and says, "We're all out for defense." Mary Peg, who died of leukemia in 1999, wrote essentially to thank my dad for a book he had sent to her. "As you know, I'm related to a worm—a book worm."

She also told about her first date, going to the St. Anthony Hotel for supper as a part of four couples to celebrate one boy's birthday and then to a late movie, getting home after midnight.

She said she had asked her dad (Max) if she could invite Uncle Hal to come visit. She said that her dad replied, "He'll come whenever he comes by here."

"Now isn't that a good answer? That might mean tomorrow or next year. Oh well, whenever you can, PLEASE come and see us."

She included a lock of her hair just to show him just how long it was. "This is how long my hair is now. Brag, Brag. See that knot? Take the pin out and hold on to the knot; that's how long my hair is." The strands of her hair are still as brilliant red-gold today as I always remembered them to be in childhood.

McCords and the Manhattan Community

Family was important to my father—it seemed to just be a part of the McCord culture. The McCord family has been a significant part of the Manhattan historical scene as well.

Carrie McCord Roper, a sister of Hal, Sr., had a column in the Manhattan Mercury-Chronicle during the years of 1940-41 titled "Gram Sez." Here she wrote poems, historical notes, family stories, and opinions on current affairs and other subjects. Her grandson Dick Young says she did have opinions. She, like my father, was a nature lover and was informed and inquisitive about all species of plants and animals.

A cousin of my dad's, Henry Landon McCord, is noted in Dad's ROTC story as also being an engineer and a cadet colonel of the KSAC regiment. Another cousin, Fred Irwin, later a member of the

Secret Service of the U.S. Treasury Department, shows up in Dad's story of being investigated by the Secret Service.

The <u>Nationalist </u>of Jan. 31, 1912, less than a week after my father's birth, told of the sign placed east of the Kaw Bridge where both the Union Pacific and Rock Island passenger lines could see it.

This is Manhattan

Population 7000

The greatest in the world.

More miles of paving than any town of its size

Electric Street Railway and Interurban to Fort Riley

Full Schools and Empty Jail

The Best Town on the Kansas map

The place to grow healthy, wealthy and wise.

Manhattan was founded in 1855 by a group of riverboat traders who hoped to establish a trading center that would rival the Manhattan of the East. When my mother was clearing customs in New York City one time, the customs agent was astonished. "Manhattan, KANSAS?" "Yes," she beamed, "and we call it the Little Apple!"

Manhattan lies seven miles north of Interstate 70, a feat seemingly accomplished by businessmen more interested in quality of life than in overflowing cash registers. The Flint Hills give rolling contours to the basin where the Big Blue River comes down from the north to join the Kaw River then heads east to join the Missouri River at Kansas City.

Prairie landscapes here feature some of the most magnificent sunsets anywhere in the world. It was a great place to grow up.

I remember once, as a child, calling my father "Nature Boy" because he seemed to know every nook and cranny of those hills. Where to find Dutchman's Britches and Dogtooth Violets blooming in the shade along Wildcat Creek. Where to find old Indian beads along a creek bed north of town, east of 177 on the way to I-70. Deep Creek. McDowell Creek. Pillsbury Crossing. Stargazing summer nights on a blanket at the hill northwest of Manhattan called Top o' the World. Able to recognize and name all of the local birds and sing their calls. One of my great joys as a child was our family picnics around the area and the opportunity to experience my dad's reverence for the special places he loved.

Part Two: Growing Up in Manhattan
1912—1930

Hal H. McCord, Jr. was born January 25, 1912. A brother, Max Worrel McCord, came along two and-a-half years later on August 8, 1914. Both would attend K-State, major in engineering, and have significant military careers.[17]

Current Events in Manhattan Circa 1912

The Manhattan Daily Mercury and the Daily Nationalist of the months near Dad's birth had many stories about women's suffrage. For example, a Dec. 6, 1911, dateline from Los Angeles: "Women not only outvoted the men in most precincts but needed less aid in handling the ballots and worked harder for their favorite candidates … against a prohibition measure to make the city 'dry as a bone'."

Women were considered instrumental in other election victories, such as defeating Hiram Gill for mayor of Seattle. Opinions for women's suffrage in Kansas ran both ways, but I think more were for the measure, at least in the Manhattan papers.

On Dad's birthday the Daily Nationalist wrote about a suffrage tea, had Palace Drug Store ads saying "When you're cold, try a hot chocolate at the Palace Drug Store," and had a large ad for the Marshall Theatre featuring moving pictures and vaudeville, "12-Big

---

[17] Max died August 19, 2000 after several illnesses; his ashes are interred at Arlington National Cemetery.

Fire Exits-12," seating capacity 1,100, no standing room. The pictures that night were "The Right Name But the Wrong Man," "A Football Hero" and "Western Chivalry." Two shows, 7:30 and 8:30 p.m., 10 cents admission, 5 cents for children under 12.

In the November 30, 1911, <u>Daily Mercury</u>, the addition of 150 new books at the library made the front page and listed every title. Dad grew up with an appreciation for many things, and books were definitely one of them. If I, as an adult, wanted to borrow a book from his personal library, he might tell me, *OK, but it'll cost you three fingers if you fail to return it.*

Details and Quality

Dad learned to pay attention to details. That must be a family trait. Whether remembering someone's name, rendering an architectural drawing or creating an experience for soldiers in his care, details mattered. If I'm buying ice cream for him, it has to be a certain brand. I've gone all over Springfield, Missouri, in search of exactly the right one.

When he and his late wife Noni attended the final performance of Richard Harris in "Camelot" in Kansas City, he had formal Spencer jackets made for both of them and hired a limousine. They attended in style, turned heads and had a ball. Every detail mattered.

My father still has a keen eye for quality, whether it be cameras, clocks or coffee—or wine, women and song. Or antiques. I used to know little about them, but now I have some, including the three large solid walnut display cases made for Eastman Kodak in Philadelphia in the 1880s. Dad acquired those from an antique dealer, Mr. Feldman, in the 1960s, driving back to Philly to pick them up.

He designed a couple of rooms in his house around those cases, cared for them and hated to have to part with them when he finally sold his home in Pittsburg, Missouri. I am delighted to have them in my home now. The largest unit is 149" long, has the Eastman seal carved into the top and retains remnants of its former life, such as an Eastman label in a drawer and the sale prices inked in one of the lower shelves: "200 ft. 8 m Reels .60; 200 ft. 8m Cans .60 .70"

Hal's Photo Album

Dad's photo album, assembled by Oma with obvious loving care, has lots of photos of Dad as a baby then as a toddler. There are also photos with Oma's younger sisters, Grace and Viola Worrel. Photos showing four generations: Dad as a toddler and Max as a baby, Oma, Oma's mother Carrie Worrel, and Carrie's mother, Dad's great-grandmother Hull.

My great-grandmother was a sweet gal—not as big as a wink—very perceptive. She was quite alert at 86 and might have lived longer but fell on the back porch at Carrie's, broke her hip and never recovered. Then Carrie later fell on the steps to the basement at her church and injured her kidney. I remember driving Mother to Colorado Springs for my grandmother's funeral.

There are a couple of photos with Hal, Sr. on his bicycle and baby Hal in the basket on the front. Dad told me that he once fell out of that basket and landed on his head. *I don't think it hurt me, but I understand Mom put a stop to that activity.*

They had an Irish setter named Bon, who was Hal's companion in many photos. Bon sired six pups—the female was owned by a Worrel relative—and there are pictures of the puppies in the back yard.

Uncle George gave Hal a Shetland pony in a specially designed May basket when Hal was three years old, another cute photo. Hal could not say pony clearly; it came out *Popo* and so the pony was named. Popo lived to be 28 years old.

No doubt the birth of a baby brother made life a bit busier for Oma and left less time for photos. There seems to be a higher concentration of photos before Max was born than the volume displayed after he arrived. She did manage to get first day of school photos for first and second grades at Bluemont Elementary School.

My favorite of those photos was later used in Dad's senior year Blue M with the caption "Our Blue M Business Manager." Two other photos show the family car decked out with placards and streamers to advertise the store, McCord Clothing, for the 4th of July parade. My dad is in the front seat of one photo, but says he was just there for the photo op as he was too young to drive then.

There is a second photo album, but judging from its state of incompletion, the organization here was the responsibility of a busy high schooler not a doting mother. Some photos are mounted, but most are just loosely inserted, awaiting that free "some day …"

46

Babe Hal

As a young child, Dad once decided to run away from home. Davis, the woman who lived a block south of 601 Thurston, had been the midwife and assisted the doctor for both Hal's and Max's births. She still helped Oma out when the boys were little, spending days doing whatever Oma needed.

After Max was born and Hal discovered he was no longer the center of attention, he decided to dramatize his hurt feelings by running away. He enlisted Davis' help; she assisted him in packing a three-year-old's special treasures in a bandana and put it on a stick, *like a little hobo.* Dad told Davis, *Babe Hal goin'...* He defiantly walked out the door and down Sixth Street toward Kearney. *She watched as I sat on the curb. When it was time to eat, I came back home.*

The 601 Thurston Street house had four rooms and two porches. The parents' bedroom was on the southwest corner; the two little boys slept on the screened-in, bug-proof porch on the south facing the backyard. The other rooms contained a kitchen in the northwest corner and living and dining rooms off the entry on Sixth Street. Dad still remembers their phone number there—824—now the number on the license tag of his Honda Civic.

The McCord family also had a lot across Sixth to the east of the house. Enough land to pasture two Jersey cows and a couple of goats. As Dad grew older, his chores included helping milk the cows, picking bugs off the potato plants and weeding the vegetable patch. *For 10 cents an hour. And I was glad to get it.*

Learning to Hunt

I mentioned earlier that the McCord men liked to hunt. Dad was a typical McCord man in this regard. *Oliver W. Broberg, a captain in the US Army Air Corps, was a friend of the family and a particular friend to me. His parents lived at 1719 Leavenworth in Manhattan. He was killed in 1927 in an accident in Panama.[18] He would come over to the folks and say, "Mrs. Hal, I want to take little Hal out for a week." We'd go out camping using sleeping bags. He taught me how to lay a snare, catch a rabbit, dress it, cook it. I was around 10 to 12 years old then. My dad's hunting philosophy was, "You clean and dress what you kill." We'd find a rabbit run in the snow. Set a noose snare on a limb so that when a rabbit would run into it, the limb would snap the noose up. It was a humane way to kill the rabbits. I also learned to hunt quail, which were plentiful, squirrel, ducks and geese.*

Tucked into the old photo album was this note, written in about a 12 year-old's childish cursive on a page from an old Big Chief lined tablet, that scrap now torn and faded brown with age:

---

[18] There is a photo in Dad's album of Capt. Broberg standing in front of a pyramidal tent, and a news clipping titled "Impressive Rites for Dead Aviator" that tells about the accident in Panama in which Broberg died at age 33. Broberg was commander of the 24th Pursuit Squadron in the Canal Zone and considered the foremost machine gun marksman in the Army Air Force. The plane he was flying crashed into Gatun Lake. A formation of five airplanes circled above Sunset Cemetery in tribute at his burial.

Dear Folks,

I got sick cleaning rabbits when I had 5 cleaned and I went on to bed—if you want to you can clean the other two which are in the basement. Mamma please don't wake me up because I didn't take my bath because I'll take it in the morning. We have not fought at all.

Good night

Your loving son, Hal

I can imagine how much that note would mean to Oma, with the assurance that Dad and his brother had not been fighting, that he would finish his responsibilities later, and that he was indeed a loving son. I asked about the fighting. Dad said that one time when he and Max had fought, Max got so angry that he tore the phone off the wall. Their father explained to both of them *in no uncertain terms what might happen* should they continue fighting. Dad said he did not fight again. And his mom did not wake him that night.

Plenty to Do

The neighborhood kids played football in a nearby empty lot. In the summers, Dad played baseball, progressing through the years from Little League to City League. His position was catcher. Once a ball split his right hand between the middle and ring fingers, ripping it open. Dad holds up his hands as he tells me this. Both hands are significantly twisted now, and the crippling has affected what he can do with them. He buys sweaters and turtlenecks to avoid the pesky buttons on shirts.

Summers also brought opportunities for fishing and swimming. Dad's father taught him to swim, mostly in Wildcat Creek at the Irwin's but also in Deep Creek at Dad's Aunt Mary "Mattie" and Uncle Elijah "Lige" Worrel's place. Lige was born in Kentucky in 1856.

Fishing was particularly good on the Wildcat between the first and the second Rock Island bridges, the Dave Russell place. And the area of the Tom Hanagan place. The creek was spring-fed, and the water was cold. Besides prolific fish schools there was a lush stand of Dutchman's Britches and Dogtooth Violets there. We would have Easter breakfasts in that place. Ham and eggs on an open campfire. One time when we were at that spot, Max got scared to death. A great horned owl was up on the hill behind us, who-hooing. Max ran back down the hill, wanting to know what in the world that was. I expect he was about four or five when that happened.

In the winter, sledding was a popular activity. Bluemont Hill to the north was relatively barren in those early days, and there was some great sledding down the hill. Dad tells of his mom making a tub of French toast for all the neighbor kids when they would come in from a cold sledding day.

He also tried skiing on Bluemont Hill, using barrel staves. He fell once, rolled under a fence, and still has the scar on his back from that along with a scar on his left leg from the knee to the ankle from sliding off his pony into a barbed-wire fence. There's another scar under his chin when he delivered milk to the neighbors a block east, the Eichenhorsts, and fell while running back home. The ear of the pail where the handle attached carved out its niche. He didn't tell his mother about any of those. *She would have made a big deal about it. I didn't think it was a big deal.* All scars would be duly noted on the numerous subsequent physical exams exacted by the military.

Hal was in the Boy Scouts, and though he did not achieve the Eagle Scout rank, he accomplished many of the steps along the way. Star Scout and Life Scout. There are three merit badge certificates tucked in the pages of his photo album—for Printing, Firemanship and Scholarship—all dated April 12, 1927. He went more than once to Camp Wood[19] near Emporia and took many of his own photos of friends at camp, also tucked loosely into his album, still awaiting suitable mounting.

In junior high school Hal had a paper route. He walked the downtown route and rode his bicycle for the Houston Street portion. The family attended First Christian Church where J. David Arnold was the minister. When he was in high school, Hal, Jr. taught a Sunday school class of younger boys. Hal, Sr. was a church elder.

My mother would later become one of the early woman elders in that same church and my brother Don, raised in that church, held his services of ordination there when he entered the ministry.

---

[19] Camp Wood was a Hi-Y and Boy Scout Camp near Cottonwood Falls, west of Emporia and south of Herrington. Bruce Tallman ran it in Dad's day. Dad later drove my brother to Camp Wood when Don was in junior high school.

The McCord family drove to Colorado Springs for several vacations after Oma's mother, Carrie Worrel, moved there. Christmas dinners were usually with extended family, commonly at B. Roper's (611 Vattier) or the William Irwin's (RFD #2) home *since both Aunt Carrie Roper and Aunt Mayme Irwin had big houses. There were about 21 first cousins that would gather. Some of the older cousins had already left home. The big holiday dinner was served cafeteria style. The kids would play hide-and-seek. Those big houses provided reasonable challenges for hiding places, were warmer in the winter than playing outdoors, and the game was a lot of fun for all.*

Cousins Remember

Phyllis Irwin told me that her family often stayed at Oma and Hal's house when visiting in Manhattan because her mother didn't think Phyllis' Grandmother Irwin was a very good housekeeper. I can verify that Oma kept an excellent house.

One of her highest praises came when anybody kept their kitchen floor so clean you could eat off it. Phyllis also reported to me, "Your grandfather, father and uncle were ALL snorers of the most violent kind. It sounded to me like many electric carpet sweepers.[20] The basement had all sorts of duck decoys and a mangle; Oma put all her sheets through that mangle."

Phyllis also remembers playing with 3-D Chinese puzzles the McCords had around the house. When Hal was in college, she

---

[20] Having stayed at my dad's in recent years, I can attest that he now snores no more than I do, which isn't much.

remembers seeing on the dining room table his exquisite 3-D renderings of buildings for his architecture classes. "I was so impressed with those drawings with little trees all around." Phyllis later visited Hal when he was stationed at Randolph Air Force Base and got a ride in his J-3F50 Piper Cub. "We saw wild turkeys all around—it was wonderful!"

Phyllis' Aunt Pat, the only surviving sibling of Fred Irwin, was born in 1912 the same year as my father. She remembers when her grandfather Henry Jackson McCord stayed with them at the farm. After his wife died, Henry stayed with one or the other of his daughters. "That's the way they did things back then," said Pat. Henry was living at the Irwin's when he died, and the funeral was held at the home.

Even though she wasn't quite five when Henry died Pat remembers what he looked like, that he had "bushy white whiskers." Pat remembers more clearly, "Aunt Oma and Uncle Hal and their two boys, Hal and Max. When the children were all little, we would have picnics in the front walnut grove at our (Irwin) home."[21]

Dad said that the Irwin's had a watch-gander that could put any watchdog to shame. *He was big, gray, and indiscriminate. He would nip anybody who dared to invade his turf. Or failing that, he might beat you to death with his wings. Believe you me, he got your attention. Aunt Mayme and Uncle Will laughed about it.*

---

[21] The William Irwin home was on RR #2, on Wildcat Creek, just above the Rock Island cut southwest of Manhattan. Lt. Col. and Mrs. James Towner now live in Bonham, TX; Pat will be 90 years old Dec. 26, 2002 and says they are still going strong.

Patricia Devereaux Irwin went to Kansas State for two years, where she was a Tri-Delt. Her husband Jim Towner was in the military; he taught in a school in Florida and did not see overseas duty, "thank goodness." They did see a lot of Hal and Ivalee, my mother, who was Hal's first wife, in Houston before the war and Pat remembers seeing me as a baby. "The war broke us up," she lamented of the friendship she and Jim had with my parents.

The Great Street Commissioner Race

In 1932, there were 11 candidates for the city post of Streets and Utilities Commissioner. In depression times almost any job looked good. Hal McCord and Hurst Majors, then Manhattan's mayor, polled the highest number of votes in the primary. From the March 9, 1932 Manhattan Chronicle, page 1:

"Hal McCord and Hurst Majors were the two men receiving the highest number of votes in the primary election held Tuesday to select nominees for commissioner of streets and utilities election. Their names will appear on the ballots in the general election April 5. McCord polled 684 votes and Majors 675 votes out of a total of 2,510 votes recorded."

Although he polled the most votes in the primary, Hal, Sr. lost the April 5 vote to his good friend, Hurst Majors. The April 6 newspaper story on the general election contained a statement from Hal, Sr. "I would just like to express my appreciation to my loyal friends for their very fine support and congratulate Hurst Majors on his victory."

Both of them belonged to the Co-op Club.[22] Donald Parrish told me that, at the Co-op meeting following the election, both men left the meeting room at the Wareham Hotel for an adjacent room. A shot was heard, and J. David Arnold, minister at the First Christian Church, ran in exclaiming, "I believe we've had a murder!" Hurst had poured ketchup on himself while Hal ducked out a door. I knew as soon as Dr. Parrish started telling the story that it was all a set-up and that J. David was a part of it. Any other explanation would have been inconsistent with all I had ever heard about my grandfather. Besides, my dad had to get his great sense of humor from somewhere.

I remember Dad's telling of stealing the banner of another square dance club one time, cleverly hiding it and pretending innocence. "Hal McCord," they exclaimed when the truth was out, "we would never have believed this of you!"

Military Musings

Dad loved the military life. The honor and the excellence of it. Doing a job right. Attending to every detail. He expected much, but was always ready to give credit where credit was due. This in spite of a somewhat patriarchal chauvinism about which we can and do tease

---

[22] The Co-op Club ran into name infringements with the Farmer's Co-op when they were incorporating chapters in New York. At that time, 1951, they changed the named to Sertoma Club. Dr. Donald Parrish was researching Manhattan history at the Riley County Historical Society one day when I was also there working on this book. He kindly shared this story, and my father verified it. Dr. Parrish also played in the City Band with my father.

him. He bought me a cap and a T-shirt with "Women Fly" on the front when I got my private pilot's license. And I got him a cap that said, "The Father of a Pilot." I know he was properly proud.

He once was bemoaning all that he had done or could have done for my brother, Marc[23], and still Dad felt Marc had not been able to find himself. Marcia said, "Daddy, why didn't you do any of those things for me?" He turned to her and said, very innocently and sweetly, *Well, honey, you wore the wrong kind of skirt...* All three of his daughters have ended up in computer science fields, without any of the mentoring he might have so ably provided. Probably a reflection on the times and general societal values more than any intentional act on Dad's part.

Dad began his military career very early...

An Eight-Year-Old's Cannon

We had a place in Manhattan called Smith Brothers. They were the Bass Pro Shop for that area. You could get everything there, even a little canister of black powder. And they sold it. I mean, it wasn't anything that anybody complained about. Until it went off...

We had decided the 4th of July (about 1920) should have a proper celebration. I took a two-inch pipe and screwed a "T" on the one end of it. It was about, oh, 12 or 16 inches long. That "T" had a plugger on the back side, but a three-quarter inch pipe actually extended on

---

[23] Marc and Marcia were children from Dad's second marriage to Thelma Holuba. Thelma was born in St. George, Kansas, graduated from Manhattan High School, ran in the same crowd as my father and my mother, and had her own military career in the Navy. She died April 13, 1983, at Whiteman AFB, Missouri.

the side. That would just accommodate a spark plug, so we screwed a spark plug in there, put a plug in the bottom of it and put about this much black powder (measuring with his fingers) *in the one end, and covered it up about that much with sand.*

Next we dug a little trench to set it in so that it would point up through the elm trees there in the back yard at 601 Thurston. Then we wired a Ford spark coil connection to that plug and had it all primed and ready to go for a proper salute the early morning of the 4th.

Daybreak came and all we had to do was to throw the switch. Whoomp! I mean, we woke up the north half of Manhattan. My dad came out in his big flannel nightgown ... and the telephone began ringing. Everybody wanted to know what was going on.

Well, we had properly saluted the 4th of July, and it really was a loud boom. Louder than we had thought it might be. We looked up to the tree where this pipe was pointed, through the tree. The leaves were stripped from every limb. The sand had acted like shrapnel and created a nice viewing hole up through the elm tree. It was like a telescope looking up through this tree.

I got a lecture then about not <u>ever</u> doing this again and what the outcome would be if I ever did. I got what they call campused, grounded for two weeks. I found out there were more uses for the razor strap than sharpening the razor. My brother Max really didn't have too much to do with it. He was very helpful in running the wire to throw the switch, and he enjoyed it as much as I did, but he didn't get the razor strap.

My dad was sure put out. Not to mention that my mother couldn't show her face outside her door for a while. The neighbors thought those McCord kids could really raise the roof.

In the summer of 1924, the family bought a new house and moved to 1504 Houston. I knew this house well as my grandmother lived there until the 1970s. Then it began to be too much upkeep for her, and she moved to Alabama where my Uncle Max then lived.

I remember the little bean-shaped goldfish pond she had put in the northeast corner of the back yard with a little limestone bench in front and the many beautiful flowers she was so skilled at growing providing a backdrop. The west side of the back yard was reserved for her vegetable and tomato garden.

There was a detached garage on the alley to the north. Wasps insisted on nesting on the west side of the back porch, and Grandmother had terrifying reactions to wasp and bee stings so this was a real issue. Roosevelt Elementary School, where my mother later taught kindergarten, was almost kitty-corner across the intersection to the southeast in front. There was a large weedy empty lot on the west side, and an unsociable neighbor we grandchildren decided must be a mean old man.

Dad has a great sense of humor and loves to tell a good story. He is also a problem solver. The budding young engineer/militarist pulled off yet another spark plug spectacular at the new house …

Our Poster Cat

About the time I turned 14 I learned more about spark plugs. We had one of those old Ford spark coils and a six-volt battery. You'd be surprised what a good spark you could pull off that spark coil with a six-volt battery.

Mom raised little Rhode Island red chickens. She had an old mother hen that usually took 'em on and took care of 'em, but the hen didn't raise all of the little chicks. We had an incubator and used it to help hatch the little ones. As the little chicks came off the incubator, Mom put them inside a small enclosure in the back yard, a chicken wire-netting fence around an area about half the size of this room (gestures around the room). *There she would feed them and take care of them until frying time.*

Our family also had a cat. That cat kept creeping up on those little chicks. About the time it'd get up to where the chicken wire fence was, Mom would rap on the window and the cat would turn around and streak away. We decided there ought to be a better solution to that. My little brother and I took the problem under advisement. We fixed a connection from the Ford spark coil ... to the wired enclosure ... and grounded it. Anybody on the ground that touched the fence would close the circuit. It was hooked up so that when the cat touched it ... Zap! (Dad is laughing so hard at this point that he can barely finish the story...:)

We had a square house, and on the south side of it there was a porch all away across that front side. We waited until the cat was in stalk mode and almost about to get into the fence, then turned the switch on. The cat touched the fence while standing on the ground. All of a sudden, every hair on that cat's back was standing up straight, and its tail got real big. And the cat let out a wild scream and ran out, up the back porch screen, over the top of the house and down the other side, dropping over the front porch. The poor thing took off to leave that part of the country. It was one of the funniest things I ever saw. That cat got about that big around. (Makes a big circle with his arms.) *Probably cured the cat of being interested in those little chicks.*

Have you seen the picture published about the wet cat, the mad cat? It had had a bath, and wasn't happy. It was what Marcia calls a tuxedo cat, with its black and white markings. That was a famous poster, and on the bottom it says, "Don't tell me what kind of a day to have!" We could have had our own poster cat. Those were great growing up days.

Music Appreciation

The McCords appreciated and valued good music. Oma owned a McPhail upright piano. "The best I ever worked on," said their piano tuner. According to Dad, Oma was an excellent pianist. One Christmas Dad's parents got him a clarinet. They opened the case and put it together that Christmas Eve to try it out, and confessed to being scared to death they would waken Hal. He later became first chair clarinet in the Manhattan High School band and orchestra.

Max played both trumpet and saxophone in addition to clarinet. The May 17, 1929 <u>Manhattan Mercury</u> had a front page story on "Student Recital Saturday" that ended with "A trio composed of Catharine Colver, flute; Bill Fitch, oboe; Max McCord, clarinet will play one selection." Max was later in a German band with Hap Mathias' younger brother and Tom Goody, a doctor's son. *The band was pretty decent, was in demand, and they had a lot of fun.*

Dad remembers R. Harry Brown as a significant figure in music education for Manhattan youth, both those in band and in orchestra. Mr. Brown owned the Brown Music Company, later acquired by Matt Betton, whose dance band was locally famous when I was at KSU.

Although Mr. Brown was not officially on the Manhattan High faculty, he and his wife Sarah were, in Dad's words, a *gift* to the school organization. *If any student needed an instrument, they would loan one. And Mr. Brown would give them lessons. He also played in the City Band concert every Sunday afternoon.*

In Dad's junior year at Manhattan High, Kansas State needed an oboe player. The KSAC music department purchased an oboe and Dad took lessons from Myron Russell, a faculty member at K-State. He then played oboe those two years in both the high school and the K-State Orchestra. I will always remember the several times when Dad, reminiscing, would sing to me various melodies he had once played on his oboe. The oboe, made in Paris, France, by F. Loree, became mine, was loaned to Phyllis Irwin, daughter of Dad's cousin Fred Irwin, for her friend's prodigy son, and is now back with me.

Marilyn McCord

Secondary School Memories

Dick McCord, my cousin and I were in the same math class in junior high, Miss Kjellin's[24] class. During the spring of the year when the cottonwoods were bearing these little cottonwood seeds, we'd take those seeds and flip them. They would pop somebody just like a paper-wad, pea-shooter style.

Dick hit me in the back of the head with one. I straightened up as Kjellin was writing on the backboard. Without even turning around she said, "Dick, you can leave the room." We never knew how she would react, and we always thought she had eyes in the back of her head. But she laughed afterwards ... It was a mischievous three or four of us that she could always count on. I never will forget that. Miss Kjellin's brother, Art, was chief of police of Manhattan at that time. She always threatened us that if we got really out of hand, she'd have her brother come in and take care of us.

At that time Carruthers was the principal of Manhattan Junior High; W. E. Sheffer was the superintendent of schools. There's a story about Sheffer that we always enjoyed. We used to have a whole school meeting in the auditorium for a 30-minute assembly fairly regularly. Sheffer, who had a big tummy and liked to wear vests, would get up in front of the student body. He stood up there on the stage, put his hands in his vest pocket, like this, and tapped his tummy like this with

---

[24] I would later have Miss Kjellin for my seventh grade mathematics class. In college, I would have other mathematics teachers who had previously taught Dad—Teresa Mossman, who taught Advanced Algebra; and William "Wild Bill" Janes for Differential Equations.

his fingers, and said, "I've seen this school grow from a small ... I've seen this grow into a big institution." And he couldn't quite understand why everybody broke out laughing. But he patted his tummy and said, "I've seen this grow into a very, great big institution." And we just exploded.

That really was quite a period. We had good schools. At that time, the school curriculum included geography as well as American history. This was when E. M. Chestnut taught American history. You know what E. M. stood for? "Early Mass Chestnut." Today in the curriculum of schools, I am disappointed somewhat that they have dropped geography as a credit course. I think it's needed. And history is needed. Chestnut did a beautiful job of keeping it interesting. Teaching interesting American history is easy to do, but too many teachers go by the textbook and do it in a dry fashion. That's why people hate it. That's so unnecessary and such a waste.

High School in an "Ideal City"

In the 1927 <u>Blue M</u>, Mabel Roepke wrote a piece on the "Evolution of an Ideal City." That was Manhattan. Dick McCord, Dad's cousin, was president of the sophomore class in '27, and another first cousin, Maxine Roper, was also in that class at Manhattan High. Intramural sports were emphasized, and the physical education requirement jumped from two years to three.

The stated purpose of intramural athletics was *to develop boys to be clean, to be courteous, to be square.* The motto was *Athletics for*

All, and activities that could carry on into adult life were stressed: speedball, basketball, baseball (more than 300 boys participated in baseball), basketball free throw, fall and spring tennis—both singles and doubles, horseshoes, bicycle racing, track, handball and roller skate racing.

A year of plane geometry and a half-year each of higher algebra and solid geometry were offered; Dad took them all. He bypassed the official college prep curriculum, which included Latin, to take mechanical drawing and woodworking. Fred Ernst ran the print shop and Dad operated the press that printed the school newspaper, The Mentor. *I did a lot of job press work; Fred Ernst was the printing instructor. He was great.*

In his senior year Dad was business manager for the yearbook, the Blue M. Although official credit for the air view of MHS was given to Manhattan Flying School, Dad actually took the aerial photos. *It was easy. I borrowed a camera from the photography store in Aggieville, strapped my legs in, and set up in the back compartment of a two-seater, open cockpit biplane, a Laird-Swallow[25]. The pilot, J. H. Boyles, would tilt the plane up so I could get the good aerial shots of both the junior and the senior high school.* Dad's brother Max was one of those credited for making linoleum cuts for that yearbook.

Hi-Y (for boys) and the Girl Reserve Club (GR), branches of the YMCA and YWCA, were going strong. Dad was in Hi-Y and Mom was in GR. Hi-Y sponsored a book exchange, a Thrift Week, a

---

[25] See appendix 3 for additional notes on the numerous aircraft mentioned in this book. There are two photos of the Laird Swallow at the end of this section.

watermelon feed for the entire school, a health campaign and an anti-tobacco campaign. Both had conferences and banquets with parents (Father-Son, Dad-Daughter Banquets, etc.).

The program from the March 11, 1926, Hi-Y Father and Son Banquet says "Printed by Hal McCord, Manhattan High School" at the bottom right. Member's names are listed on the back. The clubs sponsored a Thanksgiving morning service and a Christmas assembly play. Dad was Hi-Y publicity chairman his junior year, and Dick McCord was program chair; their senior year Dad was social chairman and Dick was treasurer.

The 1928 Blue M Hi-Y page indicated that "nineteen boys from Manhattan attended the second 10-day session" at Camp Wood in early summer. It was the largest delegation present. "Of four shields offered as awards, the local club brought back three: for supremacy in athletics, programs and all-round camp honors. Manhattan's Chapter was also presented with the Camp Wood banner and Gold Shield for being judged the best delegation to attend camp throughout the entire season."

Although my mother, Ivalee Hedge, was in the same sophomore class as Dad in 1926-27, she would take extra studies and graduate in 1928. I later did exactly the same thing when I was in high school. The 1928 Blue M says of Mother: "Ivalee Hedge received a scholarship letter and was a member of the orchestra, student council and Girl Reserve Club. Continual cheerfulness is a sign of wisdom and 'Hedgie' is cheerful."

The best summer job Dad had was being a lifeguard at the City Pool. Dad was an excellent swimmer. His father's friend Hurst Majors recommended him for that job, and he was lifeguard for three summers. Dad also helped his classmate and friend Fred Seaton[26] edit copy for Fred's dad's newspaper in the summers.

Dad played football in high school. From the '29 <u>Blue M</u>: "Although Hal was one of the lightest men in the line, it didn't hinder his fighting spirit. McCord played at both right and left guard positions." He earned a letter his senior year. This letter, along with excellent grades and "the highest type of citizenship and sportsmanship" allowed him to become a member of the National Athletic Scholarship Society. This was in addition to being a member of the National Honor Society. Dad was one of three charter members at Manhattan High chosen by Principal H. Leigh Baker.

Russell Smith, who was on the <u>Salina Journal's</u> All-State Second Football Team, and Lisle Smelser, who led the Hi-Y *Inner Circle* each Wednesday, were the other two whose names appeared on the framed charter and these four—the three young men and Principal Baker—are pictured in the 1929 <u>Blue M</u>.

---

[26] The Seaton family had the <u>Manhattan Mercury</u>. The 1929 <u>Blue M</u> in the archives at the Riley County Historical Society had belonged to Fred Seaton, and Hal autographed his senior picture in that copy.

SENIOR HIGH SCHOOL

H. LEIGH BAKER

MANHATTAN, KANSAS

Mr. Hal McCord Jr.
1504 Houston St.
Manhattan, Kansas

Dear Hal:

I am very happy to inform you that you have
been elected to membership in the National
Honor Society of Secondary Schools.

Election to this society is indeed an honor
as the qualities of Scholarship, Leadership,
Character, and Service are the basis of election. Election to this society is an honor
in that you have been true to these qualities
in the past; it is a responsibility in that
you excel in these qualities in the future.

I congratulate you upon your past record;
it is my wish that these ideals may be your
guiding forces in the future.

Very sincerely yours,

H. Leigh Baker, Principal

HLB:WS

National Honor Society membership letter from H. Leigh Baker

Earning the football letter earned a place in yet another activity. I
found this old memo tucked into a corner of Dad's photo album:

"As our star guard, you are required to bring to the gym Fri. nite these articles. (dressed for action.)

1__ 1 tube caposline

2__ 25# ice.

3__ 2 sheets of flypaper.

4__ 1 live sparrow.

5__ 4 apples.

You will wear on Fri. a girls gym suit, black stockens & tennis shoes.

You are to tell us Fri. morn what H. S. girl you got it from.

You are to carry a medicine ball. (GET at check room)"

I asked Dad about this little scrap of paper. I guessed right that it was a Blue M Letter Club initiation event. *Capsolin was the hottest stuff in the world! It was the father of Ben-Gay. You used it on sore muscles after you had bruised them, and they used it on me. They sat me on my cake of ice. If I complained about being cold, I stood up and they paddled my butt. Warmed it up.*

"So you mean bare butt?" I asked.

Yes, this whole thing was a stripped operation.

The medicine ball was a big ball. Heavy, but not air filled—a solid, soft ball.

I asked if he remembered whose gym suit he wore. *Alta Their. She lived in the Eureka Lake area. She was a popular girl and ran with our crowd.*

"Who was your crowd?"

The two Ramey girls—not twins but like twins—Edith and Marjorie, Alta, Thelma Holuba, Louise Rust, Virginia Peterson, Ivalee Hedge. Besides me, Dick McCord, Dick Fleming, Lisle Smelser, Bertrand "Bud" Harrop, Charles "Chuck" Robinson ...

He didn't remember the significance of the other items—the live sparrow, the flypaper, the apples.

In Dad's senior year, the 63-piece boys' band led one of the largest parades staged in Manhattan to that date. They also played at all home football games, prior to all basketball games, and the away game at Abilene in their first out-of-town trip. Dr. Donald Parrish, another Manhattan resident who played in the band several years after Dad, insists, "The band was the best band around. They used a shuffle step that no one else did and sounded like sandpaper coming down the road."

The so-called Oriental Band in their brilliant Chinese uniforms played at the American Royal Livestock Show in Kansas City. There were operettas; Dad always played in the orchestra. There were plays—Cousin Dick was in many of those. In "Passing of the Third Floor Back" Dick McCord played "Harry Larkcom, a cad"; Thelma Holuba (Dad's second wife) played "Miss Kite, a cat."

In 1928, Manhattan High won the Northeast Kansas orchestra contest. Besides Dad on oboe, my mother Ivalee Hedge played cello both in the high school and the composite Northeast Kansas orchestras.

At the Old Settlers Reunion in the gym given by the 1929 seniors for the junior class, the <u>Blue M</u> records: "Hal McCord was barred

69

from shooting arrows in the archery booth because he hit three bull's eyes in succession, and the stability of the target was rapidly decreasing." Dad was an excellent marksman. In college, he was on the rifle team and he would later earn his expert pistol (dismounted) rating in the military.

The Dating Game

Dating was not much done when Dad was in high school. The kids would *gather as a bunch.* Ken Olsen, whose father had the Ben Olsen Shoe Repair at 107 N. Fourth for years (and in my day a location on Moro in Aggieville), was a classmate of Dad's. *Louise Rust, Virginia Peterson and Ivalee Hedge were good friends and could be found together most of the time.* Rust's and Peterson's fathers were both faculty at KSAC; my mother's father, Noel Irvin "N. I." Hedge, was a partner in the Diehl-Hedge Furniture store. Dad said, *The whole high school turned out to donate blood when N. I. got leukemia.* My mother would lose her father when she was only 16.

There was some dating in college, especially during the summer. The crowd was generally a mixed group, though. They spent a lot of time in Aggieville, the student shopping area adjacent to the southeast corner of the campus. Popular hangouts were the Palace Drug, 704 N. Manhattan, that also had a downtown store, 112 S. Fourth—beside McCord Clothing, and College Drug, across the street from the Palace, then between Varney's Bookstore and the Campus Theater at 621 N. Manhattan Ave.

You could get a Coke or a 7-Up for a nickel then. A "400" was a chocolate milk drink in a small glass—the big glass was an "800" and cost ten cents. The Palace introduced the "Green River," a carbonated lemon-lime type beverage with green syrup and a cherry. The Campus Theater provided movies. Then and also through my own childhood and college years and beyond.

Manhattan was a great place to grow up. About 7,000 population. I knew everyone and everyone knew me, and liked me. You never had to lock a door. I could leave my bicycle in the yard.

It is still a great place to grow up. Bigger. With a population of around 40,000, Manhattan is the trade and cultural center of a five-county area. You should probably lock your doors and chain up your bicycle, but it is still a great place to grow up.

HAL'S PHOTO ALBUM

As Assembled by Oma

601 Thurston, Manhattan, Kansas—Jan. 25, 1912

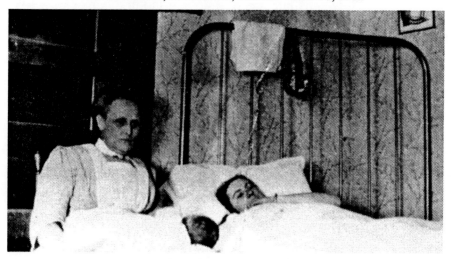

Davis the midwife, new baby Hal, Mother Oma McCord—Jan. 25, 1912

Grandmother Carrie Worrel and Baby Hal - 1912

73

Grandfather Leif Worrel and Baby Hal - 1912

Hal, Sr. and Hal, Jr. going for a bike ride - 1912

Hal, Sr. and Hal, Jr.: The hunting lesson—1912

Hal & Max, 601 Thurston, July 4, 1915

Vacation in Colorado Springs: Max, Oma, Hal (on pony) - 1915

Four Generations: Oma, Grandmother Carrie Worrel, Great-grandmother Hull; Max and Hal — Colorado Springs, 1915

The May Basket with a Pony

Popo and Hal, circa 1916

Hal and Popo at 601 Thurston

Hal spraying his Aunt Grace Worrel

Hal, learning to dive early—Wildcat Creek

Hal at Pillsbury Crossing, a popular picnic spot near Manhattan

Hal gathering daisies on Kimball property NW of Manhattan

First day of first grade; corner of 6th & Thurston—1918

First day of second grade, corner of 6th & Thurston—1919

First grade class at Bluemont Elementary School, 1918-19

Nora Hungerford, second grade teacher and Hal in front of Bluemont School

Grandmother Carrie Worrel and Hal, Bluemont Hill in background

Max, Hal, Sr. and Hal, Jr.—601 Thurston, south side

Marilyn McCord

Hal on bicycle with Bon—circa 1922

Max with a nice string of fish - 1504 Houston

A neighbor boy, dog "Bon," Max, Hal - 1504 Houston

McCord car advertising the clothing store, Hal posing inside, 4th of July parade

Boy Scout Hal salutes—1504 Houston in background

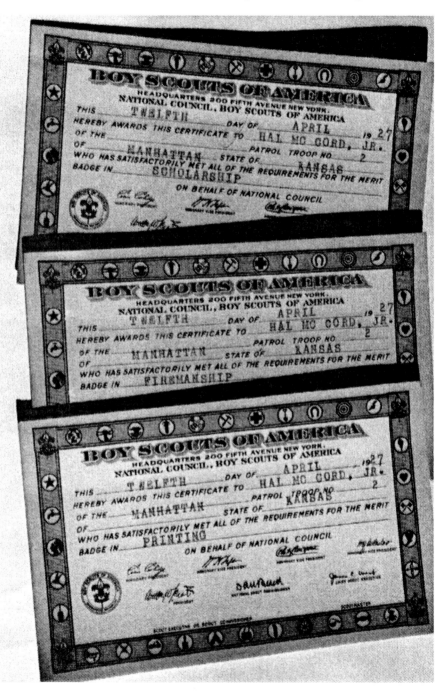

Three Boy Scout Merit badges earned by Hal, Jr.

Hal (left) and Russ Smith, lifeguards at the municipal pool—circa 1928

Hal with Laird Swallow—circa 1928

Hal (left) and J. H. Boyles with Laird Swallow—circa 1928

Hal letters in football - 1928

Hal's Senior Photo - 1929

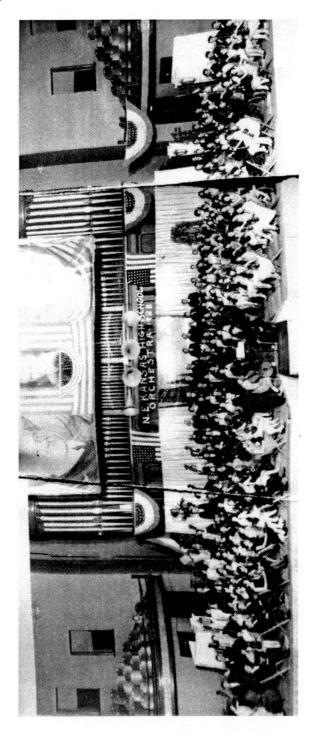

1928 NE Kansas Orchestra: Ivalee Hedge on cello, second row, right of podium; Hal McCord on oboe, center, four rows back of podium

Part Three:

Kansas State University and Marriage

Royal Purples

"Kansas State College, the first state school of higher education established in Kansas, has lived and grown for 'three score and ten' years." Founded in 1863 as the nation's first land-grant college, KSU now has a student body of around 20,000, four times the student body size when I graduated in 1961.

As I paged through Dad's 1933 Royal Purple, I was struck by all the faculty names I knew. This 25th edition yearbook was dedicated to J. T. Willard, the first K-State alum to become a faculty member. This 70th year of K-State marked Willard's 50th year of service to the college. He was then vice-president; Dr. Francis David Farrell was president. I would later have my chemistry classes in Willard Hall.

Margaret Justin was Dean of Home Economics in 1933. My mother had her office in Justin Hall when she was on the K-State faculty. Mother was once voted "favorite teacher," an honor she tossed off with a smile, saying, "Home Ec. students are probably more sensitive about voting for such distinctions."

Mary Van Zile was featured in the '33 yearbook. She began as a professor of domestic science in 1908 and became Dean of Home Economics when the divisions reorganized the following year. In 1912, she was also Dean of Women; that became her fulltime job in

1919. In 1926, she was instrumental in building the women's dormitory named after her. A young Kenny Ford was, in 1933, the executive secretary of the Alumni Association, a position he would occupy for years.

Alf Landon had just been elected governor of Kansas and had the tough job of providing more for less in depression times. The Royal Purple also had to do with less. The previous two yearbook issues had both lost money, so in 1933 the RP staff eliminated several organizations, individuals and activities that "ordinarily fail to pay for their space."

Rodney W. Babcock, who began in 1930 as the new dean of the division of General Science, was noted as "a mathematician and physicist, young, scholarly and genuinely interested in students, especially good students." Dr. Babcock later instructed one of my math classes.

From the 1931 Royal Purple: "Engineers received practical experience when the 'S' was laid alongside the 'K' in the spring of '30. Specialization was rampant. Crews mixed cement. Other groups taxied rocks to a new resting place in the 'S.' Freshman engineers complained when the time came for them to give the 'KS' a bath, but smiled while doing it." Dad participated in the party to add the 'S' to the hill overlooking Manhattan. He said they moved a five-sack mixer to the location, built the forms, moved rocks and mixed up the concrete. *All were quite pleased with the results. Putting in the 'S' made quite a difference.*[27]

In 1931, Dick McCord was president of the sophomore class and Maxine Roper was secretary, so the McCord cousins had 50 percent of the class offices that year. In 1932, Dick was a cheerleader and is pictured doing "the flying squirrel" for the cheering section, a move that I might have called the "spread eagle." The March 6, 1932 Manhattan Chronicle had a front page headline "Boom Boom Cast Selected." The program and principals of the Manhattan Theatre Musical Revue detailed 19 comedy acts with a central motif. The cast included Dick McCord and Alice Irwin. Dick, Alice and Maxine "Mackie" Roper were all favorite cousins of Dad's.

I found a page of photos in the 1932 Royal Purple called Campus Royalty. Photo Number 3 is identified as "Hal McCord." When I showed it to Dad, he looked long and hard at the photo, which did look like him, then commented, *That must be mislabeled. I never wore plus-fours.* The young man in the photo was wearing knickers, a sweater vest and a tie. Dad said he never wore that style of clothing. And clothing was the family income so he should know.

My Father's College Years

Dad commented on his extended family's association with the local college. *In Manhattan, pretty much everyone went to college in*

---

[27] For readers not familiar with Manhattan, "KS" hill is the hill above the Kansas River just east of town. The viaduct bridge across the river connects to the hill on its eastern side. This signature landmark is visible from most locations in the town and is extremely well known.

those days. I think all but one of the 23 first cousins in my family went to Kansas State at least some. Lora Irwin was retarded—we never knew why—and she was the only one who didn't attend some college classes. College was affordable and a key item in that area. The cost was $25 per semester matriculation fee.[28] *It was and still is a good value education for the money. There was wonderful cooperation between the town of Manhattan and the Kansas State faculty; they were really an integral part of the community rather than being a separate community. You knew everybody and everyone worked together.*

Dad majored in architectural engineering, "Ark-E," as my own son would later call it. Although Mother graduated in 1933 and Dad was a senior that year, he did not graduate until 1934. Dr. L. E. Conrad had him take some graduate level classes toward another degree, one in Civil Engineering. He remembers Dr. Conrad and Reed Morse as the additional instructors for that effort. *They were great.*

Dad had started his freshman year in straight architecture. One of Dad's architecture professors was Linus Burr Smith, who apparently, according to Dad, was determined to *bring culture to the provinces from Haw-vawd.* He was very demanding, but that was not the issue. Smith had given the students a problem to design a ferry landing, the slip and approach. The solution involved a lot of drawing board work and took nine 3-hour periods in the classroom. Preliminary sketches

---

[28]Tuition was up to $104/semester when I was an undergraduate from 1957-61. I worked in the Comptroller's Office and often helped with enrollment as well as with student and faculty insurance.

were required along with figuring out the structure to carry the traffic adequately and safely.

Smith was seldom in-house during class time. When Dad was 25 hours into the assignment, Smith finally looked at it. "Mr. McCord, nobody <u>ever</u> builds structures that size. You can start over." He took the drawings and tore the sheaf of papers in two. Dad was devastated. He took the torn hours of labor to Paul Weigel, the Dean of Architecture, and spilled out his frustration. That's when he switched majors.

For two years during college Dad worked at Varney's Book Store in Aggieville. *I swept out, unpacked books and worked with Ted Varney to acquire used books and put up the used book section. Ma Varney, Ted's mom, ran the place. She was a good businesswoman. I would sometimes get free samples, such as watermark paper, from the salesmen. They gave me some excellent paper I could use for drafting and projects requiring watercolors.* Varney's now takes up that entire block frontage on Manhattan Avenue plus another store on Moro for children's books. A dominant presence in Aggieville.

Acing Activities

My dad's list of activities in college was staggering. In fact, Dad remembers that Cotton Durland, then Assistant Dean of Engineering, had the Registrar send Hal's grades to him every six weeks for review. He would frequently call Hal in and counsel him. "If I'm not pleased with your grades, Hal, I'll confine you to study rather than let you be so heavily involved in activities."

M. A. "Cotton" and Lorna Durland were very good friends of Dad's parents, and they played in the same bridge club together. There were four tables that met every month for dessert and bridge with rotating hosts. Other bridge club members besides the McCords and the Durlands included Doc and Maude LaShelle (Dr. C. O. LaShelle was a dentist), Ruth and Lucian Hobbs (L. E. Hobbs was a veterinarian), Jimmy and Iva Ryan (James E. Ryan had a funeral home), Dick and Margaret Bennett (R. R. Bennett was the president of Citizen's National Bank), Dr. John and Nettie Peterson (Dr. J. C. Peterson was chairman of the Psychology Department at KSAC), and Walter and Faye Gage (Walter was the Riley County Attorney).

This bridge club group would often meet with their entire families for a day's outing at Lost Lake, a famous weekend recreational spot. Lost Lake was south of the Ashland Bridge in the Hunter's Island area. It was very sandy, and the level of the lake varied with the level of the Kansas River. Someone would package a basket of fried chicken, someone else potato salad. We'd have watermelons. Pitching horseshoes was a favorite pastime. Maybe Doc LaShelle owned it; he seemed to be the guy that gumshoed everything. They had two daughters—Goldie was the oldest, Marjorie was Max's age. Others besides the bridge club would be there, too. Ivalee Hedge, Louise Rust, Virginia Peterson. Families and kids. It was very congenial. The picnics were fantastic. It was excellent entertainment. There were sand plums in the same area, red, not too big. Dad and Mom would harvest those, and Mom would make some of the best preserves and jellies out of those.

On page 33 of the 1933 <u>RP</u> Dad was one of seven K-Staters on the student council. Members were elected every April for the following year. Nomination required 25 endorsees, then a ballot was made and a vote taken by the students. Ruth Stiles was another student council member. Dad remembers her as a *very attractive redhead from Kansas City,* and one of my mother's best friends and Alpha Xi Delta sorority sisters. Ruth later married one of Dad's favorite friends of those years, Sid Brady. I remember that Ruth and my mother participated in a round-robin letter writing that involved around a dozen Alpha Xi's. That letter circle lasted for more than 40 years.

Dad played oboe in the band every year, in the orchestra for three years, and was a member of the national music honorary, Phi Mu Alpha, organized to "advance the cause of music in America and in the Alma Mater." The double-reed oboe is difficult if not impossible to play while marching, so Dad played bass drum with the marching band under the direction of Lyle Downey. His sophomore year he was a member, and captain, of the Varsity Swimming Team. Besides the backstroke he did a lot of diving. I asked him what his best dive was. *The back flip. I also did a jack-knife, a back jack-knife and a gainer. I went for the higher point dives in competition yet tried to do an excellent job on all of them.* He also earned several intramural letters playing soccer, tennis, handball and swimming. *It was a miserable soccer game we usually had, hard body contact. Lisle Smelser and I were guards.*

Dad assisted in the Physical Education Department, was on the YMCA Board and its Activity Fund Budget Committee, and a member of Alpha Phi Omega, a national coed service-oriented fraternity partnered with, among others, the Boy Scouts of America. For three years he was treasurer of the Gargoyle Club, a group composed entirely of architecture students and organized for their support. I wondered if the selection of that name, Gargoyle, was any sort of reference to the self-images of architecture students back then.

Dad was also in many engineering honoraries including Sigma Tau, the national engineering honorary fraternity to which he was elected as a junior when most students were elected in their senior year. He belonged to Steel Ring; two representatives were elected from each engineering department and the organization "symbolizes the welding together of the seven departments" with membership limited to a very manageable 14. Hal was a member of Scabbard and Blade, national honorary military society for cadet officers. In ROTC, he was the lieutenant colonel of Battery "B" and he was on the rifle team.

He worked on the Engineering Open House Committee years 2-3-4. His fourth year he was on the military sub-committee; on the monthly periodical the <u>Kansas State Engineer</u> his junior year; on the Engineering Council his senior year; and was secretary of the K-State Engineering Association.

Oma usually kept two or three girls during the Greek rush week as a favor to her friend, Ruth Hobbs, a Kappa. The girls otherwise would have had to find a place to live for that one week as they planned to move into whichever sorority they ended up pledging as soon as that association was formalized.

Dad, of course, loved this. There was a flute player from McPherson, Helen Pickrell–a niece of Walter and Faye Gage, members of his parent's bridge group, and Eugenia Leighton. They both pledged Kappa Kappa Gamma. He also said, *They were good kids, smart kids. Otherwise they would not have been in rush. Ruth told me not to influence them. I was proud of Mom for boarding them. But the Kappas didn't have a particularly high regard for the Kappa Sigs.*

Dad said of several of the pretty young girls ... *and I was in love with her.* He told me he saw Helen after his graduation ceremony. He had already given his fraternity pin to my mother, who was gone that year, and Helen asked him, "Why didn't you wait?" *You open some doors and you close others.* One little change and the rest of your life is different.

Kappa Sigma Sagas

Kappa Sigma fraternity was, and still is, important to Dad. His younger brother Max was also a Kappa Sig. My father and my uncle would both exemplify the Kappa Sigma motto: "The sun never sets on a Kappa Sig." Dad said he was the *GMC*—Grand Master of Ceremonies. I asked if that meant he got to deliver the secret handshake. He chuckled.

I suppose so. I was a townie so didn't stay in the house. It was a long walk from 1504 Houston to the campus. The other guys were probably glad of that. I did have bids from other fraternities. Hurst Majors was a Kappa Sig and influenced me greatly. Lisle Smelser pledged Kappa Sig also; we were very good friends.

He remembers Mother Amis (Mrs. J. W. Amis) as *a fine lady and a very good house mother*. The Kappa Sig house was then at 519 North 11th Street. The 1931 <u>RP</u> had a section called The New Yorker Shorts and Hee Haws:

"Kappa Sigma seems to have made up their (sic) mind that they are going to make a place on the hill for themselves, one way or another, and they don't seem to care whether this place is famous or notorious. A few members and the annual Roughneck party event have somewhat successfully achieved this latter distinction."

And again…

"In good old Kappa Sigma language, the party was a 'fair go' and 'plenty slick.' It seems to be their idea of an honor because they delight in broadcasting the fact that they nearly got kicked out of school."

From the similar *Razzberry* section at the end of the '33 <u>RP</u>:

"The [Kappa Sigma] pledges, from the start, mind you, are instructed to seek their rendition on the parlor harpsichord. … the boys lost their rushing privileges this year by concealing some Phi Sig and Sig Alf prospects in their basement, so they immediately put in a bin full of Johnathans and waited for the trouble to blow over. This saved half the male populace of Centralia from Kappa Sigmaism."

Still quoting from the *Razzberry* section:

"Among the notable Kappa Sigs are the Hancks boys from Wamego. They startled the conservative element of the school by wearing bull-necked sweaters (turtlenecks) to formal parties. Two months afterward every fraternity man this side of Fourth Street had a duplicate of the Hancks boys' garment."

One cartoon indicates the Kappa Sigs would hold "many open houses each year: one in September for new students to raise money for the rent; several later with the sororities, to raise their social standing." Dad was the Kappa Sig representative along with E. F. Peterson from Yates Center to the Freshmen Men's Panhellenic Council.

Strong Family Ties to Kansas State

Our family love Kansas State. We have a long history of involvement with the university, and my children are fourth-generation K-Staters. My mother was on the faculty in the Family and Child Development Department for 20 years, 1957-1977. I have three degrees from Kansas State: BS in Mathematics—graduating summa cum laude; MS in Curriculum & Instruction; and MS in Computer Science.

My sister Janice has a degree in Modern Languages—German—from K-State and had nearly completed a master's degree in linguistics when her husband of three months, also a K-Stater, was tragically killed in an auto accident just off campus.

My uncle, Lawrence Hedge, also a K-Stater, was a member of Sigma Alpha Epsilon fraternity, a pilot and a practical jokester. As an undergraduate, he and his buddy Harry Wareham made several flights over the campus of rival school Kansas University located at Lawrence. On one of those flights they draped the KU Bell Tower with toilet paper. Another time, more destructively, they poured K-State-Purple paint around the campus.

Dad said, *Lawrence was a gay blade. He had a good voice—sang in a quartet, was probably in the 1928 "Mikado" production on campus.*

My brother Don's wife, Ann, from Stafford, Kansas, transferred from Phillips University in Enid, Oklahoma, to Kansas University—K-State's arch-rival—to complete her nursing degree. She has never heard the end of it, being a Jayhawker, the KU mascot.

Ann's brother, Dale Hunter, gave Ann a little stone Jayhawk several years ago, personally hand-carried in his lap on a flight to visit them in Chicago. When Don's and Ann's then three-year-old granddaughter Emma was visiting, the child went into the garden, saw the Jayhawk, and inquired, "What's with the *duck*?" We just won't let that one die.

During the 1980s while I was working for the Geophysical Service Inc. (GSI) subsidiary of Texas Instruments, I represented GSI on the K-State campus. Employers coveted K-State graduates—"they have such a great work ethic"—and I participated in several recruitment efforts.

Students in computer science, engineering, math, geology and geophysics were our targets. The trick was to ascertain which students were actually willing to leave Kansas and relocate to Dallas <u>before</u> we paid their way down for a site visit.

I remember SWE (Society of Women Engineers) Career Fairs and a couple of Engineering Open House events, one in particular. A GSI colleague, also a K-State Computer Science graduate with whom I shared some classes, and I took our materials for a "show and tell" exhibit at the Open House. I had in my suitcase a four-foot section of the cable towed behind the GSI boats, a two-to-three-mile long cable that was used to record sounding reflections from the ocean floor. This section featured a cut-away and revealed the interior electronics. Boy, did we confound the airport security folks! "What in the world have you got in that suitcase, lady?"

Growing Up With KSAC

When I grew up in Manhattan, Kansas State was then known as KSAC. Kansas State Agricultural College. We three McCord children lived at 1413 Laramie, a house then owned by our maternal grandmother, a block away from campus and a block from Aggieville.

What a great location! We were always interested in what happened on campus and thoroughly enjoyed the annual homecoming activities and walking the rounds to see all the fabulous homecoming house decorations.

The annual Engineers Open House with all its exhibits was especially thrilling to my brother Don. The Artist Series concerts always brought wonderful talent to our campus.

We knew the campus buildings, the grounds and many of the special places. The formal rose gardens with reflecting pools and Kansas wildflowers around the edges and its many native species of plants. We learned to buy great ice cream cones at the dairy barn. We visited the second floor of Fairchild Hall that housed a natural history exhibit with stuffed animals and birds, some of which I have now learned were donated by my great-uncles. The great horned owl with his tufted ears and the slender bobcat were my favorites, though I often wished the owl could turn his head and blink his big eyes and the bobcat would show off with a graceful pounce. I am not a hunter and dislike guns. A camera is my weapon of choice.

I took piano lessons from Robert Hayes through the eighth grade. That's when we moved to Nebraska for three years when Mother taught at Wayne State Teachers College during 1954-57. I was never that good on the piano and would often try to make up for lack of skill with my memorization ability. I had to watch where my fingers were going in something like a Bach two-part invention, which was probably the epitome of my piano progress.

Like many others in my day, I slid down the spiral fire escape at the old KSAC auditorium where Mr. Hayes had his office on the second floor near the entry to the slide. Just lift the window and step down. Sometimes we would use wax paper in attempts to polish the slide and improve its aerodynamic characteristics. Don remembers playing ditch-em in the trees, towers and fire escapes of the campus.

My sister Janice is the best musician of the three children in my family. She believes that music is the soul of life. She still plays piano, organ and cello doing them all justice. In concert band she played the tympani; in high school marching band she was a twirler then drum major. Her teachers were all K-State faculty members.

Jean Hedlund, wife of the band director Gene, was Janice's first real piano teacher. Taking lessons from our Grandmother Hedge, who taught piano as a profession, apparently didn't count in our young minds. Mother once asked Janice how old Mrs. Hedlund was. Elementary-school age Janice responded, "Oh, middle aged." Mrs. Hedlund was then 26.

Janice then studied piano and organ under Marian Pelton. Whenever Janice visited our mother at Meadowlark Retirement Center in recent years, she always visited Miss Pelton as well. During her college years, Janice was organist at the First Baptist Church in Manhattan. In graduate school she gave an organ recital concert that one of the music professors, Dr. Thomas Stuenenberg[29], called "the best student performance he had ever attended."

---

[29] When I asked Janice what Dr. Stuenenberg's first name was, she laughed and said "I always just called him by his first name: 'Doctor'."

Warren Walker was her cello teacher, and they are still in contact. Janice played her cello for our mother's memorial services at First Christian Church in February of 2001. The *Intermezzo Sinfonico* from "Cavalleria Rusticana" by Mascagni has been played for many special occasions in our family, including this celebration of the completed life of our mother. Warren attended and Janice pressed him for some useful cello tips afterwards.

We learned many of the trees around campus by reading the little plaques that identified them. This was a catalpa tree, that was a ginkgo, and so on. We remember building snowmen and snow women on campus. Once, some college students were building a stunning Victorian snow lady. She had a hat, a muff and a bustle and her long skirt flowed down in carefully sculpted snow curves. The snow artists let us add bits of snow and make some strategic pats, so we became members of the building team. Our usual childish snow people were much less elegant than this snowy-cold dame.

The Children's Storybook Parade

On Saturday mornings we would go up to the KSAC radio station, which was established Dec. 1, 1924, located on the third floor of Nichols Gym.[30] Don, Janice, Skipper, our Cocker Spaniel, and I were regulars on the hour-long "Children's Storybook Parade." Once we even showed up on a Saturday morning when the temperature outside

---

[30] Nichols was later destroyed by fire, but the castle-like shell retained and the interior rebuilt.

was 20° below zero. The director, Miss Marian Kirkpatrick, was sure no children would come, but there we were, bundled up to the hilt.

The program was broadcast across Kansas, and we had a certain fan club following around the State. Miss Kirkpatrick would initiate conversations with the children and we would sing songs and act out many different children's stories. Don was perhaps best known for being Peter Pan—"I want always to be a little boy and to have fun ..." Skipper would bark on cue and do tricks, such as sit-up that we would describe to the radio audience. Miss Kirkpatrick later taught ninth grade English at Manhattan Junior High, though to our mutual disappointment I moved away just as I was ready to enter ninth grade.

Nichols Gym—from a set of postcards with 1929 postmark, courtesy of Dad's friend Joe Mobley

The Children's Storybook Parade. Marian Kirkpatrick, director, at left back, near banner. Beginning at lower right: Don McCord, dog Skipper, Marilyn to his left, Janice in the middle with braids. At KSAC radio studio, third floor of Nichols Gym, circa 1948.

K-State's Basketball Glory Days

In the 1950-51 school year, I was smitten with the entire Kansas State basketball team. Coach Jack Gardner used a two-platoon system, so there were at least 10 outstanding players. I knew them all.

Lew Hitch[31] was the 6' 7" center. Ernie Barrett was an all-American guard and later Athletic Director at KSU. Jack Stone broke

---

[31] Lew was later on staff with my first husband, Ed Dillinger; they opened up Wichita Heights High School in 1961. And yes, there may be a family relationship to the infamous bank robber, John Dillinger. Once, when I boarded a bus in Chicago with my name-identified suitcase, a fellow passenger quipped, "And what's in that

a school individual game scoring record with 29 points against Illinois. Jim Iverson was the shortest man on the starting line-up and had the best free-throw average. Bob Rousey was voted outstanding sophomore of the Big Seven. Ed Head helped Lew control the backboards. Defensive ace "Hoot" Gibson was known for stealing the ball and also for pulling down rebounds. Hoot's fraternity's backyard adjoined ours, so getting an autograph from him for my scrapbook was easy.

Ernie Barrett was also easy to find as his future wife Bonnie lived in the Alpha Chi Omega annex housed at my friend, Janet Krider's.[32] Other autographs were a bit harder to come by, and I wasn't above knocking on the front door of the Sigma Alpha Epsilon house to see if Bob Rousey, my personal favorite, was in and would sign my latest newspaper clippings.

For my birthday that year the only thing I wanted was a ticket to the K-State vs. K.U. basketball game. When there was none to be had, my mother magically found one. Jack Gardner's son Jimmy was in my class at Eugene Field, but I don't know if that factored into the equation. Ecstatic with my birthday present ticket, I attended the game and stomped on the bleachers in old Nichols Gym with the rest.

The away game with K.U. later was also particularly exciting, a last-minute thriller. "Big Lew" stole the ball from Jayhawker star Clyde Lovellette to tie it up, then Barrett hit one of his famous 30-

---

suitcase, lady?" My daughter-in-law, whose last name is Dillinger, named her Labrador "John."

[32] Janet's father, Alden Krider, was in the Architecture Department at KSU. Janet was my best summer swimming buddy.

footers. Free throws by Iverson and Gibson clinched the victory. We were glued to the radio and cheering like mad.

When that splendid team lost to Kentucky 68-58 in the NCAA finals that spring, the faithful fans nevertheless turned out a large crowd in drizzling rain to welcome them home and express appreciation for such a wonderful season. The reception was held at the old auditorium, later burned by vandals and replaced by McCain Auditorium. The team was lined up on the auditorium stage. I went all the way from the back of the building, which seemed huge to me, and up the stairs to the stage to shake the hand of each one. The top of my head barely reached Lew Hitch's belly button. When I asked for yet another autograph, Ernie Barrett's comment was, "I waste more pencils this way ..."

I adored them all. Brother Don also remembers that the Manhattan High sports team members had the opportunity to do ushering and so get into K-State games. It was easier to get into the nearly empty football stadium than the crowded basketball arena in those days.

Flight Connections

I did not know until recently that Lloyd Stearman attended Kansas State College during 1917-18, studying engineering and architecture. World War I interrupted his studies when he enlisted in the US Navy Reserve Flying Corps. After the war, he returned to Wichita and the site of the first commercial airplane company, E. M. Laird Co., that was then turning out the Laird Swallows that Dad flew as a teenager. Stearman hired on with them as an airplane mechanic.

Another Laird employee, Walter Beech, taught Stearman the finer points of piloting. By 1925, Stearman and Beech teamed up with Clyde Cessna to incorporate the Travel Air Manufacturing Co. A year later Stearman went to California and formed his own company, the Stearman Aircraft Co. but brought it back to Wichita in 1927.

There were a lot of permutations in companies and associations that included Boeing, Lockheed, Hammond, the Bureau of Air Commerce (forerunner of the FAA), Transair, Harvey Machine Corp, National Aircraft Corp. and others. Stearman's planes have flown countless hours training military pilots worldwide and doing agricultural tasks such as crop dusting. I love seeing the old Stearmans still flown at air shows.

The 1931 <u>Royal Purple</u> yearbook reported that "The first glider built on the hill was a success; it flew."

Dad educated me on his early interest in the military, shared by his brother and a cousin, Landon. Another cousin, Fred Irwin, served in WWI in France after enlisting in the Signal Corps at the completion of his freshman year in engineering at K-State.

Beginnings of a Military Career

There were three McCords who took engineering at Kansas State. Landon "Mick" McCord,[33] Eleanor's big brother, was the first McCord to be cadet colonel of the ROTC regiment there. I came along some time later and I too was cadet colonel of the K-State regiment. Four years later, Max, my younger brother, came through, also took engineering and also became cadet colonel of the regiment.

Camp Training Certificate
Reserve Officers' Training Corps

This is to certify that *Mr. Hal H. McCord, Jr.*

member of the *Coast Artillery* Division, Reserve Officers, Training Corps,
has successfully completed the *Coast Artillery Advanced* course
at this camp, from *June 17*, 1932, to *July 28*, 1932.
Remarks *Marksman – Rifle; Sharpshooter – Pistol*

Headquarters *Ft. Sheridan, Ill.* R. O. T. C. Training Camp,
July 28, 1932

W. D., A. G. O. Form No. 189
June 18, 1924

F. C. BOLLES *Brig. Gen. Hdl.*
Commanding

C. A. Chapman
Major. Cav. (AO) Executive

ROTC Training Certificate from Camp Sheridan—1932

---

[33] Landon was a son of Will and Ellen McCord. He was commissioned as a first lieutenant honor graduate in the Army and died of self-inflicted .45 wounds in Panama in 1929.

We all had a military interest and background. I got my commission as a second lieutenant the first of June in 1933 at the age of 21.

I had worked pretty hard on the military end of it. The summer between my junior and seniors years at KSU, I was assigned to the 61st Coast Artillery Anti-Aircraft (CAA) and I attended a 30-day session that trained at Fort Sheridan, Illinois. After graduation, I tried to get into West Point but was then too old for the entry class and gave up on it at the time. My dad, however, was a good friend of Charles Curtis, the Vice President of the United States.[34] Through his connections I later got an appointment, but again I was too old to enter the Academy when the vacancy was available. So, West Point was out. As a second lieutenant, I was sure there was a possibility I could make some sort of a military career with the regular Army in active assignments.

The last year of college I worked as an assistant to the Riley County Engineer in the design and construction of county bridges. Right out of college, I got a job with Mont J. Green, a contractor in Manhattan, Kansas. Mont was the person who had talked me into going into architecture. Once when I had lunch with my dad and Mont, Dad said to Mont, "I thought today was fish day." To which Mont, a Catholic, replied, "Yes, but my stomach's a damn protestant." They were eating ham.

---

[34] Curtis, a Kansan, served under Herbert Hoover from 1929-1933. His great-grandmother was a Native American from the Kaw tribe.

I worked for Mont for a year. In my first job, I was a junior superintendent for the State Hospital project in Winfield, Kansas. The next contracting job assigned had me working with the Kansas State Highway Commission. Specifically, it was the bridge department, out of Topeka, helping in the design of a conservation project in northeast Kansas. It was a special overpass-type, flow-through for the Walnut Creek Dam, and we had to sign our names on the end of the design sheets. I would later get a chance in the Civilian Conservation Corps to work on that project I had designed.

Courtship and Marriage

During the summers Ivalee Hedge and I would date. During the winter, the school year, we would date others. There was a Delta Tau Delta whom Ivalee dated quite a bit, which made me very unhappy. So, when I was cadet colonel of the ROTC in my senior year, I decided to get back at Ivalee. I invited Winifred Wolf to be my date for the Military Ball. Winifred was also an Alpha Xi Delta. I had a corsage and when I went to pick Winifred up, the Alpha Xi's arranged for Ivalee to be the one to answer the doorbell. It was a dirty trick, and they assisted me in pulling it off. Our relationship was overshadowed by the military even then.

Before Ivalee left to teach at Syracuse for the 1933-34 school year, I had given her my fraternity pin. That was as good as an engagement ring then. The official pinning ceremony took place at the Alpha Xi house after the Sunday noon meal. My father had written a special poem that I read to her—he did an absolutely super job on many poems. Ivalee had that pin a long time. We thought that maybe a maid took it when we were living at Randolph Field in the early 1940s.

The year Ivalee was in Syracuse her brother-in-law, Herbert Schwardt,[35] was a faculty member at the University of Arkansas at Fayetteville. I managed to hitchhike to Fayetteville to see Ivalee during spring break in 1934. Well, I hitchhiked to within 30 miles, then phoned them, and they came to pick me up.

Family of the Bride

My Grandfather Hedge had directed the choir at church in Norton, Kansas, and Grandmother Hedge played piano and gave piano lessons. They moved to Manhattan in 1922. The family store located at 304 Poyntz Avenue was simply Hedge Furniture then. It became Diehl-Hedge sometime prior to 1929. Several years after my grandfather's death the store would become Diehl Furniture.

My grandmother's maiden name was Bower—Maude LaBelle Bower—also spelled Baur and Bauer in past generations. She was the only girl among seven brothers; she was born along the way to Kansas from Ohio in 1879 in a covered wagon. All of the seven brothers were embalmers and most also were in the furniture business across the state of Kansas.

---

[35] Herbert received the first Ph. D. in entomology ever awarded at Kansas State. Dad says he did a tremendous project on box turtles. Uncle Herbert was later head of the entomology department at Cornell University in Ithaca, NY.

Her father, my great-grandfather, W. J. Bower of Norton, had a furniture-mortuary-hardware business. He helped found the Norton Christian Church, went around the state producing cantatas, and in 1912 was elected President of the Kansas Funeral Directors Association. The 1932 <u>Manhattan Chronicle</u> contained an ad that had to represent some part of my mother's family:

W. H. Bower – Undertaker

Coffins & Caskets of all sizes

and prices constantly on hand.

Tombstones furnished.

Furniture Repaired!!

Pictures Framed.

303 Poyntz Ave.

On July 7, 1934, my dad and my mother, Ivalee Beryl Hedge,[36] were married in her mother's neighbor's backyard, 222 South 17th Street in Manhattan. The Hedge's lived at 216 S. 17th Street. My mother used to say, "The seventh day of the seventh month, Saturday—the seventh day of the week, at 7 o'clock in the evening,

---

[36] My mother was born June 14, 1911 in Norton, KS. After my parents were divorced and after the children were grown, my mother in 1979 married Glenn W. Long, a retired KSU sociology professor. Glenn died in 1990. Although she had hoped to die like her mother, Maude Hedge, who walked six blocks to church the morning of the day she had a coronary, Mother died at Meadowlark's Health Care in Manhattan January 27, 2000 after several years with increasing Alzheimer's symptoms. I believe that the death of her oldest grandson, Paul McCord—my brother Don's son—in a blizzard in Alaska in 1996 affected her greatly.

and the year, '34, adds to seven." She used to think that was lucky. Lucky sevens.

Ivalee and Hal's wedding, July 7, 1934—backyard of 222 S. 17th Street

It was a garden wedding with Mother in a long pale pink dress and a large pale blue picture hat. She looked lovely, and my dad looked so handsome. Rev. J. David Arnold read the ceremony amid arrangements of peonies and ferns. Music was by a string trio. Mother's sister, Bernice Schwardt, sang two numbers. Esther Smiley and Merle Mark, sorority sisters, were bridesmaids; Dad's younger brother Max was best man. Cousins and friends assisted with greeting, ushering and serving.

The next noon Grandmother Hedge hosted a bridal dinner in her home for close family and a few friends, especially those who were from out of town.

"Mr. and Mrs. McCord will be at home in Winfield."

A Casualty of War

It's a shame that events conspired to break this team up in later years. They both had so much to bring to a family. Joining their separate gifts would have made the combination very powerful; one plus one would have equaled more than two.

I always figured that our family was another casualty of the war years. My mother did not enjoy being a military wife. In those days she was a teetotaler. I suspect that the military wives' milieu in which she found herself was just not her thing.

She played an excellent game of bridge. In fact, she was often the partner with whom I would score the best. Certainly not afraid to redouble, and she generally made her bid. However, she would tell of holding a single glass in her hand for hours at a cocktail party to avoid having someone continually refilling it. She was bright, talented, energetic and probably needed her own career, and additionally, my father was gone most of the time. In fact, when he returned from the War in 1946, I remember my sister Janice, then not quite three years old, saying, "Mommy, who's that nice man?" She didn't even know her own father.[37]

Mother's mother, my Grandmother Hedge was, I think, overprotective and never thought my father was good enough for her little girl. Remember that her husband, N. I. Hedge, died of leukemia when my mother was 16. In addition, my mother was her baby. Of the six children born, only three survived to adulthood.

Mother has told us about her hydrocephalic little sister who died at the age of two and was carried around in a basket because she couldn't hold up her over-sized head. After these losses, I can understand my grandmother wanting to hold on to what was left. Even though parents need to let go.

Ivalee accelerated her high school studies and started college early. She finished ahead of Hal, who took an extra year. After graduation, she left to teach school at Syracuse University in New York. Grandmother Hedge went with her. Dad stayed that year in

---

[37] I live 800 miles from the nearest of my grandchildren; the farthest two grandchildren are now in a remote Alaskan village. I think my children are smarter about managing physical separation than my mother was. My children keep photos of me on the refrigerator so that the grandchildren see my picture regularly. And they talk about me, so when I phone, the grandchildren know who I am. Granted, long distance phoning was a big deal when I was a child.

Manhattan and worked on a Master's degree in civil engineering. He earned extra credits but not the degree.

He later earned an MBA at Eastern New Mexico University in Portales, New Mexico, in 1966 and a Master's in engineering management at the University of Missouri in Rolla, Missouri in 1973. Although he had 44 hours toward a Ph.D., he never completed the work or the dissertation.

Dad received the same advice I would later hear. "Unless you want to teach in a university, don't bother. The Ph.D. will only price you out of the jobs you really want to do. Unless you are driven or want the degree simply for the ego boost..." He admitted that it did bother him some that Ivalee finally earned her Ph.D. and he didn't. There's that competitive drive again.

After my parents were married, *Mother Hedge* moved in with them for several months. *A mother hen with her favorite chick,* said Dad. Their housing was one-half of a duplex in Winfield, Kansas, where Dad was working in construction for a state institution. Including utilities it cost $15 a month. They drove my grandmother's car.

My father corroborated that the continual presence and bad press he got was a definite factor in making it difficult for him to stay. He was a believer in setting clear limits with his children, and his mother-in-law had her own ideas on discipline. It made for an uncomfortable situation.

However, I have never heard him say an unkind word about my mother. In fact, he recently told me, *I loved Ivalee. I always loved*

Ivalee. I still do. In spite of all—and there is a lot of all—I believe him. He said that the real difficulties in the marriage began only after he returned from overseas. *The war cost me that family.* I believe that, too. Just because we love someone doesn't mean we don't hurt them deeply and irreconcilably.

After Winfield came a job in Topeka with the State Highway Department. Then the CCCs followed by the war. By 1948, Dad was working in Topeka for Servis and Van Doren, an engineering firm. Home only on weekends. *Commuting was not an option.*

In 1951, he returned to active duty from the Reserves and was off to Washington, D.C. and an office in the Pentagon. *There was no possibility of NOT accepting that. Cal Phillips said, "I'll give you 30 days to get here.*

The passion that was not poured into a family was transferred to a job and eventually into a second family. There was an eight-year period of my life, 1952-1960, when I would not see my father once. I do remember a gift of wine corduroy fabric he sent me that my Grandmother McCord made into a lovely jumper. I wore it with a soft pink sweater.

There was an interval when Mother, out of a combination of anger and depression, sort of went into a funk. One of her old-maid friends reminded her that, unlike her situation, Mother had three wonderful children. Mother snapped out of her despair, decisively took charge of her life and again became the warm, responsive parent we had known and always loved. Being a single mom is not easy, but she did it with style.

The summer after I completed my first year at K-State, 1958, Mother began work at Purdue University, receiving her Ph.D. in 1961. Not many women received Ph.D.s in those days, much less those just turning 50. She retired from the Family and Child Development Department at K-State in 1977 after many contributions to early childhood education. In addition to being the director of the laboratory nursery school at KSU, she had a hand in many other projects and published articles in several home economics journals.

She was president of the National Home Economics Association one year, on the President's Council for Fitness and Youth, overseer of an Air Force preschool started at Randolph Field, and regularly visited many of her students in the field across the state of Kansas. Her three children set up a scholarship at Kansas State University in her name when she was still able to appreciate that honoring of her efforts on behalf of children. It is known as the Ivalee McCord Long Scholarship in Human Ecology.

Sometimes I wonder how my life would have been different if I had been able to be a part of a two-parent family. Would Dad have taught me how to fly? Might I have gone into a different career? I'm sure I would have known my cousins and extended family much better than I did, although Mother did keep in touch with some members of Dad's family the rest of her life. Certainly my images of the role of a father would have been vastly more concrete, hopefully more positive than the negativism intimated by my mother and grandmother. It would have been so much easier for Mom to have had Dad's help. The way it was, it was painful for everyone.

Growing up, the subtle tension between my two grandmothers, both of whom lived in Manhattan, was so heavy you often could have cut it with a knife. They were jealous and territorial. I sometimes wondered if they timed us in the amount of a vacation that we spent with one versus the other. But life is too short for regrets, and I really have none. I have heard two different tellings of reasons. The accounting of each of my parents is definitely their own personal true story. The real truth is probably both and neither. And it no longer matters.

Part Four:

Civilian Conservation Corps (1935-1938) and Flight Training (1940-1943)

The Civilian Conservation Corps was my entrée to a military assignment. I was in the Cs for the better part of three years, including commanding the Headquarters Company at Ft. Leavenworth, Kansas.

Years in the Cs

Camp 728, Indian Trails State Park, east of Salem, Missouri

1 September 1935 to 8 February 1936

Part of Franklin Roosevelt's conception in developing the depression era Civilian Conservation Corps (CCC) was that you should make do with what you had. Those were tough years for a depression-weighted country and a dust-bowl-plagued Midwest. Sometimes I wonder how we did all that. I was a commander, a new ROTC graduate with a commission. My fellow officer and I, both military types in uniform, peers, were on our own, making it up as we went.

It was critical that the two of us worked well together and complemented each other. When I discovered that just wasn't going to happen satisfactorily, I asked Ft. Leavenworth, headquarters for the Missouri/Kansas district, for a transfer for my junior officer and got an excellent replacement. Ivalee, my wife of less than a year, joined me in Salem, Missouri, and I could see her every other weekend. But during the week I lived in and supervised the administration of the camp.

Our administrative staff included an educational adviser, a general practitioner doctor, technical staff and itinerant inspection staff. The technical staff members all were young chaps out of Cornell University. They supervised the work staff in tasks such as decisions about road service, location of fire lanes and so on. The inspection staff was primarily composed of WWI veterans who were senior officers; they would do things like audit the camp expense accounts. The pay was room, board and clothing plus $30 per month; $25 was sent home to the family and $5 went to the young men in the camp. We had a sort of commissary where the kids could spend part of their monthly allotment on items such as shaving equipment and candy bars. We had to teach them how to keep the books.

It was quite a period and the program developed a good bunch of kids. Training included discipline, reading and writing, and trade skills for the 270 youngsters that made up a camp. There were many different types of CCC camps: soil conservation, earth dam building, forestry, public works. The work solved the potentially serious personnel problem by giving the kids something productive to do. We were organized into groups with good training and a job to be done. The kids learned how to handle trucks, bulldozers and other construction equipment.

Our barracks were tar paper shacks, 20 men to a shack, folding army cots for beds. We had a common shower and common latrine facilities. Mosquitoes were a problem.

Breakfast came early. We worked until noon, then broke for lunch. After lunch, we would finish work and after the evening meal it was time for games. For fun we had a baseball team and competed with other camps. Movies provided entertainment many nights—16 mm films. We designated a film-master to run and change our well-patched supply. Some were training films, some educational and some entertainment and music.

There were rules and regulations. One rule was "don't generate any babies." Medical care for wives was not provided, and it took a special leave to be able to be present for the birth of a child. Since I was on military active duty, the rules were a bit different for me. Near Christmas time that year Ivalee said, "Hal, I want a baby ..." Donald Hal arrived in Manhattan, Kansas, almost exactly nine months later, on August 26, 1936, Oma's birthday.

Our monthly shipment came from the quartermaster at Ft. Leavenworth. We had to submit a menu for 30 days in advance and put in our order: so many sacks of potatoes and flour, so many sides of beef. It was fascinating to figure out which kids had the moxie to cook and then train them. I remember signing inventories for shipments—china, utensils, several trucks, other equipment and supplies. Salem was at a railhead and carloads of items would come in from Leavenworth at a time.

We were set up so those on the administrative staff ate at a separate table but ate the same food as the kids were served. A nutritionist wrote the menus, and we had some guidance from the home economists at universities such as Kansas State. The kids learned how to set up and how to use each utensil and piece of dinnerware, heavy-duty military-type china. Sometimes the lessons were pretty primitive as some kids had zero experience with these items. The food service was interesting. Hog jowls and corn pone appeared on the menu with regularity. I remember the first time we served grapefruit, one young man commented, "Lew-ten-ant, I like that grapefruit but those rinds are certainly bitter."

It was extremely fine training for those of us on the administrative staff. Very diverse. I'm sure these experiences were helpful to me later when I served as chief of staff personnel with the US Army Air Corps during WWII in the USA and overseas. We sometimes had to play god—judge, jury and hangman. Though we were in uniform we had to exercise reasonable restraint as we were also surrogate parents. It was our job to keep the kids out of trouble.

For example, at Ft. Leavenworth some kids were visiting the red light district in Kansas City. We had to help the few doctors we had to make sure medical problems such as VD were suitably served. Another time, during a shakedown inspection, we found a tow sack or gunnysack full of knives and brass knuckles. The kid knew how to use them, too. We couldn't have that. Good discipline was essential. The kids themselves really took care of anyone who didn't shower adequately. Offenders were given a good washing with a harsh brush and harsh soap and scrubbed down but good.

Our camp was filled with 18 to 26-year-old kids from the Ozarks. Many of them had never worn shoes before. Most could not read or write. We had to teach them to sign their name—trace it out—so they could sign the payroll. One young man had an aunt in Poplar Bluff and he wanted to write her a postcard. He asked me to help him with some spelling. "Lew-ten-ant, how do you spell we-unses? Like, we-unses is goin' somewhar?" It was sometimes a completely different language to me. Another young man remarked, "Why should I learn to read and write? They ain't nobody at home what kin read and write, so who'm I goin' to write to?"

From the <u>Manhattan Republic,</u> Nov. 7,1935, p.2

"MCCORD DIRECTS CCC WORK

"…He has the job planning the menu for the camp along with his other work. He is also teaching classes in charcoal drawing and sculpturing in accordance with the educational work in CCC camps.

"McCord writes that his camp is located in Indian Trail state park and that their work is building two lakes, three large houses, and miles of roads."

Our first assignment at Salem was to build the park and recreational facilities at the State Park, but our camp was primarily a forestry camp. The kids did a good job; they were used to working in the forest. In that part of the Ozarks, it was common to do a burn in the spring to eliminate weeds. With the lack of rain during those years, we were tired of having to fight the fires that got away from the folks starting them.

There were some squatters in the area with a couple of cows and some minor livestock. They lived off the land. One night, we caught someone torching the dry grass in the national forest. We ended up not being able to prosecute; we couldn't get a jury because in that area everyone was kinfolk.

One of my young truck drivers was bound and determined to keep his elbow out the window, an unfortunate decision for him. One day he was driving across a narrow bridge in a fairly congested area and a hayrack came by. A bolt extended from the wagon. It caught his arm, breaking the arm and tearing out the elbow, and we had an emergency situation.

Later, it was my responsibility to tell his folks about the accident. "Don't wear a uniform when you go." I was told that in uniform I'd be identified as a revenuer and likely shot. So, I set out on foot in my fatigues to find the young man's family. "Watson's? Over yonder. About two looks and a holler." That meant peak to peak, then down a draw.

I found the Watson place. A one-room cabin but good-sized. Beside the young recruit in my charge, there were four to five other youngsters, and the whole family plus livestock—chickens and pigs—lived in the cabin. I told them about the accident. It seemed to me that they were as interested in the monthly disability allotment checks they would now receive as they were in their boy's accident. Twenty-six dollars a month, $5 to the boy, $21 to the family, must have seemed like a lot of money to them.

When the boys wanted to see a locomotive, we posted a trip to the nearest railroad, Doniphan, Missouri. Later, as we transferred some kids to the forestry camp in Bemidji, Minnesota, those young men got a long train ride. Even though it was June, the weather turned cold; I *had to have the kids check in their cottons and issue woolens to them. I remember, during that ride, the engineer saying, "Watch!" at a certain mile marker. He blew the whistle and a bunch of wild turkeys flocked in. Apparently they had been routinely throwing out some corn along this point about 90 miles south of Duluth.*

Among other CCC posts I worked in was a camp on the waterfront of St. Louis. Again, senior leaders with 270 recruits. Not Ozarkians but this time boys with a little better education. In another assignment I was transferred back to Ft. Leavenworth to be in charge of the headquarters company. It was a mixed company with both juniors and WWI veterans, both black and white in the same company, which was unusual for that time. In '38 the Cs administration changed from military to Department of Interior.

Many of these CCC kids became good leaders. During WWII, I ran into one of the Salem CCC senior leaders in Europe. He had received a field promotion as a lieutenant and also did a hitch in the Marines. The Cs were good training for kids, for the officers, and we accomplished a lot during what were some otherwise pretty bleak years for our country. I'm proud to have been a part of it.

Besides the CCC Camp at Salem described above, Dad worked at these other CCC Camps, serving as company commander in each:

8 Feb 1936—1 Jun 1936, Bardley, Missouri.

1 Jun 1936—1 Jul 1937, Ft. Leavenworth, Kansas,

Headquarters Company.

1 Jul 1937—1 Feb 1938, Seneca, Kansas.

1 Feb 1938—1 Jun 1938, Union, Missouri.

The Seneca CCC Story

At the time I finished college, the military were doing the administrative oversight for the Civilian Conservation Corps. When I was in ROTC at Kansas State, one of my instructors was a chap named Broderick, Colonel Lynn Broderick. He was with the Corps of Engineers after I graduated, and the Walnut Creek Dam project I had worked on under Mont Green with my name on the design sheet had to pass through the Corps for approval. They were looking for ROTC graduates who had commissions to work with the CCC.

Colonel Broderick called and asked O. J. Ideman, who was a bridge engineer with the Kansas State Highway Commission, if he would recommend me for working on that project in the Cs in Northeast Kansas. O. J. called me and asked me if I wouldn't be interested in doing the job we had designed. He said, "I suggest it." I said, "Fine, I would love it." And I enjoyed working for the CCC in Seneca on the project I had designed.

Les Droge was one of the men who worked under Dad in 1937 at Camp SCS 16, Co. 2735 at Lake Nemaha in northeast Kansas. An account of Mr. Droge's experiences in the CCCs is posted on the Nemaha Valley High School Internet site.[38] The high school students did an extraordinary job of interviewing and writing up his memories:

---

[38] http://www.geocities.com/nvhsccc

"We were assigned to a company, platoon and squad. We lived in barracks, [were] assigned a bunk, saluted our officers, wore military clothing, fell out for reveille, stood retreat, did K.P. and stood guard and became efficient at military drill. A pass was necessary to leave the post.

"… The officer in charge was 1st Lt. Hal H. McCord. My work assignment was with the survey crew. We checked everything including the compaction of the dirt as the dam was being built. We were in the process of damming off the Nemaha River to create a reservoir consisting of approximately 350 acres. The dam is located five miles south of Seneca, Kansas, and the lake has since been drained. However, the rock pillars are still there on both sides of the road where Highway 63 crosses the dam.

"There were two companies of men and all the men except the cooks and administrative people worked on building the dam or other soil conservation projects in the area. The dam building went on around the clock, three eight-hour shifts. I worked two shifts part of the time, either driving an Indiana dump truck or driving a D6 Caterpillar pulling a packer, packing the dam. One night I went to sleep and ran [the caterpillar] off the end of the dam, a gradual slope, into the Nemaha River. I woke up in a hurry and was able to back out okay. By working two shifts, I could take the time I had built up to help my parents with wheat harvest or whenever I was needed at home."

Mr. Droge also talks about being center on the camp basketball team and playing other teams at Fort Riley, Fort Leavenworth, Highland College and the Seneca town team. He agreed with Dad that "the military training turned out to be valuable to most of the men in the CCC" as many either volunteered or were drafted when World War II commenced shortly after the termination of the CCC program. He was one of those who volunteered.

I talked with Leslie A. Droge in January of 2002. He also went to Kansas State, was in the ROTC program and finally retired a lieutenant colonel in the Army Reserves. After volunteering in 1941, he went first to Ft. Leonard Wood then served in the Philippines with the 11th Airborne Division as a paratrooper. He commented that he had to do some convincing to be accepted as a paratrooper—they have a 6-foot height limit and he is a too-tall 6' 6".

After the surrender of Japan when his division flew to Japan, he was left back to bring some of the 11th Airborne wounded via ship. His ship was docked alongside the Battleship Missouri in Tokyo Bay on September 2, 1945, and he watched the signing of the terms of surrender. The 11th Airborne stayed and comprised part of the occupation troops in Japan. He returned to the family farm in Seneca and later served 12 years in the Kansas State Senate.

Moving On

Dad left the Cs in 1938 when the military no longer administered the program. He took a job as a structural engineer with Walter P.

Moore doing construction in Houston, Texas. This lasted for 18 months, during which time he designed and did detailing for residential and commercial structures; and supervised construction, layout and field surveys. In his words …

I had originally gone to Houston the summer of 1938 to work for W. G. Ferrington Construction Company, on various projects at or near Houston, Texas. Walter P. Moore was the chief engineer. Work consisted of constructing commercial and residential units, designing and supervising construction of highways and bridges and creating the approach for the Galveston-Bolivar Ferry. I was plans engineer for the US Housing Authority in Houston and in charge of the preliminary work for the $11.5 million USHA program for that city.

From the Cs to Active Duty

At Ft. Leavenworth as commander of the CCC Headquarters Company, I wrangled an appointment as a non-empowered freshman to sit in on the Command General Staff School Program and attend all the non-classified classes. One of the instructors at the Staff School was a fellow named Donaldson. Colonel Donaldson was my main mentor. He not only helped me with the Staff School Program, but we also played golf together on Friday afternoons.

In '40, Donaldson was moved to Omaha as Chief of Personnel for the Seventh Corps Area Command at Fort Omaha. In looking down through the available people, a name he recognized was McCord.

I got a telegram in August of '40 asking if I would be interested in and available for assignment to Omaha. Under the Thompson Act inactive reservists assigned to inactive military units had to serve a year because of the impending problems in Europe. There wasn't any choice really when Donaldson asked. I said, "Sure, I would enjoy it." This was then my first start in, supposedly, a year under the Thompson Act, and I went to Omaha.

The duplicate of the telegram received at Ft. Sam Houston on October 3, 1940, and telephoned to Dad, is sparse in details but specific in assignment. The extract from SPECIAL ORDERS No. 186 listed others from the 960th Coast Artillery as well as several officers specifically identified as "ROTC Kansas State College."

Getting Back to Texas

During that time, my second child, Marilyn, was born October 27, 1940 in Houston, Texas. I think I still have the telegram that Lawrence Hedge, my brother-in-law, sent me. He advised me to "be careful of Father Dionne's record ..." insinuating that we had quintuplets. He teased that he was suddenly Uncle to five more. It was a humorous telegram. I was able to get back to Houston from Omaha by the time my daughter was brought home from the hospital.

Shortly thereafter, in January of '41, I had orders to go to the Pacific as a part of the contingent destined to go to Bataan. I wasn't finished with the project that Colonel Donaldson had set up for me, and he'd radioed or talked to the director of personnel in Washington

143

to have my orders delayed until such time as I finished the project in Omaha. So my orders were canceled—that shipment to Bataan— thank goodness.

It wasn't until the spring of 1941 that I got a new option. Col. Donaldson, my mentor at Ft. Leavenworth, was reassigned to Australia with the military there, and the war was getting hotter all the time. He called us in and said, "I've got to leave. What do you want to do?" He said, "I'll give you whatever orders you want— you've done a fine job, and whatever you'd like to do, I will fill you. Write your own ticket." At that time my family was still in Houston.

I told Donaldson that I'd like to go to the Army Air Corps, preferably at Randolph Field, Texas, which was as close to Houston as I could get at that time. I got the orders and went to Randolph, where Colonel Holden was Chief of Staff at the Flying Training Command. They were just activating Ellington Field in Houston with Colonel Wally Reed as the commander and I had a couple of sessions with him. A short time later, he looked at my record with the long experience in Administration with CCCs and the job that I'd had in Omaha with Colonel Donaldson, and he told Colonel Holden that he wanted me as his adjutant at Ellington. So I did get back to Houston in a matter of months after initially being at Randolph Field.

Col. Walter "Wally" Reed, a WWI pilot and the first commander at Ellington, and 1st Lt. Hal H. McCord at Ellington AFB in 1940

Randolph Field

Randolph Field in San Antonio, Texas, was named in memory of Capt. William Randolph, U.S. Army Air Corps, a native of Austin, Texas, who lost his life in an airplane accident in 1928. According to a 1941 pamphlet on Randolph Field in Dad's files:

"The purpose of the field is to train the young men of America in the principles of military aviation. The entire course of training lasts about nine months, and comprises flying, academic and military training. Classes start every five weeks. The first 10 weeks of the course is spent at one of the many civilian flying schools that have been selected by the Air Corps to cooperate in the elementary training of the future pilots. Then the Flying Cadets are transferred from the civilian schools to Randolph Field for their basic training, the second 10-week period. After successful completion of basic training, the class is again transferred, this time to Kelly Field, also located near San Antonio. There the Flying Cadets receive advanced training in formation flying, cross country navigation and night flying."

Then there is an invitation to young men between the ages of 20-27 to join up for the privilege of this training.

A Ticket to Fly

Dad learned to fly in 1928 at the age of 16, in an Alexander Eagle Rock at Manhattan, Kansas. The flight instructor was from Kansas City, and Dad's memories of any pilot's license requirements, whether he actually got one then or not, and the ownership of that plane are vague. He has no idea where his logbook might be, or even if logbooks were used at that time.

They flew out of the #1 fairway of the Manhattan Country Club golf course north of town. There were no obstructions, and the grass provided a good strip. However, Dad says the real training came later. His instrument rating was a part of that; he earned that rating at the flight school in Bryan, Texas. I am truly amazed at the number and variety of aircraft he actually ended up flying.

Although I learned to fly a biplane at Manhattan when I was in high school, I didn't get my ticket until I got to Randolph. There I probably had more experience gathered from flight testing various kinds of airplanes they had put through the maintenance section than from any other experience. Chuck Heidingsfelder was in charge of maintenance at Randolph Field. He'd call and say, "Hal, I've got such and such airplane; it needs to be flight tested. Can you come down to the field?"

My job at Randolph was training and familiarization with different kinds of aircraft anyway, so I'd check them out. Sometimes it took an hour, an hour and a half. I thoroughly enjoyed doing it. It gave me quite a variety of aircraft with which to become fairly familiar. The Vega Vultee,[39] for example, was a twin-engine bomber type made for the British as a sub hunter to do submarine eradication. Randolph had two of them. "Beau" Cornett (John Beaumont Cornett),[40] a 1933 graduate of Texas A&M, and I had learned to take it off, and we flew it quite a little. It had R-2800 engines in it, which were big Pratt & Whitney engines. Those were very capable, very good airplanes. Lots of power. We took one to Big Springs and out-ran a terrible sand and dust storm—we could see the top of the storm when we got to 14,000 feet. We were risking needing oxygen.

---

[39] See aircraft notes in Appendix 3.

[40] After finishing the Army-Navy Staff College in Washington, D. C., Beau was sent overseas to MAAF (Mediterranean Allied Air Force) in Italy, Combat Operations Headquarters for all the allies in Italy. Later he was assigned to the 15th AF, then given the 485th Bomb Group in Venosa, Italy. On a mission late in the War, Beau was shot down by flack over Vienna. He crash-landed in a no-man's land between the Russians and the Germans and was finally captured by a German patrol. He remained a POW of the Germans until the end of the War, not too long a time. Beau is currently living in Dallas, Texas, where he cares for his wife, hospitalized with Alzheimer's. He and my father have corresponded, picking up a friendship almost where they left off 50 years ago.

Outside Club Bali, Miami, early 1940s. Left to Right: Capt. Lund of PanAm; Col. Ben Starkey, A-4; Beau Cornett, A-3; Hal McCord, A-1; Col. Brown, Commanding Officer at Miami; Steig, Asst. A-3.

I also flew the P-51 Mustang, a beauty of a plane. We had aircraft of almost every type. At one time, I figured that I had flown every one of the prop-driven aircraft that the Air Force had in its inventory. These were not experimental aircraft. Our job was just to make sure they were airworthy after maintenance, and those guys were good maintenance people. There was a period in the early part of the war operation when the military had an awful lot of civilian airplanes turned over to them for training.

Esco Obermann, who was on the staff at Randolph, had gone in with me to buy a J-3F50. A Piper cub, with a J3 Franklin 50, a 50-horse engine. High-wing. A little monoplane type, all fabric-covered and very light. We bought it for $500. It was so much fun. You could take it up to 6,000 feet, deadstick the prop and fly like a glider. Then, dive enough to get the prop windmilling, which would start the engine. I flew an awful lot of tail draggers.

Owning a T-6

The T-6 was a tail dragger. I bought the T-6 from the disposal center at Albuquerque in '46, I think. For $1,800. They were disposing of what they called surplus aircraft. A friend of mine, Colonel Booth Harriston, was in charge of aircraft disposals at the depot at Albuquerque. We had been together a lot during the training days at Randolph, and I'd also met up with him at Caserta, Italy, during World War II. He knew I was interested in a T-6.

When I was doing instrument training at the flight school at Bryan, Texas, I got acquainted with Major Hubbard, Operations officer. He had been the original owner of that T-6. Hubbard had flown it from the time it was delivered. He kept it on the flight line, and it was then his airplane. It was in perfect shape. Of course, it would be. Here was a director of operations who had a couple of guys who groomed it every day. I mean it was really taken care of. Lovingly.

Harriston knew I would be interested in that plane and contacted me. "This airplane is a real good one—has only 3500 hours time, airframe time. And it's been hand-polished all the time. It's in fine shape."

I remember the number on the plane, the one that was assigned to me by the CAA (Civil Aeronautics Administration): 61328. The only thing we had to do with that T-6 was to change the flight indicator lights on the wing tips from on top and underneath to the outer edge in order to conform to CAA regulations. The navigation lights had to be more visible by having them out on the tips of the wings, on the edge, rather than on the top and bottom of the wing surface. It was no big deal. The other thing that they required was to change the radio frequencies from the military to commercial frequencies. Other than that, there was no requirement to make any changes.

Three T-6s in formation. Hal is in the middle, Henry Bailey is in front and Ed Potter is in the back. *Potter was a tad high and too far forward, but overall it was pretty good. This photo was taken at Ellington Field by the base photographer in 1941 or 1942. The T-6s had been delivered and several of us got checked out in 'em very early.*

I had a lot of experience in the T-6, logged quite a few hours. At Randolph, for one place, in the early '40s. One of the things we did down there on Sunday afternoons was what we called a round-up. South and west of the field was a private field. A guy who was very gung-ho for the Army Air Corps invited us all over for sandwiches and a picnic. Those of us who were invited would find a way there on whatever plane was available at the time. Chuck Heidingsfelder flew the T-6 over, and I flew the J-3F50. When we got there, we just traded off. We initially picked up whatever plane was available to fly, and returning we just traded round and all of us took turns in flying something.

On the way home, Heidingsfelder wanted to fly the J-3F50. He said, "You take my T-6 and fly it home, back to Randolph." I agreed that that was fine, so we just traded off and headed back home.

At that time, General Luke Smith was in command at Randolph. We landed, and I taxied up to the ramp. I threw my parachute over my shoulder and started to walk back into operations. I had returned in the T-6; the J-3F50 had come in ahead of me. When I came in and landed, General Smith was still in operations. He came out and said, "McCord, I want to talk to you. Did you bring that T-6 in?" I said, "No, Yuhudi did."[41] He looked at me, then said, "Well, you tell Yuhudi I want him to be at my desk at 0900 in the morning."

I went in and reported to him at 0900 the next morning. Someone else was responsible for that plane. Why had they let me fly it? He wanted to know what the deal was. I told him we had had a picnic over at wherever it was—I don't remember those people's name. They were fine people and very interested in aviation. He explained to me that he didn't think I was in a position to fly an airplane at that time, and the T-6 was still an active advanced trainer. And he gave me a lecture about what would happen if I scratched that airplane. All in all, he didn't give me too much trouble.

---

[41] Dad's form of a joke, a response when the response was obvious.

Then he said, *"Well, if Heidingsfelder traded planes with you, what did he fly home?" "He flew my J-3F50." "That kite?" I said, "Sure!" Smith said, "I want to fly that kite, too." "Fine, General."*

The Swimming B-23

There is another story about General Luke Smith, and this actually happened. He was the only one who ever took a converted B-18, one that had been changed from a B-18 to a B-23, and sank it.

This happened at Bolling AFB, right along the edge of the Potomac River. The B-18 had a big, bulbous nose and quite a body; a cumbersome looking aircraft, but it was a bomber. The B-23 was a slimmed down bomber. The only difficulty was, there is a characteristic of those airplanes that the way the motor rotated would provide a torque, either right or left. No matter, General Smith wanted to fly that B-23. They tried to tell him, "General, you've got to be careful. It'll turn the opposite direction of what you're used to."

General Smith knew all of the answers to start with. He was kind of a hot rock. He started to take off and dove right into the river. They fished him out and got the airplane out, but he got a reputation for being the only swimming B-23 flyer in the Air Force. He never lived that one down. And, he didn't slow down a minute.

Meeting Jackie Cochran

Jackie Cochran[42] *managed the Woman's Air Force Service Pilots (WASPS) flight training school at Sweetwater, Texas. The school was sometimes referred to as "Cochran's Convent." At that time, I was at Randolph Field as chief of personnel for the Flying Training Command under General Luke Smith. Jackie had made several personnel requests by name for people she wanted on her staff to assist in training the women's flying command. Luke called me in and said, "Hal, I can't make that trip. Whatever Jackie wants, give it to her." I said, "Well, you should go." He confessed, "There's no way I can go. I'm in her little black book."*

So I made the trip and met Jacqueline Cochran. She had specific people whom she wanted. I hedged a little bit about a couple of them, but she said, "I really need these people." "All right, you've got them." And that was when I got to fly her green Beechcraft with-a-negative-stagger biplane.

---

[42] Cochran was the first woman to break the sound barrier. When I got my wings, Dad gave me his copy of her 1954 biography, The Stars at Noon. It tells of her childhood poverty. She had no shoes until she was eight years old; her bed was a pallet on the floor; and at age eight she was working a 12-hour shift in a cotton mill. By age 13, she was an expert beauty shop operator. In 1953, she was voted Business Woman of the Year, then owning three cosmetics firms. She began flying in 1932 when few had pilots' licenses, and even fewer of those were women.

Cochran won more than 200 awards and trophies and holds many men's as well as women's world speed records for both jet and piston engines. In 1945, she was awarded the Distinguished Service Medal for her work as Director of the WASPS, who flew over 60 million miles in wartime. In 1954, she received a unanimous vote for the International Flying Organization's gold medal for the outstanding accomplishment by any pilot, man or woman, during 1953. She has been called the "Airborne Cinderella." Chuck Yeager, the first man to fly faster than the speed of sound, sometimes flew chase plane to accompany some of her test flights. In the foreword to her book, Yeager salutes Cochran's courage and skill.

The lower wing extended out past the upper wing. It was powered with a Pratt & Whitney 450, and it was great. The only problem was—they warned me at that time—that her landing gear was high tech with a coil type spring on those gears, a coiled landing gear suppressor. When you came in with it, it would feel like you were ground looping, as if the ground was moving. You didn't have real good control. I remember the first time I flew it and came back in to land. You didn't quite feel secure with the way it reacted when you set it down.

Dissoway Disguised

Barksdale Field in Shreveport, Louisiana, was one of the early Army Air Corps flight schools. Gabriel P. "Gabe" Dissoway was one of those who instructed the instructors. I happened to be at the flight school at Barksdale for an open house. As people milled through the exhibits, they were given a ticket with a number on it. The lucky winner was to receive a free airplane ride in one of the old biplane types, maybe a T-3, I'm not sure.[43] As the afternoon went on, the time came for the drawing. The pilot brought the plane up, and the emcee called out the winning number. A dowdishly dressed old woman spoke up, tickled as could be, "I've got it! I've got it!"

The pilot then apologized that he had to go do something that had just come up, but assured her he would be right back. He left. The old woman, not to be denied her free flight, went ahead and climbed into

---

[43] Our best guess now is that this was a Douglas BT trainer.

the plane. Then, to the amazement of all, she took off. Bounced around, but got off. The crowd was scared to death and watched in stunned silence. The plane tried to come in for a landing, but had to do a go-around. The old woman finally managed to land in a practice field. Folks didn't know what had happened and were getting quite worried.

The pilot was Dissoway dressed as an old lady. We kidded him a lot about that, and he said he had a great time himself. I was chief of staff personnel at that time and recommended to General Harmon that Dissoway be given command of the instructor school at Bryan, Texas, even with the increase in rank. He was an excellent instructor, a good pilot. Gabe Dissoway eventually became a full general and commander of the Tactical Air Command.

Kelly Field Stories

Here's another Air Force or Army Air Corps story that is a classic. There was a balloon hangar over at Kelly Field. A couple of young pilots, Army Air Corps types, delighted in flying what they called a P-26, a peashooter. It was a pursuit-type aircraft and a hot machine, a good airplane. One of these young flyboys would make sure that both doors were open on that balloon hangar, then he'd get up in the air some place in that thing and come down and fly through that hangar. Just scattered everything in the place. He was banished by the mechanics in there who were working on the aircraft. It would just burn 'em up that he would do this.

Marilyn McCord

One day he took off and went back up. He had a habit of getting back up before he'd come in and not give 'em much warning before diving on that hangar. The mechanics waited until he got up there and then they went to the opposite end and <u>just about</u> closed the door. They left just enough room that he might get through ... without clipping the tips of his wings.

This kid had to think pretty fast when he got in there and saw he had a restricted flight space. So he turned the P-26 wings up just a little bit and went through this way, at an angle (Dad slanted his hand at about a 30° angle), *instead of flying horizontally. I don't remember his name. This was just one of the stories. And it cured him of flying through the balloon hangar.*

Another tale that was a characteristic little classic of Kelly Field days: They were training pilots and the dual-control trainer type of aircraft had a stick control. (Aside to me, *"Like the T-6 that we flew out to Denver."*) *This particular instructor couldn't get one of his student trainees to solo. That student pilot just wouldn't take it over and fly the airplane.*

So the instructor arranged to take an extra stick in his flight suit. He got this kid up there, pretty well up at six, seven thousand feet up, and motioned for him to take it over, fly it. The kid shook his head. He wouldn't do it. So the instructor took the control stick out of the aircraft and dropped it over the side. He wanted to get that kid to fly the airplane. Well, the kid took his dual control stick out and dropped it over the side, too. They were up there with no control sticks. Had none for a little bit. They only had their rudder controls.

Finally, the instructor grabbed his flight suit and took the extra stick he had with him out and inserted it, and flew the aircraft back. It cured him of any tricks. The story goes on to say that when he got down, he headed for the nearest laundry. What happened to the kid? Oh, he finally flew.

Defeathering the Guineas

Once we made a trip in a B-25 from Randolph up to Fort Leavenworth to pick up some records. We finished that task and started back to Randolph. We were bucking a very high, southerly wind, a head wind. In checking the winds-aloft charts, we discovered that there was a west wind at the surface, and as we got up higher, not only were the winds from the south, but they were also considerably stronger. So, we filed a flight plan for what is called VFR—visual flight rules—and flew a corn-picking route, close to the ground.

As we came south across Kansas from Fort Leavenworth down towards the Walnut River area, there was a fairly high plateau on each side of the river. We came across a plateau, and one of the passengers in the back end called up to us and asked, "What in the world did you drop back there?" "Why?" "Because, all of a sudden, there was a great explosion of feathers."

What we had done was to pop right off that plateau over a farm and put the airplane kind of in the lee of any winds. The farmer had a big flock of guineas roosting in the trees. We scared those big guineas to death. We must have startled everything on that farm. They took off and were really moving. They must have been sure a "big hawk" had 'em.

The farmer filed a complaint because he said he was picking up guineas over three counties. He was sure that those guineas would never lay another egg.

Turkey Hunting in a J-3F50

One fall, I used the J-3F50 to go turkey hunting. The location was about 20 miles northwest of Randolph Field toward Kerrville on the Albert Falteen Ranch. Eight officers had a lease for hunting. We had put in $50 each and gained exclusive rights to hunt on this ranch.

That little ol' J-3F50 was sure fun to use. It was a monoplane, very light. I expect it'd be probably 20 feet long from prop to tail and maybe a little longer than that wingtip to wingtip. All fabric covered. The "J-3" means it was a Piper Cub; the "F50" identified the Franklin 50-horse engine that was air-cooled. It had a wooden prop. You started it by getting out and spinning the prop through, then getting back in the airplane. A two-seater, one in front flying and one behind as passenger.

On this particular trip, I ended up getting two gobblers with one shot. They were lined up like this, (two fingers side-by-side) *and they both raised their heads at the same time. I aimed the .12 gauge shotgun and fired. I knew I hit one, but I didn't know I had the second one until I got up there. I had gotten the two birds with that one shot, both through the head. I picked up my two turkeys, field dressed 'em and put them over my back and went back to the plane to fly back to Randolph. They were big birds. I expect they were 25 pounds apiece. I put those two turkeys in the back seat and took off. It was starting to get dark.*

By that time the wind had laid pretty well, and I got started down on my run out. The plane was in an oat patch, and there was a fence at the far end. With that extra 50 pounds weight, I saw I wasn't going to make it, so I turned the aircraft, braked to stop it and back-taxied to start over. This time I faced off perpendicular to the wind, got up pretty good speed and made a controlled turn. Then I gave full throttle, and she cleared the fence by two or three feet.

When I came back into Randolph, Sgt. Jarris, the chap who was trying to say grace over me, was pacing like mad because it was getting dark, and he knew I didn't have any lights or the controls for flying instruments. At that time, they didn't have lights on the main field. They wouldn't have wanted to turn 'em on for me, anyway. Strictly speaking, I was illegal in my activities for that time of day, and they would have had some explaining to do. When I did come around over the field, Jarris had arranged with the tower to give me a clear signal to land. They turned on the landing lights on the ramp, the maintenance ramp.

I came in and set her down on the maintenance ramp outside of the hangars. I didn't run very far because that isn't a very big airplane and doesn't weigh very much. I turned the J-3F50 and rolled back to where I sometimes kept it. Col. White let me keep it on the flight line if I didn't demand any services of any kind. No fuel, no services, no anything. But the J-3F50 was popular, and many pilots campaigned for a chance to fly it. Jarris liked it so much he said, "I'll take care of that one."

I climbed out of the plane, and Jarris came running out, shaking his finger at me. He said, "Colonel, if you ever do this again, I'm, ... I'm going to kill you! You're never going to do this to me again." I said, "Look in the back seat." He looked back there and saw these two big birds. I said, "Pick out the one you want." He said, "You can't do this to me."

That finished my turkey hunting for that fall. The chef at the officers' mess gave me instructions on how to cook that en papier (in paper). Ivalee baked that turkey in a paper bag, and it was probably one of the best turkeys we ever had for Thanksgiving. It really worked extremely well; it was an excellent method. Well, today, of course, they bake turkeys in these plastic bags that aren't quite the same. I still like to use the paper bag method—it does the best job on turkey.

That was quite a trip. The good old days. Today you couldn't move three inches without all the sign-offs.

Bargaining for a Service Pilot Rating

Randolph Field, TX

10 April 44

Colonel Richard M. Montgomery

Room 4C1075, Pentagon Building

Hq, Army Air Forces

Washington, D. C.

Dear Dick:

With regard to my telephone call a few days ago, I appreciate very much your action in securing orders for Lt. Col. Ola because he was really wasting away from inactivity. Every now and then we have officers on tap who are scheduled for release but for whom there is apparently difficulty in securing a suitable assignment.

I had hopes that I would be able to slip up to Washington for a short visit some time within the next ten days, but with the present trend of work here, that may be impossible.

I am enclosing a copy of board proceedings and letter of transmittal covering recommendation for a rating as Service Pilot for myself. As you know, I have been interested in this for several years. I have felt at all times that I could not take time from my primary job to devote to a more aggressive prosecution of the work required in completing the necessary requirements. The approval of the board proceedings by your Headquarters may have to be done as a special case, and I sincerely hope that you can convince the necessary authorities there to approve and grant the rating. I have been doing quite a bit of travel in connection with personnel administration within the Command. Many times I have to take an officer of my division with me, and this requires using a larger airplane than would normally be necessary, and the pilot doesn't do anything but sit around and wait on us; whereas, if the rating is approved, I can take a single engine airplane and one man with me and save using one additional man and a larger airplane.

I realize, Dick, the argument is pretty thin, but I have been flying considerably. The time recorded in the application does not include any Army time, of which I have had approximately four hundred (400) hours. This is in everything from AT-6 to B-24s. I am really anxious to receive the rating because my commission at the present time is in the Air Corps. I know nothing of any other branch, and when this is over, I want to remain in the Air Corps, and I would like to be able to do some flying instead of sitting back and watching the rest of the boys fly. During the past two years, I have purchased a Piper and a Spartan. Both of them are in flyable condition now. Sometime when you are down this way, I would like to take you fishing in the Cub. It really makes a fine method of getting about the country in late afternoons.

Please drop me a note on what can be done about this application. I have discussed it with General Smith and General Hornsby, and both are very much in favor of having the thing completed. In fact, it was at General Smith's direction that I am finally submitting these papers.

Warmest regards,

HAL H. McCORD

Lt. Col., GSC

Asst C of S, Personnel

Dad always wanted a rating as a Service Pilot for himself. Attached to the letter were: a signed Physical Examination for Flying form with everything normal and no disqualifications; copies of the CAA Airman Certificate and Airman Rating Record No. 289635 dated March 25 1944, showing Dad rated for "Airplane single engine land 0-975 hp"; Exhibit G - Dad's application for Service Pilot and listing 506 hours as pilot of "heavier-than-air aircraft"; Exhibit D - showing the hours as pilot in five different types of planes—Piper J3, Fairchild, Beech, Waco and Spartan—for a total of 412.25 hours.

Capt. Tim Dacey subsequently spent a four-hour session with Dad, running him through his qualifications for the Service Pilot Rating. The plane they used was a BC-1A, a variation of the AT-6 Texan. After Capt. Dacey's favorable report, Col. Montgomery gave the okay and Dad gained a new freedom with his Service Pilot's Rating.

A Special Letter Opener

Before Dad left for the Eastern Air Command, the crew from Duncan Depot in San Antonio gave him a letter opener he still uses. It is the threaded end of a Waco end strut with a handle. Within the handle, Dad's name, rank and serial number are inscribed.

Tragic Accidents

I witnessed several accidents that I still have dreams about. A C-97 cargo carrier—a bomber converted into a four-engine carrier—came in to land and apparently lost the hydraulic system or something. Anyway, the brakes didn't work, and they ran into the abutment at the end of the runway and exploded. I sometimes still have nightmares about the screaming of the guys that burned to death in that accident. It was terrible. Pan-Am later added a lower deck to the C-97 and produced the Stratocruiser, a wide-body commercial air transport. Their main cabin was in the upper lobe of the fuselage and a luxury cocktail bar accessible via a spiral staircase was on the lower deck.

At Randolph, where I really got my flight experience, I knew a chap named Dellinger. He was an inspector for the CAA that later became the FAA. Dellinger was part of a group that was barnstorming over the country. He was killed in Mexico, trying to do a low-altitude roll. His wing caught a tree and spun him, and he didn't get out of it.

Another accident that I will never get out of my mind happened at the B-26 training station at Dodge (Dodge City, Kansas). That involved the Martin 26 Marauder commonly called in Air Force circles the Flying Coffin or the Widow Maker. There were some characteristics about it so different from other aircraft. It had such a wing-loading factor. It hung on its prop for the first four or five minutes after you got off, before it got up on the step where it could pick up enough flying speed. (American designers continued working on designs and produced a second generation of bombers, more reliable and more controllable than the Marauder.)

In this case, however, they were coming in for a touch-and-go landing, but pausing on the tarmac. The crew chief got out each time and would check the brakes to be sure that they weren't caught and locked up. The '26 props hardly cleared the ground when they were on the runway, only about four or five inches clearance. It's a four-bladed prop. Well, this guy, the crew chief, was careless and leaned up. The prop decapitated him.

I was right behind him, the next plane for departure. I was sitting there waiting to take off, and here was a body under the airplane and the head rolling down the runway. And, I lost my cookies. I called the tower and said, "Cancel my departure." I went back to the pilot's lounge and took a couple of hours to kind of re-group. It was a very tragic accident. I never wanted to get into anything like that.

Later in Kunming when I was later flying the Hump, a colleague coming back in to land wasn't paying close attention apparently, because he was over-shooting his base-leg turn. Everyone was shouting, "Pull up, pull up, pull up!" But he didn't, and ran into the face of that rock cliff. They never did get out of it, of course. There wasn't ... wasn't any way ... he was gone. Nothing but debris.

Everybody in the operations room saw it. We were all upchuck. We were ready to toss our tummies real quick, because we knew the guy.

Those accidents are things that I remember. And sometimes wake up dreaming about. It doesn't make any difference who it is, it gets you.

I asked Dad if he had been in any plane crashes. *Yes, three.* He walked away from all of them, the definition of a successful emergency landing. One incident involved an old B-10, a two-engine bomber with cable landing gear. The cable snapped and fell, just as the plane finished its roll on landing. Dad was with Col. Robert Orth of Harlingen, Texas, on this flight.

Another time, before WWII, the J-3F50 experienced what Dad thinks was carburetor icing, though he said they would never know for sure. They managed an emergency landing in a cornfield, got back in shape, and flew back to Randolph. The third incident happened in Italy, though Dad said details are too fuzzy to recall.

The question, however, triggered another memory—an accident in the Eastern Air Command when Jim Michaels, squadron leader, in a Northrop P-61 Black Widow, buzzed some native crew sailboats on the Brahma Putra River. *The prop wash turned those sailboats over and some of the crew were lost.*

A Daughter's Flying Career Takes Off

Though accidents have a sobering effect, I have always been fascinated with aviation. In listening to and working with these stories, I began to understand why. Some vague childhood memories exist of flying on a biplane at the Manhattan Airport. My memory of flying as co-pilot on Dad's AT-6 as a third grader is much more vivid.

Dad had an AT-6 back then. Fancy color schemes cost money, and Dad's plane, like so many aircraft, was kept in bare metal. Our family budget couldn't afford a plane, and it was probably another tear in the fabric of the now-fragile marriage. But I do understand the love of the plane. Dad could fly Cuban-8s in the T-6; it had strong wings and excellent flight characteristics. But noisy as all get-out. The tremendous noise it made no doubt was a key factor in Dad's later hearing loss.

Finally, realizing the impossibility of keeping up the costs for maintenance and fuel, Dad sold that plane. It was to be delivered to someone in Denver, and I was invited to go along on the trip. What a thrill! I rode co-pilot under the canopy in the seat behind Dad. We were flying at 10,000 feet. There was a bit of weather, and it got pretty rough. By the time we got to Goodland, Kansas, we had to land so we could clean up my breakfast from that morning now on the floor in the back seat. I didn't eat cantaloupe again for over a year.

The rest of the trip was uneventful and glorious. Being above the earth, seeing everything so small and far away. A high in the best sense. It gives a different perspective to life, to problems, to priorities. There is something freeing about being up in the sky in a small plane—as long as you have someone competent at the controls.

From Denver we took a train back to Kansas. Dad had some business in Lindsborg, an interesting and delightful Swedish enclave in central Kansas. Bakeries, coffee shops, gift boutiques, quaint little stores. We stayed several days in a hotel there. I remember that he rented a typewriter for me. My third grade class at Eugene Field School was at that time doing an experimental unit with typewriters, and I was delighted to continue my practice. Besides, it kept me happily occupied while Dad did his business.

This was my first long plane trip, and as with the 1950-1951 K-State basketball team, I was smitten. Dad has since given me the clock that he had cut out of the panel of his T-6. It still keeps good time when properly set. I go to air shows every chance I get, and the AT-6s are always a wonder. Even in little Durango, Colorado (population 15,000), we have had some wonderful air shows. It is a thrill to see all of the old aircraft, but especially the Thunderbirds, the Air Force ace precision flying team, four abreast wingtip to wingtip plus two "chase" planes. Taking off from the same runway I take off from in my rented Cessna 152. We are close enough to Colorado Springs and the Air Force Academy that the team enjoys coming out to Durango to put on a show, and they have been here several times. The local airport clears the airspace 30 minutes before to 30 minutes after their performances, and they own the skies. And my undivided attention and admiration.

The Air Force Thunderbirds over Durango, Colorado

Two views of a DC-3 Dakota with 3 T-6s in formation—Durango, Colorado Air Show, 1995

In June 1991, returning from an air show in Durango, the P-51 Mustang from the show circled Lake Vallecito about a mile from our home while our Labrador was swimming and fetching sticks in the lake. Seeing the late afternoon sun glint off the gleaming metal so close to home was an exhilarating sight. I tried to imagine the pilot inside, and what he was seeing from his (or her) vantage point. That area is one of the most beautiful places on earth, certainly one of the best spots in the spectacular San Juan Mountains.

I would later make that same trip myself twice: once with my flight instructor, Arngrim Jacobson[44] in a C-172 and later alone in the C-152 I usually flew, "N4568Foxtrot."

In my early 40s I made a static line parachute jump from 3000' with my then 19-year-old son Eric. We made three more the next summer. The jump school we were working with required five jumps with good form and dummy ripcord pulls of your reserve parachute before they pronounced you fit for free fall from 8000'. Shortly after our three jumps in 1983, I broke a toe on a footstool in my roommate's living room and that curtailed my jumping for then.

At age 55, I finally realized the dream of getting my own private pilot's license. A neighbor, Laureen Diephof, had earned her license a few months before I did. The two of us would often have picnics or other meals at our mountain homes for the group of eight to ten

---

[44] Arngrim is from the Faroe Islands, an excellent pilot and instructor, and a friend. He held a window open with one hand so I could take aerial photographs of my home area.

international kids who were instructors at Durango Air Service, where we learned to fly.

One of our neighbors, Gwen Crawford, now in her 80s, was a "99"[45] and flew in Powder Puff derbies. She tells of coming in to her airstrip in Enid, Oklahoma, in winds so strong the ground crew had to grab the wings and hold her plane down so it wouldn't take off again. There is not a 99s chapter near us, but it surely is fun to swap flying stories. Laureen and I formed "The Grannies' Flying Club of Vallecito," and Laureen made us T-shirts. Those early days of flying with my father made a deep and lasting impression.

---

[45] The Ninety-Nines organization was founded in 1929 by 99 licensed women pilots for the mutual support and advancement of aviation. They're still going strong today.

Part Five:

Active Military Duty and World War II 1940-1946

October 1940—June 1943

Hitler and Mussolini had taken most of Europe by 1940. By '42, the extent of Axis territory included virtually everything on continental Europe (which excludes the British Isles) except the neutral or nonbelligerent countries of Sweden, Switzerland, Portugal, Spain, Ireland, Turkey and the island of Malta.

The eastern extent was a line that went roughly from Murmansk to Leningrad west of Moscow and just west of Stalingrad. In addition, parts of North Africa were held by the Axis powers. In 1940, US President Franklin D. Roosevelt had no intention of entering the war.

German troops entered the open city of Paris on June 14, 1940. They hung a huge swastika flag beneath the Arc de Triomphe and marched down the Champs Èlysée. On June 15 the Germans took the fortress at Verdun. The next day French Premier Reynaud resigned, and a new government was formed under Henri Philippe Pétain, who asked for armistice terms.

Those terms had German troops occupying all of Northern France including Paris and the Atlantic coast of France down to Spain. The unoccupied French government moved south to Vichy. Rebel general Charles DeGaulle chose to flee to Britain, and he became the leader of the Free French. He had few followers and an amazing talent for antagonizing his allies.

Britain, afraid the French fleet would fall into Nazi hands, seized French ships in British ports and attacked a squadron of the French fleet at Oran, Algiers, resulting in much damage to ships and heavy loss of life. The next day Vichy France broke diplomatic relations with Britain.

In Winston Churchill's "This was their finest hour" speech on June 18, 1940, he stated, "What General Weygand called the Battle of France is over. I expect that the Battle of Britain is about to begin."

Hitler believed the Brits would realize their militarily hopeless situation and make an honorable peace, but there was no response to German peace offerings.

August 1, 1940, Hitler's Directive No. 17: "The German Air Force is to overcome the English air forces with all means at its disposal and as soon as possible. ... The air war may begin on Aug. 5. The Navy is authorized to begin intensified operations on the same date."

Goering was delighted with this directive and figured the Luftwaffe would wipe out the Royal Air Force fighters in about four days. England's mood was grim, but they stood ready. Churchill's motto was, "You can always take one with you."

Sir Hugh Dowding, the British opposite of Goering, understood aerial combat and the problems of men and machines; he is credited with winning the Battle of Britain. A number of factors were in Britain's favor: home turf advantage, technical skills such as radar and communications, Germany's battle fatigue—it was easier for Germany to replace planes than pilots, and pre-war German intelligence errors on the numbers of RAF aircraft. German figures were so low that when RAF aircraft were destroyed, there were still more left than Germany figured. The Battle of Britain was an epic of heroism on both sides and decided by "the few" Churchill would later memorialize.

Bombs were dropped on London by mistake during a night raid. In retaliation, Britain sent 80 bombers to hit Berlin. It wasn't militarily effective, but Goering was so angry he promised to erase British cities off the map. Thus on Sept. 7, the Blitz occurred—a massive, daylight attack on London. Many British cities, including Coventry, suffered great damage. Forty thousand British civilians died, and 46,000 were injured. These disproportionate acts against civilians served to renew flagging British determination.

The Soviet Union bore the greatest war losses with at least eight million military deaths and seven million civilian deaths. Stalin's Army purge of 1937-38 that carried out the execution of countless officers had left the Red Army of '41-'42 leaderless. Poland lost 20 percent of its pre-war population—six million—half of them Jews. More than half of Europe's pre-war Jewish population fell victim to the Nazis.

March 6, 1943, British and Allied bombers returned to Germany, bombing Essen. Goebbels wrote in his diary: "The city of Krupps has been hard hit. The number of dead, too, is considerable. If the English continue their raids on this scale, they will make things exceedingly difficult for us."

Hal McCord in Dress Whites, my favorite photo of my father

Active Duty: 4 October 1940—7 June 1946

Dad's active duty began 4 October 1940, prior to Pearl Harbor and the U.S. entry into the war. He left his job with Ferrington Construction in Houston upon assignment to the Seventh Corps Area Service Command in Omaha. My parents had built a house in Houston—3327 Oakdale Drive—at a cost of $4,700 including the lot. So many people were moving into the area when the war started that they sold the house two years later for $26,000.

My brother Don remembers particularly his fourth birthday at the Oakdale house in 1940. Our parents had rented a clown and had hung a sheet on the garage to show 16-mm movies. Not a real drive-in movie but close. It was a great party in the back yard. Don also remembers their German shepherd dog, very protective of him, who once bit Grandmother McCord when she came toward him too quickly.

Marilyn ("Blondie"), Hal, and Don in Houston, 1942

With the worsening of the war, as Dad said, *The whole damn world turned upside down.* The October 3, 1940, telegram he received in the mail was a duplicate of the telephoned telegram received at Ft. Sam Houston and stated:

"ORDERS BEING ISSUED PLACING YOU ON ACTIVE DUTY ONE YEAR AT THIS HDQRS EFFECTIVE OCTOBER 4 AND DIRECTING YOU TO PROCEED THAT DATE FROM MANHATTAN KANSAS TO OMAHA NEBR REPORTING UPON ARRIVAL TO COMMANDING GENERAL HDQRS SEVENTH CORPS AREA FOR DUTY."

In Omaha, Dad was assigned to general staff duty, G-1. I saw in his files that he received a voucher for $50 uniform allowance. There is a statement of service for longevity pay which details his Coast Artillery Corps service beginning with his commission as a second lieutenant on June 1, 1933. It was determined "Lieutenant McCord will rank from 7 October 1938." Although his original military obligation had been for one year, before that year was up his active duty would be extended for another year ... and then extended again. His active military duty would go to 1 March 1946, with the official Date of Separation being 7 June 1946.

Dad's files contain a humorous memo about the Fort Omaha Skating Rink, ready for use on Jan. 29, 1941, weather permitting ...

"For non-skaters and amateurs, the club has been exceedingly fortunate in securing as an instructor that renowned rink performer, that demon of the frozen diadem, that fugitive from a Frigidaire, none other than Lieut. Eugene Herbert (just call me Wing-foot) Snavely.

"Lt. Snavely may be reached at Ext. 162, or if after skating hours, at the convalescent ward, Post Hospital. Individual equipment for the classes (including liniment, tape and bandages) must be procured individually. Formal dedication of the rink will begin at 2:45 p.m. Wednesday, at which time Wing-foot Snavely will hold forth in a <u>short</u> exhibition demonstrating a few <u>don'ts</u> for beginners. ..."

Dad said Gene flew him to Houston for his leave in January, 1941 and started Dad's training in a C-45.[46]

Because he had just arrived in Omaha, my father was late for my birth in Houston in October, 1940. He did arrive to greet me before I came home from the hospital. Back in Omaha, he asked for and got a two-day leave of absence for Valentine's Day in 1941. Three days later, word came in that a transfer to Randolph Field (San Antonio, Texas) had been approved. That was as close to Houston as he could wrangle right then.

Shortly after that, however, he did manage a transfer to Houston when his temporary duty for seven to15 days training the next March

---

[46] See Appendix 3 note on the AT-11.

became a change of assignment on March 28, 1941. He flipped back and forth from Randolph to Ellington quite a bit, sometimes for two-week temporary duty training assignments.

In addition to being assistant personnel officer, he was the inspection and receiving officer of all buildings completed at Ellington. There is a memo in his 201 Personnel File with that assignment. Roger M. Crow, second lieutenant in the Air Corps, assistant adjutant and a fellow K-State engineer who would show up later in Dad's overseas duty, signed that memo.

Allowance for the noonday meal was $.40 except Sundays and holidays. Dad's medical history records reveal eyes 20/20, hearing 20/20, 68" in height, 160 lbs. and blood pressure of 116/78. The form's item 20 notes "slight limitation of extension, middle finger right hand, due to old injury." The residue from having played catcher in summer baseball. Everything else was pretty normal.

On June 17, 1936, 2nd Lt. Hal H. McCord was promoted to first lieutenant within the Coast Artillery Corps. November 27, 1941, after entering extended active duty, he became a captain. Fingerprint records were taken at Ellington the next day. February 1, 1942, he was promoted to major. A later 201 file memo on this promotion is dated May 30, 1942, but there is a copy on this date from the office of the Secretary of War, G. C. Marshall, Chief of Staff. "Execute oath of office and forward to TAG."

July 23, 1942 he moved from major to lieutenant colonel; again the excerpt is from Marshall's office. That was some pretty fast traveling but not atypical for those war years, especially given the experience contributed from the CCCs. Dad would become a full bird colonel on May 22, 1945, at the age of 33.

Ellington Field Duty

Captain Hal McCord, Base Adjutant, Ellington Field—1941-42

I got orders to go to Ellington Field, just south of Houston, as the adjutant of the new base there. I don't remember now how long I was there, but it was not long after[47] that I was ordered back to Randolph as assistant to Colonel Bailey, who was then assistant chief of staff personnel. It wasn't but about two months when Bailey was ordered

---

[47] 14 April 1942 Dad got a two-week leave, then reported to Randolph on 1 May 1942.

to Washington. Bailey recommended to General Jerry Brandt, who was the commander at Randolph, that I be placed in the job as assistant chief of staff personnel. General Brandt did that. He was a World War I veteran, retired and shortly thereafter was replaced by General Hubert Harmon.

It seemed like several things happened all at once. I had originally gone to Randolph Field as a first lieutenant in 1940 at Thanksgiving time. By July, 1942 I had been promoted to lieutenant colonel. At that point, I was also assistant chief of staff personnel because the higher-ups had already left, and I was the most experienced individual remaining. That's how I got started in personnel operations.

While at Randolph, Dad did take a personnel management short course, six weeks at Harvard. *It was good training.* As a part of his responsibilities in personnel operations Dad was assigned to quite a few boards. A Nov. 25, 1942, memo details officers to a board for "the final selection of EM [enlisted men] ... for detail to Officer Candidate Schools" and lists "Lt. Col. Hal H. McCord" first, the ranking officer. Feb. 10, 1943, Dad is on a board to "consider recommendations for temporary promotion of commissioned officers of this Training Center ..."

An April 1, 1943, order lists Dad as president of another board to "process applications of and to approve when found qualified ... the final selection of EM ... for detail to Officer Candidate Schools." As president of the board, Dad had the "authority to summon qualified officers of Arms and Services ... in an advisory capacity."

A December 16, 1943, letter of recommendation from Col. F. Trubee Davidson, Chief of Special Projects, expresses "enthusiastic commendation for the superior work of Colonel McCord in regard to the survey for availability for reassignment of flying officers in continental United States conducted by Special Projects Office, Hq, AAF during October 1943. ... Colonel McCord's wholehearted cooperation, unflagging attention to detail, resourcefulness, initiative and willingness to devote time and attention beyond the demands of duty while assigned to temporary duty with this office is to be commended to the highest degree." The letter was sent by command of General "Hap" Arnold.

General Harmon made the final approvals on assignments, but he often asked Dad's opinion. "Hal, who would you recommend for Base Commander at Garden City?" Dad knew every one of the 1,800 field grade officers in the command, those who were majors and lieutenant colonels. As personnel officer, he had to know their capabilities and their possibilities for assignment. *I was a good officer. I liked it. People were my forte; I loved people. Things were moving so rapidly everyone was bump, bump, bump up the ranks.*

At Randolph Field, my parents lived on the post in officer's quarters, 3 South Park. Don was privileged as an officer's brat. He got special treatment at the base pool, was allowed into a Link trainer (like the cockpit of the AT-6), and able to charge cigarettes at the PX.

The cigarette buying lasted a week until the bill arrived, and then he couldn't sit down for a while. A cherry wood paddle with a hole in it to allow more sting, sometimes a birch switch.

He also remembers going hunting with Dad. One time he wounded a bird and had to put his foot on it to finally kill it. My brother still had his Winchester pump-action .22 and a .22 pistol through high school. Don's Texas memories also include water moccasins and swamps somewhere; Maria, our Mexican maid/housekeeper; and a black cat who soiled the laundry, "a nice and warm spot, and maybe we didn't have the litter box attended well enough?"

Don also remembers attending graduation ceremonies for the young pilots trained in the P-38 Lightnings and sent off much too soon, much too young, to war in Europe. Always there was a victory celebration in anticipation of their coming victories. The base multi-faith chapel was able to change the worship center from Protestant to Catholic to Jewish in a flash.

Old E. M. T.

In thinking about this next story I couldn't help but make reference to similarities in my own work. I teach computer classes in industry, some of the newer technologies to employees who are already programmers.

The advice of the gurus in object-oriented (OO) computer technology is, "Make your software—the design, architecture, whatever—as simple as possible, but no simpler." It's advice I always include when I teach OO classes. The problem being addressed is sometimes called "feature creep."

In the C Programming Language, one of the painful realities students learn is the huge size of the executable file for the very simple classic program "Hello, World!" The lesson: You shouldn't have to pay for features you don't need.

It makes sense to match resources to needs, supply to demand. My father's take on this philosophy years before resulted in what he called Exact Manning Tables.

One of my memories of the wartime personnel operation included the sequence of commanders that I had at Randolph Field in San Antonio, Texas. When I first went there, General Brandt, who had been a World War I pilot, retired shortly after I arrived. His replacement was General Hubert Harmon, who later did a tremendous job setting up the Air Force Academy and was the first superintendent at Colorado Springs. General Harmon was forward thinking and one heck of a great guy.

I worked very closely with General Harmon. We did several projects at Randolph when the crazy expansion program was in full swing. We were activating cadres like mad, and we were short on people. I had suggested that we evaluate how many people it took to run a station, because the same contingent of troops was assigned to Harlingen, Texas, for instance, as were assigned to Garden City, Kansas. Garden City had to have people take care of keeping the place heated. Snow would be characteristic there, and they'd have coal delivered which had to be shoveled to keep the place warm. Harlingen, which is semi-tropical, had the same complement of personnel as Garden. I suggested to General Harmon that we do a study on manning those stations for the positions that had to be filled.

We then set up what we called Exact Manning Tables (EMTs) and disregarded the traditional Tables of Organization (TOs). General Harmon thought this was a smart idea. We saved 36 percent of the personnel we would normally have had under TOs by using an evaluation of what it took to run a place. Every table was different because every type of station was different.

Sam Ellis, one of the old-time colonels and commander of Big Springs (Texas) *Bombing School, was very enthusiastic about the EMTs. Big Springs was using the AT-11s to train bombers; these were big training type aircraft that they'd use to drop bombs. Harlingen school and the school at Mission* (also in Texas) *were both flexible gunnery schools, but they were different, had different requirements and different contingents of people required to run their schools. It made sense to tailor the personnel requirements.*

Many of the younger commanders on those stations—and we had a bunch of kids running stations in those days—would see me coming and say, "All right, here comes old EMT." Exact-Manning-Table McCord.

The Exact Manning Table approach made a lot of sense. The Army Air Corps staff in Washington was advised about this new approach to staffing. They called down and asked General Harmon to send me to Washington to brief them about this program of management, using people as they were needed. When we recommended this to the air staff they jumped on it because they were short of personnel anyway.

A characteristic issue of that time was who got credit for a program. One of the senior generals in the planning section at Washington really got vicious about it. He was a lieutenant general and Harmon was only a major general. He told Harmon, "This is a fine idea that I thought about, and I'll have no underling of mine taking credit for this program." That's what generals were— generals. They were not to be tampered with.

Another thing that was characteristic and interesting to me was what happened when personnel were not kept challenged and involved. I'd go over to Kelly Field and Brooks Field in San Antonio. When the students were up flying, there on the flight lines were all of these so-called handlers of the aircraft, lying on their backs looking up at the sky, watching. We had the theater put on two extra schedules of movies because kids had to have something to do or they got in trouble. AWOLs were high. The sick call in the morning was crowded. When we started cutting down the excess personnel in the base, all these things disappeared.

For Group Night November 27, 1943, several officers of the Hondo Army Air Field Officers' Club put on a short musical play entitled "Exact Manning Table, or Where is My Wandering Basic Tonight?" In addition to expressing serious concerns about the demands of the EMT approach, it was a spoof on Dad's efforts and sounds like it was a fun event.

The cast of characters listed included the following: Col. Dany (Dad's stand-in); Major Negley (The Colonel's Adjutant); Four Trained Men (Experienced Man, Very Experienced Man, Very Very Experienced Man, and Too Experienced Man); and 10 others.

The scene was set in the Commanding Officer's office. The play's action reports a training program to be completed that is accomplished by having four soldiers supporting a box labeled "Work To Be Done." The Colonel explains the ground rules of the Exact Manning Table in sequence and as each rule is explained, the succeeding action affects the equilibrium of the training program. Finally the training program collapses under the weight of extra duties and too many inspections. I'm reciting enough play remnants here to give you the general idea ...

COL DANY: "... Now the first ground rule states that when we lose one experienced man, he is to be replaced by a trained man." (Cue for piano tune "Somebody Else is Taking My Place." Enter man with sign "Trained Man" and dressed as a baby. He carries a baby's bottle of milk and has a rifle slung over his shoulder, which he will give to the man he is replacing.)

BABY: "I have had my training, so no complaining, I'm the guy who's taking your place." (The Too Experienced Man shoulders the gun and marches out to the tune "Over There.")

COL DANY: "... Now the second ground rule states that able-bodied men will be released for combat by a Limited Service Man." (Cue for music "I've Been Working on the Railroad." Limited Service Man enters in wheel chair, dressed in red hospital robe and carrying gun. Doctor and nurse continually administer to the sick man with injections and pills.) CHORUS sings "We were happy and contented. Our work was smoothly done. Then the Manning Table entered and spoiled all our fun."

LIMITED SERVICE MAN: "Here I am an eager-beaver, ready to take your place. They say I have a little fever, but I still can take up a pace." (Very Very Experienced Man receives gun and marches out to "Over There" as Limited Service Man takes his place.)

COL DANY: "… There is still a third ground rule which states that WACs will be used to replace able-bodied men fit for service overseas." (Cue for "Pistol Packing Mama" as WAC enters, very giddy and coy, with blank pistols tucked in her skirt.) CHORUS sings "Here we are on bended knee, the burden is getting tough. Anything can happen, although we've had enough." WAC: "Oh, joy and goodie-goodie, I'm a member of the WACs. I'm here to take your place, boy, so now you can relax." She shoots the man she is to replace and he staggers off the stage. CHORUS sings "Put that pistol down, Babe, put that pistol down. Pistol Packin' G.I., put that pistol down."

COL DANY: "… So there we were all replaced, after a fashion, and although the burden by this time was unbearable, what do they do but slap tons of extra duty and inspection on our collapsing organization." (Cue for "Whistle While You Work." Comic soldier enters with sign *Extra Duty*. He is carrying a huge dumbbell, a gas mask and a book labeled *Sanitation Course*, all of which he deposits on the floor.)

Extra Duty Man sings "Keep busy after work, you have no time to shirk. It is my task to give you a mask and other things, you jerk. Here's a good course on hygiene, we've got to keep it clean, and to make you strong, I've brought this along, P.T. is what I mean." (Extra Duty Man takes props to Experienced Man, deposits them on him, and exits. Cue for "Stout Hearted Men.")

Enter three inspectors dressed in pith helmets, white gloves, and carrying magnifying glasses. They sing "We are the men who come time and again to inspect this field through and through. We sneak all around from the sky to the ground to inspect everything old and new." (They inspect the block; find lots of things to be fixed.) "We're through inspecting, but don't be neglecting the things that we asked you to do. Don't start to slack, 'cause we will be back to inspect this camp through and through." (Exit with dance fadeout.)

The men holding the block are tired, complain, think they can't go on much longer, but hope for some rest. Just then the Air Inspector comes up from the audience for a final inspection to end all inspections. He ends up climbing on a chair behind the block, which is now only a few inches off the floor, and jumps into the Training Block and the whole thing collapses. (Applause, applause.)

Training the Trainers

We created other additional improvements in personnel policies after the EMT scheme. The cream of the crop, the best mental and physical specimens, came in as pilot trainees. Yet we were washing out 85 percent of those who came in because the kids doing the instruction didn't know how to instruct. Again, I made a suggestion to General Harmon. And I'm not taking undue credit for this. I did this.

"General, we can do something better than this. Let's set up a training school for instructors here at Randolph and see if we can't lower the washout rate of these fine kids." I knew the recruits who followed would not match the quality that we had been washing out. He said, "Do it."

I called in people from our assignees, those who had educational experience. Lo and behold, in that bunch was H. Leigh Baker, Harry Leigh Baker. He had been the principal when I was at Manhattan High School. He was the one who had given me a hard time about high school fraternities.[48] *I ordered him in from the station out in the field for a discussion. I planned to have him set up and manage that instructor school because he had a doctorate in education and was a graduate from Columbia. I knew he would do an excellent job with this.*

I'll tell you, this was fascinating—I knew in advance exactly how I wanted to handle this meeting. I first let him sit at Cooley Field (San Antonio) *outside my window. And, talking to my secretary, I said, "I'll have you understand I'll have no high school fraternities in this operation!" It was said loudly enough that Baker could hear it*

---

[48] My mother had also been involved in a banned high school sorority—was president, even—at Manhattan High School, and I would later have H. Leigh Baker for an education course at K-State in the late '50s.

through the open window. He stuck his head around the corner and said, "Hal McCord, what in the world are you doing here?"

I was then a lieutenant colonel and he was a captain. "Come in. It's a pleasure meeting you again." We had old home week reminiscing about our high school days. I told him what I wanted done; that I wanted a training school set up for training instructors. "You can have your choice of people to come here out of our command."

He set up the school and started the first class of training instructors. The kids really took to it. The second class that attended the training but had not graduated, and the first class that had graduated went back to Baker's instructor school for training new recruits. By the time we were in the third group our washout ratio had just reversed: we were washing out 15 percent and using 85 percent. This program became a standard for the entire curriculum to train instructors on how to instruct.

Later, at our 50th class reunion of the class of '29 at Manhattan High, Baker was among those attending. He got up and said he had a story he wanted to tell, and it involved me. He told how I had let him sit outside and cool his heels while I was relating one of the things that he had originally said about there being "no high school fraternities." About how he had gone to my dad when my dad was president of the school board and gotten his approval for limiting this type of activity in the high school. About how he thought it was divisive. And cliquish. And distracting from studies. All of that.

On August 13, 1943, Lt. Col. McCord was reassigned as acting assistant chief of staff, A-1 (personnel) until August 30, 1943; then assigned to general staff with troops as assistant chief of staff, A-1 at Headquarters Army Air Forces Central Flying Training Command at Randolph. September 1, 1943, 201 file papers show a rating for "Pistol Expert (dismounted), the highest category, over sharpshooter, marksman." He was authorized to wear appropriate insignia.

On May 19, 1944, Dad was reassigned to Air Transport Command (ATC), 503d AAF Base Unit, National Airport, Washington, D.C., effective upon completion of a 12-day leave. By the time he actually arrived in Washington the assignment was changed to the 501st AAF Base Unit (Hq ATC), and he was given another seven days leave prior to going overseas.

Meanwhile Back at the Home Front...

The separations began even before Dad went overseas; they began in the CCC Camps. Mother said that Dad was not present for the birth of any of their three children. Dad says that, *Even at Randolph, during wartime, it was not a choice. I was assigned many places where I couldn't take Ivalee with me. I was away an awful lot—you know that.*

When Dad went overseas in June, 1944, Mom gathered up her children like the good mother hen she was and took them from Texas back to Manhattan, Kansas. This was familiar territory with better support systems: two grandmothers and many friends.

We spent that school year of 1944-45 at 1731 Poyntz Avenue, renting the Wilson Tripp house while Mr. Tripp was on a year's sabbatical and took his family with him. This red brick house is the first house really up the hill as you go north in that block and has around three dozen steps from the curb up to the front door.

Marilyn, Janice, Ivalee, Don—1731 Poyntz Avenue, 1944-45

Ivalee and I set up a code before I left. We got a Mercator projection map used in the military and push pins to mark locations. Though weekly letters were censored both coming and going, we established enough communication so Ivalee could do the charting and keep a rough track of where I was. I was not allowed to clearly identify where I was and sometimes the censors blacked out words.

I remember that Don and I won rabbits in the Easter egg hunt at City Park that year. We had a cage for them by the garage that was on the alley behind the house. They were both New Zealand whites with red eyes. Don's rabbit strangled itself in the chicken wire of the cage in the first year. Mine, named "Scratchy," would live for several years, attend kindergarten more than once for show-and-tell and die when a neighborhood child forgot to close the cage door and a dog got him.

Janice ended up that year with some minor disease due to a vitamin C deficiency. Mother couldn't understand why, as she served us orange juice <u>every</u> morning. Then she realized that Janice often didn't finish her juice, Don did. He was already taking over the meal time garbage-can duty from Dad. As he became the man of the house he had the last turns on the crank when making homemade ice cream with the old hand-cranked machine.

When the Tripps returned, we moved to 1413 Laramie to a house then owned by my Grandmother Hedge. We lived there from 1945 to 1954 and that house holds many memories for our family, both good and bad.

Air Transport Command

Dad's overseas assignments were all with the Air Transport Command, ATC. Essentially the ATC was an airliner for the military. It began as an outgrowth of the ferrying command that was established to deliver US-built aircraft to Britain under the lend-lease agreement, allowing the US to provide planes yet remain neutral.

Prior to Pearl Harbor, Army Air Force combat pilots had done most of the ferrying. Although some planes made the Atlantic crossing via ship, others were flown over. Pan Am contracted to deliver US-built planes and flew them from Miami to Khartoum, Sudan. After 1942 the contract was extended to deliver planes to Cairo and Teheran. Eastern Airlines and Northwest Airlines later joined the program, flying other routes such as across Alaska and over the North Pole.

On June 20, 1942, General Henry H. "Hap" Arnold, chief of staff of the Army Air Forces, officially established the ATC and made it responsible for all ferrying and transportation tasks except those necessary for combat operations.

When the US entered the war, combat pilots were needed for combat roles. The ATC then employed civilians for both aircrews and administrative positions, and there was a scramble to train more pilots.[49] Dad was a part of this pilot training expansion. By 1944, the situation had changed; pilot training programs were cut and civilian

---

[49] One of Dad's fellow officers in the command at Casablanca, Robert E. Lee Turner, quipped that ATC stood for "all terrified civilians." The ATC has a website that I used for additional information on their activities.

instructors were again commissioned for ATC duty. The Women's Air Service Pilots (WASPS) were also an important yet often underrated part of the ATC ferrying effort.

Although nearly 90 percent of ATC flying started out as military-contract flying by the commercial airlines, by the end of the war military crews were doing around 81 percent of the flying. Finding crews was one problem, finding planes was another. Only two of the 450 C-46s ordered by the Army before the war had been built by Dec. 7, 1941, the day Pearl Harbor was bombed.

Initially the military bought and adapted commercial planes. The C-47 version of the DC-3 performed admirably but was too slow and lacked payload for over-water transportation. The C-54 Skymaster was on order but not yet available. In the meantime, C-87s and C-46s performed much of the ATC mission.

Ferrying combat aircraft was the most important ATC task; hauling aircraft parts and other material too time-critical to send by ships was also high on the list. Air rescue and weather reconnaissance were other parts of the ATC mission. The ATC was later involved in the ferrying of relief items for Berlin during the Berlin airlift operation.

Supplying the China-Burma-India (CBI) Theater where my father first served in his overseas duty was the longest and most famous of the ATC routes and the only one that came close to being a combat mission. Flying the Hump was a route from India over the Himalayas into China. After Japan took control of Burma in May 1942, this air route was the <u>only</u> way in to China. The only way to get fuel and supplies to groups such as the Doolittle Raiders and Chenault's Flying Tigers. The Hump provided some of the most dangerous flying in the world with violent storms, snow and ice in high altitudes over the mountains. And carrying heavy loads, especially airplane fuel, only exacerbated the other factors.

The accident rate was high. This was especially true in C-87s and C-109s; Liberator-type transports suffered a 500 percent higher accident rate than C-54s and other ATC transports. So many planes were lost on the Hump—more than 600—that the northern route into China became known as The Aluminum Trail.

When the war ended, the Air Transport Command was the largest airline in the world with routes that led literally all over it.

Eastern Air Command

May 29, 1944. Special orders relieved Dad from further duty and assignment with the 501st and assigned Dad to Headquarters, India China Wing ATC, Calcutta, effective June 1 and to report to 503d AAF Base Unit. There was a flat per diem of $7 authorized in the continental U.S., to be suspended when billeted and subsisted. "While travel by air, sixty-five (65) lbs. of baggage is atzd [authorized]. Baggage will physically accompany officer. … Immunization against yellow fever will be accomplished within four years but not less than ten days prior to departure from the United States."

Change-of-address cards would list his address as APO #4377. A June 2 memo increased the baggage allowance to 75 pounds. "In addition to that equipment listed in List E, this officer is atzd to draw pistol, holster and ammunition."

Dad's gear in List E included the following, quantity (1) unless otherwise specified:

"Gloves, mosquito; Flashlight; Bag, duffel; Bag, canvas field; Strap canvas field bag; Can meat, complete; Canteen, complete; Headnet, mosquito; Insect powder; (2) Repellent, insect; Necklace identification; Packet first aid; Knife trench w/scabbard; Belt pistol; Holster M1916; Pistol auto Cal..45; (3) Magazines pistol Cal..45; (21) Cartridges Pistol Cal..45; Pocket magazine double web."

Dad had hoped for a bit of extra time to familiarize himself with the Eastern Air Command where he was to be assistant chief of staff personnel. There would be no extra time. He was slated to be an official courier, transporting official documents "exempted from censorship" and "to be exempted from examination by customs." There are forms with signatures of Dad and two different Courier Transfer Officers; the form notes that "Courier departed at 2000 3 June 1944 … with pouch 43-358 APS 1549-69." He would not arrive in Delhi until June 10.

General, You've Got Mail

When I got my orders to go overseas, General Tom Handy was director of plans for the Department of Army. He would check the overseas orders that anybody had, and he knew who was headed overseas and where they were going. His assistant was Milburn Huston, a chap that I had been on CCC duty with. Milburn called me and said, "Hal, I understand you're going to take a trip?" I said, "Yeah, I was planning on it." He said, "General Handy would like to talk to you."

Handy was a four-star general, and I didn't know what in the world was going on. He said, "Be here at 1400 hours." I went from my office to my quarters and got into a freshly pressed set of summer clothes, khakis, and polished my shoes and polished my brass. I was at General Handy's office at 1400. I checked in and Milburn took me in to General Handy. I saluted, "McCord reporting as requested." "Fine. I understand you're going to take a trip?" "Yes, sir." "Where are you going?" "I believe you probably already know, General." We had been instructed not to talk. He laughed and said, "I think you'll do."

I didn't know what he meant with "You'll do," but he said, "I have a mission for you. How are you traveling?" "I'm traveling on a priority three." That was going to give me time to see some of the stations along the way and observe their operations. I needed to get a little bit more familiar with what I was going to be facing when I arrived at the Eastern Air Command, which was, at that time, at New

Delhi. I was going to be placed in a position of assistant chief of staff personnel.

"Well," he said, "I don't believe that's going to be quite the way you're going to travel." He called his secretary in and said, "McCord is making a trip overseas. Amend his orders to provide priority one." And to me, "How much baggage do you have?" "Well, I have two foot-lockers." At that time, they were limiting everyone to 65 pounds. "Is that going to be enough?" "I think that's all I have, Sir." "All right."

He told his secretary to make the orders for unlimited weight allowance. "And," he said, "make it concurrent travel. I don't want the baggage to come along some time two or three weeks later. They'll travel with McCord."

I didn't realize what he'd done to me when he said priority one. When we finished, he told me, "You've got to go back and get an hour or so of rest. You're going to leave fairly quickly. The next available southbound airplane—you're going to be on it." The next available aircraft left about 2000 hours. "You'll also need a sidearm. Do you have one?" "Yes sir, and I know how to use it."

I went back to my quarters and gave a copy of my orders to the transportation section. Then I sacked out and went to bed. I hadn't been in bed more than an hour or so after having something to eat when the sergeant came in.

WAR DEPARTMENT
WAR DEPARTMENT GENERAL STAFF
OPERATIONS DIVISION
WASHINGTON 25, D. C.

2 June, 1944.

SUBJECT: To Identify Lieut. Colonel Hal H. McCord, O-302922,
A.C. as an Official Army Courier.

TO: Collector, U. S. Bureau of Customs.

1. The above named person is acting in an official capacity
as courier for this office and is carrying one (1) mail sack.
The sack is numbered S4934 and is addressed as follows: "Deputy
Theater Commander, USAF, CBI, New Delhi, India, from Assistant
Chief of Staff, Operations Division, War Department General
Staff, Washington, D. C."

2. The above mentioned mail sack is further identified
by the inscription: "Official United States Army Communication
Exempted from Censorship", followed by the signature of the
Chief, Asiatic Section, OPD, WDGS.

THOS. T. HANDY,
Major General,
Assistant Chief of Staff.

W. N. WOOD,
Colonel, G. S. C.,
Chief, Asiatic Theater,
Theater Group, WDGPD.

War Dept. Letter from General Thomas T. Handy, 2 June 1944

*"I didn't realize," he said, "you're on a priority one." "That's
right." "Your aircraft leaves at 2000 tonight. Get everything ready
because we'll load you on that airplane. You're going to ride that
airplane all the way to Delhi." "Ooh. Am I not going to have time to
stop anywhere along the line?" "No, you're not."*

General Handy had given me a brown parcel. He said, "I don't want you to have anything else to do but deliver this. I'm giving you a handcuff and a chain to that item. Don't let it out of your sight. If anything happens to the aircraft you're on, it has a self-destruct connection to it. Destroy it." He emphasized, "That's first. I don't care what happens to you after that."

It was a contract flight, one of TWA's such flights going to Miami. We landed in Miami, and again I checked in and went to bed. I hadn't been in bed 30 minutes before one of the sergeants came by. "Colonel, you're en route on the next flight out. It leaves in 30 minutes. Get everything ready." I inquired, "Well, where is my baggage?" "We've already taken care of that. It's on the airplane."

The military contracted quite a few commercial airlines then and especially ones with transoceanic capability. This was a Pan Am flight. They were carrying two 3350 Pratt and Whitney engines, replacements for B-29s. I was going to be riding with the cargo so I was back in the cargo hold in a bucket seat though I didn't stay there very long. We were headed toward Belém in Brazil. I'd met the crew en route down to Miami from Washington, D.C.

The radio operator for that flight was a chap named Ben Cooper. We had been on the ground about an hour when Ben came back and said, "The captain says that you're going to be awfully lonely back here. Come on up and ride with the crew." They moved me up front where they had bunks set up for the crew. So, I got a little more shut-eye.

206

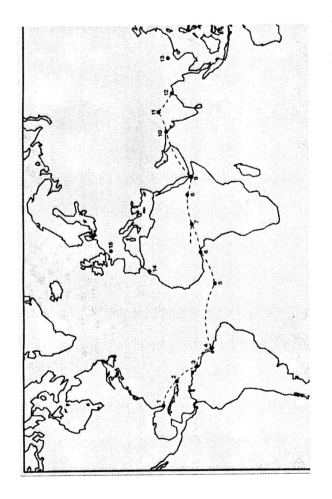

Dad's Route to India (connect the dots): 1-Miami, Florida; 2-Puerto Rico; 3-Atkinson in Guyana; 4-Belém, Brazil; 5-Ascension Island, mid-Atlantic; 6-Accra, Ghana; 7-Nigeria (Kano-Maiduguri loop); 8-Khartoum, Sudan; 9-Eritrea, Ethiopia; 10-Karachi, Pakistan (still India then); 11-Delhi, India; 12-Calcutta, India. Also marked are 13-Kunming, China; 14-Casablanca, Morocco; 15-Paris, France.

We went into Borinquen, a Coast Guard Air Station in Puerto Rico, and from there jumped to Atkinson Air Base in British Guyana along the east coast of South America. We got into Atkinson sometime during the late night or real early morning. I remember that they had to circle the field two or three times to clear the green parrots off the field. There was a red alert out because the green parrots could be devastating and were a hazard to the flight. The Pan Am was a four-engine type aircraft, a DC-4. We got up at Atkinson and headed into Belém across the Amazon delta through the Ornoco area.

I remember the co-pilot saying, "Well, you've got to work your way across; you can't just sit back there and sleep. Here's a set of charts. I want you to plot a course to Belém." I started plotting. He said, "How are you on your navigation? Can you recognize marks of information that you might enjoy using and get necessary data from these instruments?" I said, "I think so." So he had me check their compass settings and other instrumentation and estimate arrival at Belém.

We were on the ground at Belém just long enough to service the airplane and get a bite of breakfast. When we got up and started off, this same crew was going to fly me to Ascension Island, located in the Atlantic midway between Brazil and Africa. Then Cooper really put me to work. He wanted to know how my astronomical observations were. I told him I'd had a little experience with this sort of thing. "All right," he said, "I want you to do me a sun shot."

He wanted me to plot 20 seconds before we crossed the meridian, 10 seconds before we crossed the meridian, the second we crossed meridian point, then ten seconds and 20 seconds after, and plot those on the map. "When we are 'in the box' for that location, we'll have an absolute fix for our position. I want to know exactly where you plot that to be."

This was a Mercator projection map; it's a little different than a Polyconic projection and much more accurate on mileage. "Also, I want you to give me an estimate of when we're going to be into Ascension." They made a bet. If I gave them within 10 seconds of the actual arrival time into Ascension, either plus or minus, they'd buy me lunch. If I missed it, I'd have to buy them lunch. So, they made it a pretty good game, and we had a lot of fun out of it.

Finally, as we were getting close to the target point, the Pan Am captain said, "Look over to the right there. What do you see?" "Well, I see some clouds over there." "Do you know what they are?" "No, sir." "What do you estimate Ascension?" I gave him a figure. He said, "Those clouds, they cover Ascension." They were on the projection of whatever mountain peak it was. The runway at Ascension had been cut out through the sides of two mountains; you came in over the water and you landed and you took off over the water. They bought lunch that day.

I never will forget that place. Over the mess hall a sign said, "Take all you want, but eat all you take."[50] *The reason for this slogan*

---

[50] As a child, I grew up hearing that phrase regularly, perhaps more than any other. The bodies Dad saw swept up each morning in the Calcutta area also contributed to this gospel.

was that everything had to be flown in—every supply item took effort to acquire.

I got a new crew to fly from Ascension to Accra in the Gold Coast. Ghana, just under the western hump of Africa. The Captain was Johnny Rogerson, an old-timer with Pan Am; he had something like 12 or 13,000 hours. He'd flown boats, the big sea planes, most of his life. When the previous Pan Am crew turned me over to him, they said, "McCord's been checked out on his piloting; he's also been checked out on his sun shots—on his astronomical observations." Rogerson said, "I'll take him. He's OK." Then they told me, "Now, you get this plane into Accra."

We were getting into some southerly winds, and we had to observe and correct for the effect of the winds. They would drop a smoke bomb to see the direction of the wind, and estimate the intensity so we'd know what our drift was. Captain Rogerson had me give him a heading that would compensate for the drift. This was interesting, and I enjoyed doing the navigation. We were pretty much on course. The thing I didn't know until we landed was that they had a radio beacon, and the radio operator was tied in and locked into flying the radio beam in. It really didn't make any difference what I told him, they were going to fly the radio beacon anyway.

We got into Accra and were on the ground maybe three or four hours. I had really wanted to see the place and see what their operation was, but I didn't have time. As a matter of fact, again I got back in the bunk and was asleep for a while.

When we took off from Accra, there were two stations in Nigeria that we were supposed to check on going into Khartoum, Sudan: Kano and Maiduguri. The pilot on that flight asked if I'd ever been through that area at all. "No, I know nothing about it." "All right. We'll divert just a little bit. We've got some time."

We got down on the deck, and he asked, "Have you ever flown four engines?" I said, "Yes, I have. I'm checked out in a B-24." He responded, "This plane is much like the B-24. All right, move over there, and you take the controls. I want you to drop down to a thousand feet. Then you can better observe what you're seeing."

So, we went down to that level and were on the south edge of the Lake Chad area. We saw a lot of wildlife. Elephant herds and all sorts of African beasts. It was fascinating. Unfortunately, when we dropped down on that one area—this was between Kano and Maiduguri—we frightened a herd of elephants, and they stampeded through a village. That herd just pummeled the thorn-type fence that they had up around the village, and we could see the poor natives running off like mad in all different directions. We don't think the elephants killed any of the townspeople, but we never did find out for sure.

We went into Maiduguri and checked it out, then dropped into Khartoum. Khartoum was interesting. We hadn't been on the ground an hour and were not quite fully serviced, when one of the natives came in. "La Haroof! Sahib, La Haroof! La Haroof! La Haroof, Sahib!" The big storm, a sandstorm, was blowing in. They covered the engines with protective covering to keep the sand from getting into them. Then we went into the quarters, and they gave us wet towels to put over our heads and faces so that we could breathe without getting loaded up with sand.

It was about, oh, maybe 30 or 40 minutes after that, that this wall of sand coming in off the desert hit Khartoum. We were on the ground 12 hours. It took that long for the storm to blow out. Then, of course, they had to really clean out the aircraft and the engines and check everything before we took off.

We left Khartoum and flew from there into Eritrea on the east coast of Ethiopia where we had a station and changed crews again. We flew down over the mouth of the Red Sea. There was a British station there that we checked in with en route to Karachi. We landed and again refueled so that we had enough to get to Karachi. Karachi was then in India; now that area is Pakistan. All of the time I was feeling like I was a prisoner. And I really was. They were careful to take good care of me, but it was kind of a lonely trip. When we were over an island off the coast of Saudi Arabia out in the Arabian Sea, they pointed out that this particular island below us was only about six miles off the coast of Saudi Arabia. Nobody ever tried to swim it because it was full of sharks; there had never been anyone who made it. It would've made a good prison to put somebody on. They'd never have left.

We cruised from there into Karachi. The crew had warned me that when we got to Karachi there would be some interesting operations when we landed. There would be hanger's-on that made the arrival of every trip. And here she came, a diseased little gal with a baby slung over her shoulder in a rag, like a big tea cloth. This woman was a habitual greeter to incoming airlines. Her approach was "Baksh sish, Sahib, baksh sish. No momma, no poppa, no pilot, no co-pilot. Baksh sish, baksh sish." Begging alms. The crew said, "Don't have anything to do with her; she is one of those poor, diseased women that is ... running sores and all this horrible stuff. One of the pitiful low-cast people." She greeted our airplane, and it was true. She was as they had described.

We weren't on the ground long at Karachi. Just long enough to get service, then we flew on to New Delhi. I still had the package tied to my left arm. It was going to be a little difficult to get my clothes changed.

I got into Delhi and had a shower and shave, clean clothes and went in and asked for an audience with General Stilwell's backup man in Delhi. His adjutant, a young major, said, "Colonel, fine, I'll take that for you." I said, "No you won't." "Oh yes, I'm going to take it. I'll take it and give it to General Sultan."[51]

I just reached down and undid the holster to get at my .45. And he said, "You're serious, aren't you?" "Absolutely. I was told by General Handy to deliver it to nobody but General Stilwell or his deputy, and you aren't one of the ones on his list. Thank you. Now will you please announce me? I'll appreciate it." He went in and announced me.

---

[51] Major General Dan I. Sultan was Deputy Theater Commander, USAAF, CBI.

I didn't know how else to handle it. I was under orders, and I wasn't going to do any violation of that order. He took me right in. That's what I intended to have happen.

I said, "McCord reporting from Washington, sir." And, General Sultan said, "What's the mission?" "I have a package here from General Handy for War Plans Division, and I am to deliver it to General Stilwell or his deputy." He said, "I am his deputy." "Do you have proper I.D?" "Yes, I do have." "All right, fine. Then you will have the key to take this off and take it." "Yes, I do have." "Fine," I said, "you take it."

He took the package and opened it and disarmed the destruction device that was in it. When he opened the mail he said, "My God!" And he called his adjutant to bring in his people. He said, "I've got the war plan for China." And that was my first idea of exactly what it was—it was the plan of operations against the Japanese in China.

Then he looked up and noticed me and said, "What are you doing here?" I said, "Sir, you have not signed my receipt yet. I can't leave until I have a receipt for that package." It was in the package. He said, "I'll take care of that right now." And he did. He signed the receipt on it. And he said, "Thank you very much, Col. McCord. I appreciate your delivering this, and it would be helpful if you forgot what you heard." I said not to worry about it; I saluted. "You're dismissed." "Yes, sir."

From there I went to my quarters and thought about what it was that I had been charged with delivering.

CBI: The Neglected Theater, 1943-44

The "Bloody Tarawa" battle on a V-shaped atoll in the Gilbert Islands of the Central Pacific taught us some lessons. At the end of 76 hours of savage fighting that November 1943, 4,690 of 4,836 Japanese were dead and 3,301 Marines were killed, missing or wounded. In fact, the Marines lost over 1,000 men, 20 percent of the invasion force. It became painfully clear that the Japanese were fanatical, tenacious, willing to go to the death. American losses were going to be heavy. It was not worth taking every island in the Pacific inch by inch.

During the height of the Tarawa battle Churchill, Roosevelt, and Chiang Kai Shek[52] met at Cairo. The emphasis of this conference was the Pacific theater with special attention being given to yet another forgotten war front in the Far East—China, Burma and India (CBI). Burma was the key to China's supply lifeline; unfortunately it was in Japanese hands. Admiral Lord Louis Mountbatten headed the Southeast Asia Command, and Lt. General Joseph W. Stilwell was his deputy.

Stilwell was chief of staff for Chiang Kai Shek as well as commander-in-chief of all American forces in the CBI. Stilwell

---

[52] I was teaching at the American School in Taipei, Taiwan, at the time of Chiang's death in 1975. Along with colleagues I attended the memorial services held for Chiang, who was considered a father figure by many of the Mainlanders who had found refuge in Taiwan and still hoped Chiang would lead in retaking the Chinese Mainland. In 1976, Chiang's granddaughter, Chiang Yo-Mei was in my high school geometry class. She was white, blond, looked Western and spoke excellent English, but when she asked me questions, her notes in the margins of her text were always in Chinese. She was a delightful student.

contemptuously called Chiang "The Peanut"—they were not on the best of terms. Chiang was in fact stubborn, uncooperative and demanding. Stilwell, forced to fight with little in the way of supplies, troops and top-level understanding, became a bitter critic of one and all and earned the name "Vinegar Joe."

Churchill and Roosevelt had decided to relieve the Soviets, who had suffered immense losses on the Eastern Front, by diverting Nazi attention. Their plan was to invade Axis-held North Africa with Operation Torch. A squadron of bombers in Florida, originally designated for China, was diverted to Egypt along with 10 American bombers then in India and also intended for missions over China. If they could break Hitler's grip on Tunisia, the Allies would be able to use the short sea route to Egypt and India instead of being forced to go all the way around the Cape.

Claire L. Chennault, a USAAF captain and an adviser to the Chinese Government since July 1937, had been active in the CBI Theatre since shortly after Pearl Harbor. On December 8, 1941, the day after the Japanese attack in Hawaii, he flew three squadrons, then based near Mandalay in Burma, across the mountains to the Chinese city of Kunming. He was promoted to colonel that day.

On December 19 the Flying Tigers[53] intercepted 10 Japanese warplanes on a bombing raid from Hanoi and Kunming in their first

---

[53] During the summer of 1974, I taught school with one of Chennault's pilots. Between the two of us, we were charged with taking five 7th grade youngsters—four Chinese and one Thai—in an English-speaking school in Taipei run by Filipino nuns and improving their English skills sufficiently so that they would be able to move ahead with their age group to the ninth grade. One of the subjects I was to

combat mission; nine of those 10 were shot down. On December 24, 54 Japanese bombers and 24 fighters raided air installations in Rangoon, the Burmese capital, and destroyed many allied aircraft on the ground.

The Flying Tigers managed to take off safely in the midst of the bombing and strafing and shoot down six of the Japanese planes, losing two of their own. Chennault's pilots provided a visible and highly able US presence in the defense of China against further Japanese inroads.

By April 1942, the grip of Japan on Burma had intensified. The Japanese had seized Lashio, the terminus of the Burma Road used by the Americans and British to send supplies to China. General Stilwell's position inside China became untenable, and he withdrew to India taking with him 100,000 Chinese troops. Four days later, the British were forced to abandon the port of Akyab on the Bay of Bengal, less than 100 miles from the border of India. Much had been lost. "Triumph and disaster marched together."

The Japanese then began a railroad link from Burma to Thailand, using British, Australian and Dutch POWs as work crews. Lt. Col. Lindsay Ride, an Australian surgeon, escaped from captivity and was subsequently appointed a representative of the British Military Intelligence escape organization.

---

teach was French. The French was only a token subject, thank goodness, as I only had 9 hours of French from Kansas State and no other practice with it. My colleague spoke excellent Chinese; I only knew a few words and the students were forced to speak English with me.

Disease was taking an extremely heavy toll among the POWs. Col. Ride helped organize the return to India of POWs who managed to escape and provided medical help for tens of thousands of Chinese in an area where the Chinese Army had no medical service at all. From his base at Kweilin, China, Ride also issued weather reports twice daily and was of inestimable help to the Allies.

Decisions following the November '43 Cairo conference were to have the British begin working their way back into Burma at the Western front, and Stilwell, with Chinese troops and special American units, begin operating in northern Burma. That campaign opened December 21, 1943.

By 1944, the Allies began pushing the Japanese out of positions they had occupied in Burma since early in the war. Stilwell, aided more by Merril's Marauders, an American commando-like unit, than by his own Chinese troops, took the airfield at Myitkyina, Burma, May 17. It was a tough battle that could have gone either way. They retook the Ledo Road, the western section of the Burma Road, and reopened the land route to China.

By the close of 1944, B-29s flew against Japan in their home territory from strategic Saipan in the Marianas.

CBI Air Theatre

My assignment after delivering the war plan for China was to the Eastern Air Command at Delhi. General Stratemeyer was the commanding general at that time—June 1944—and I was to report to

218

him as the assistant chief of staff personnel. It was an interesting change for me from the stateside duty. We then moved from the base at Delhi to Rishra, about 80 kilometers northeast of Calcutta on the Hooghly River, the most westerly channel of the Ganges in its delta. We had under our supervision the air command units in China, Burma and India, known as the CBI Air Theatre. The 1300th AAF Base Unit. This was a broad area geographically to cover—all of India, all of Burma, all of Southeast Asia and all of China. I was there from June to October of '44.

In my assignment to Stratemeyer's command, I was replacing Colonel Gordon, who was anxious to return to the States. He was in fact, ready to go and hoped to catch the next westbound flight back. He'd been in India quite a while and apparently he had had a belly full. I didn't get much briefing from him, so I had to learn a lot of things from his staff and his people there in short order.

They were good people. They accepted me readily and briefed me on everything that they felt I needed to know immediately. There were a lot more things I would learn as I became familiar with the command. I covered a lot of territory. There were a lot of stations. The war was really on at that point.

The Airborne Chinese Corporal

Once, I needed to get to the China side of our area because we wanted to make some personnel changes there which General Strat and I had discussed. His staff flew me across the Hump on one of the transports that was delivering material to Claire Chennault's 14th Air Force, the Flying Tigers. We went first to Kunming, then up to Chungking where the 14th was located. They wanted to move a Chinese regiment into the Ming Swa Salient, a military area of operations in the southeast part of China.

The plan was to solidify the Allied positions and start moving the Japanese out of that area. This particular Chinese regiment had been assembled at Chungking for the purpose of assisting in this movement to oust the Japanese. We loaded the regiments on Gooney Birds, C-46s, to transport them down to the Ming Swa area on the border.

During the flight an interesting thing happened. The Chinese had a corporal whom apparently they didn't like. I mean, he was bad news to them. We had loaded him on the manifest but he never made Ming Swa. We found out later that they'd pushed him out of the airplane at about 10 or 12,000 feet without a parachute. His life was the cost of their not being very happy with him. We had to account for that. The Chinese had no compunction whatsoever about getting done what they wanted to have done. Our crew on that flight didn't know that the Chinese troops had opened one of the cargo doors and kicked him out.

Chinese Bandits

The Hump was the air route across the Himalayas from Calcutta to Kunming to service forces such as Chennault's Flying Tigers. I was working at the Kunming end of The Hump out of Yunnan Yi, the western Yunnan province bordering Indochina and Burma. One of the guys who flew for Chennault was a fellow named Tott. He had quite an operation, and the Japanese were fearful of him. The P-40s had sharp noses on 'em; they were scared to death of those.

A plane had gone down on the eastern side of the Himalayas. We pretty well had a fix on it because of the search-and-rescue radio that became an automatic type beam we could follow in on. The ELT— emergency locator transmitter. We found the airplane. There was nobody there alive. Just bodies that had been completely stripped of everything.

All three of us in the search party had United States flags on the back of our jackets. As we started to fan out, searching the area to see what else we could find, bandits came out of the hills and started after us. They were the dirtiest-looking humans you ever saw. Dressed in furs and this type of stuff. And were they big! They carried typical folk-country knives, crude-type machetes—we're talking a foot and a half long here! And they could really operate 'em.

They started coming after us. There were two of 'em. I remember I was a little isolated from where the other guys were, and the bandits were coming at me. I told 'em, "Ti Kai Joe. It's OK, don't bother me." They didn't pay any attention to that or they may have not understood it or whatever. I could tell what they were going to do though. They planned on separating me from whatever I had.

That's when I found out just what my .45 could do. I drew it. They didn't pay any attention to it, just kept coming. I hit one dead center. I never saw anything fold up like he did. The other one paid no

221

attention. Apparently that made him even more eager to get to me. So I had to do both of 'em.

There was a village not too far away. We went back by the village and explained to the headmaster of the village that these Chinese bandits were up in the nearby hills, and they were dead. That I had killed them. The villagers wanted to give me the keys to the kingdom because these guys had been harassing them and terrorizing them. Stealing them blind about everything. The headman was very happy that they had been dispatched. It bothered me quite a while but there ... there wasn't any choice. I found out what .45s will do.

Search and rescue missions there were an ad hoc assignment, meaning there was no particular designated search and rescue unit. Whoever was available at the bases nearest the point of loss of any aircraft would do the search and rescue. We were equipped with finder radios that could track the emergency locator transmitter— ELT—signal from a downed aircraft.

That area was kind of like a rain forest, and the tree canopy from the top of the trees to the base was some 200 feet. If an aircraft went down in it, the forest opened up and took the plane and closed up again. We had a real challenge in trying to find anything. We did, however, have jeeps available at that time. We got as close as possible by jeep, on a road if we were lucky, then by foot. We didn't have helicopters. Not like today's search and rescue.

A Theatre Ribbon with a Gold Star

I thought about the ribbons I've had when that Navy Admiral shot himself a while back over questions about an award of some sort.[54] *He had a V for valor from the Viet Nam operations, and there was perhaps some mistake about his really earning it. "Zoom" Aldren and other senior generals now retired knew the operation and knew what he was doing and said it was an absolutely useless thing for him to shoot himself. It was tragic; he was an outstanding officer.*

I've thought about that many times. There wasn't any question about what I had. I had the specific theater ribbon with a gold star on it, representing one combat operation. This combat event happened when the Japanese attacked us as we were building the airport at Chanyi. That's when a slit trench full of water and snakes became a fairly welcome place to hide. It was like, snakes get out of the way—I need this place.

Chanyi, southeast of Kunming, was an interesting air base. It was set up to provide emergency landing and fuel for the B-29s when they were flying out of India across The Hump and bombing Tokyo and Japan. We had a fuel dump there and supplies for the B-29s.

I'm grateful our communication system with the Chinese worked. When a group of Japanese Betties (Betty was a name we had assigned to this type of bomber) *were headed our way, the Chinese in that area advised us they had observed a flight of Betties on a course that*

---

[54] We were recording these stories in May 1996 about the time a top Navy officer, Adm. Jeremy Boorda, killed himself after medal inquiries about the legitimacy of his combat valor pins.

223

would take them to Chanyi. The fuel dump was on the east side of the Chanyi base, and we had dummy camouflage on a dummy fuel dump on the west side. Well, the Japanese just bombed the bedevil out of the west side. They didn't get the east side, didn't bother with the dump at all.

When they were coming in, we then alerted the 51ˢᵗ Fighter Group that we had "ducks on the pond coming in." The commander of that unit was a boy from Kansas City named Louie Hughes. Louie had joined the English early in the game and flew for them in the Battle of Britain. Later, when the United States got into the war, he transferred back to the U.S. Army Air Corps. Louis had the 51ˢᵗ Fighter Group, and they flew P-51s, Mustangs. He just loved them, and he knew how to use them.

When these Betties were coming in—we had radioed the 51ˢᵗ that we had varmints approaching—the 51ˢᵗ was about 30 to 45 minutes away. The Ps at that point were equipped with six 2.5-millimeter rockets, three on each wing. Louie's people knew how to fly those babies. When that group of Betties came in, his people caught up with them. They made an interception after the Japanese had bombed Chanyi and were starting back. He never let one of them get away. He got 'em all.

As the Japanese hit, we dove into that slit trench to avoid being caught by the shrapnel and the bombing. We didn't lose any of our people. The Chinese lost some people, but our American forces there—there weren't too many—came out virtually unscathed. We had all of these Chinese coolies assisting in building that air base for the B-29s, and they either didn't understand the gravity of the situation or thought they were immune. It was too bad. Perhaps some of them decided they were going to go to join their ancestors anyway, and this might as well be the way. They did have safe areas that they could've gotten into, but they were awfully hard to communicate with.

We would show them what we wanted done, and they would do it. They were excellent workers but would do the strangest things in building an air base or building a runway. The women would carry good-sized rocks on their heads and bring the rocks in where the coolies were. The coolies would sit there with hammers and break those rocks up into pieces, then hand-place these in the runway they were building. They had a roller—a great big hunk of stone, a round-type roller—pulled by a team of coolies. Like a team of oxen in harness. It was almost as though they had an axle through it. They'd start that thing moving, and if one of the coolies fell, they didn't pay any attention to him. They'd just run over him. Never stopped moving.

Another odd thing would happen when the B-29s came in to land at those bases. The Chinese had a philosophy that every one of them had a personal devil, and if they could break that chain between them and their personal devil that was always chasing them, they'd be rid of that devil. So they'd try to run across a runway ahead of a landing airplane to break that chain between them and the devil that was chasing them. Very few of them ever made it.

Maybe their buddy would get chopped up with the aircraft landing, and the props would cut him to pieces. But that was just too bad, he didn't make it. If they did get across, and the chain between

225

them and their personal devil was broken, then they were happy as bugs in a rug because they'd gotten rid of the devil that was causing them all their trouble. It was amazing. It was, of course, a crazy philosophy.

I don't know what their religion was, whether they were Taoists or what. There are 50 different religions that they professed to know something about. Most of their beliefs were superstition. Maybe Confucius wasn't too good a teacher; maybe he was just misunderstood.

The Deli-Belly Special

Hal in India: I grew a mustache to show the Brits they weren't the only ones who could grow them.

Our joint command in India was located in an old jute mill that had been converted into military headquarters. We were all in one big office, so a whole bunch of little railings had been set up to identify different sections and different activities. From where the English staff was divided off, they had a long hall to go down to get to the latrine at the end of the building.

Everybody that came over there got what we all called "deli-belly" within the first six weeks. The surgeon was in on the action. He fixed the newcomer up with a pretty fast-acting laxative. We waited until the new arrival had been there two or three days, then we raised the curtain and watched the show. The pantomime was fantastic if they had to go to the latrine.

A very dapper-type Englishman, new to the command, arrived in his shorts and his precise English dress. We helped him out, set him up, with something in his oatmeal. When that laxative began to take good effect, he started down the hall and started stepping. Then all of a sudden he'd start stepping real quickly down the hall. Finally, he'd get about halfway down and stop real quick, and walk stiff-legged back to his quarters. He had to change clothes.

We didn't do this to everyone, only to certain guys. Certain proper, British arrogant types. The ones who thought they knew better than anybody else did. This chap was one of the types who carried a swagger stick and was very exacting. After he decided to head out of the place to go back to his quarters, we just had to get into the aisles, holding our sides, laughing like mad. We brought him down to our size real quick.

Bidets, Brides and Other Battles

A personnel officer sees a lot of things. Sometimes we know more about people than we really want to know. Being a personnel officer—think about it—seeing all of the shenanigans. Never a dull moment.

One WAC detachment came to India by boat. They'd crossed the Atlantic, had come through the Suez Canal and across the Indian Ocean. Then they rode the train to their detachment at Rishra. Their assignment was to take over all of the stenographic and filing operations, replacing warm-bodied American men who could then be used on combat duty.

A young warrant officer who had been working in my personnel section, a good-looking kid, was one of the men the WACs would replace. The first night these young women were on liberty, they decided to have a mixer-type dance. One gal grabbed this young warrant officer of mine and said, "Come with me. I want to talk with you." When they got out there on the floor she said, "I've been on the water over 30 days, and I've been waiting to get in a position where I can enjoy a good man and you look like a good man. Now, let's get at it." He came to me and said, "Colonel, what am I going to do?" I said, "Good luck, man."

I remember a gal from Tennessee. She had received a message via the Red Cross that her folks were separating, and she felt she needed to be home. She was sure she could take care of that home problem if only she was there. But the commander said, "I'm sorry. The only way you can get back to the States is if you're pregnant." So two weeks later, she came up pregnant.

We put her on a westbound aircraft and sent her back to the States where they discharged her. She headed back to Tennessee. I know that she rejoined her family. Whether she straightened out the family problem or not, I don't know. It seemed to me that her parents would not be helped any with the addition of her pregnancy to the rest of whatever problems they had. Of course, she didn't marry the guy, which wasn't the requirement. It was just being pregnant. Just being pregnant.

Getting married wasn't always a solution, either. Sometimes a man on my staff wanted to marry a girl from overseas. Of course, way back then during the war, it was much more of an issue than it is now, a mixed marriage. At one stage of the game, as the commander's representative, I had to approve or disapprove the request for marriages overseas. I was the yea or nay guy. That was not a comfortable job. I had to take my chaplain and the State Department people into consideration, and get everybody assembled so they could counsel the participants before there'd be any approvals granted.

One young chap from Stuttgart, Arkansas, became enamored of a WAC-I, an Indian WAC. She was a good-looking gal, and black as the ace of spades. Not a Negro but the oriental-type black. I tried to convince him that this was certainly not the way to go. I had the chaplain take him aside and try to get him to change his mind. He refused. He said that he was very much in love with this woman, and she apparently was very much in love with him. So I had the sergeant in his section pack his bags and baggage, and I put him on the next plane back to the States.

Later, after I left Europe in '46 and came back to the States, I saw this same young man at Washington National Airport. He was enroute back to India. International Harvester had hired him to be their representative there. He had kept in correspondence with this girl, and he was going back. He planned to marry her and live in India. He wanted to be accepted by her family and friends. I couldn't see it. I asked him what his folks had to say about it. He said, "They're going to disown me."

When the first unit of WACs was sent to North Africa from the USA, we agreed to take them at Casablanca. The Sea Bees built their quarters, and General Stowell, commanding general, ordered impenetrable fences built around the quarters "just to protect the WACs."

Their water closet contained a bidet, and that bidet created some real interesting situations. Here was an item that was not a part of the common experience of most women from the United States. Initially, they simply took the bidet for another regular water closet. But of course when they got in there, they got a real good, quick, violent bath. Totally unexpected.

The major of that WAC's detachment probably had sat down on that bidet herself, probably was getting her pants on, when it blew on her for the first time. Oh, she was hot! She was sure we'd pulled a fast one on them, that we were having fun indoctrinating the new kids on the block. She came over to personnel and demanded, "Colonel, you've got to do something about this. That toilet isn't hooked up right." It really had the flavor of a M*A*S*H scenario. I'm sure we could have provided some copy for their scripts.

Dad has in his files a thank-you note signed "Ash"—Carol Ash, one of his enlisted personnel. He had arranged her transfer back to Chattanooga to be with her mother, who was dying. "Dear Col. Hal, Due to the rapidity with which you arranged my transfer, I was fortunate enough to be with Mother on her birthday, the first we spent together in four years. Her condition is rapidly growing worse and now she is in a coma. The doctors expect her to last only a few days."

Another thank-you letter is from Francis Dealy, written in Paris and dated Oct. 1, 1945. He thanks Dad for assistance in getting him to Lisbon, a neutral area.

Paddy, the Earl of Banning

The English complained about the Americans. I'm sure you've heard how they said, "The bloody Americans. They're over paid, over ranked, oversexed, and they're over here!"

In Calcutta we had a suite, two bedrooms and a drawing room, where they had the joint command, the English and the Americans

231

together. My compadre from this country was "Pinky" Alden; Pinky and I were the colonels. The two Englishmen with us held the rank termed group captains.

One of them, Jack Leather, had been a survivor of the blitz in England. He had been a fighter pilot and had been shot up pretty well, but he was over in India still in service.

His buddy was an Irishman named "Paddy" Daniel. Since I was assistant chief of staff personnel, the orders for promoting Paddy came through to me. The English had promoted him to brigadier. Paddy was out on a mission at the time, over with Sir John Baldwin of the Third Tactical Air Force. He was on the way back when I got the orders that he was promoted.

The other three of us set up quite a deal in our suite. We really bedecked the apartment for the announcement event. Across the mirror in the bathroom we placed a banner: "This is where the Brigadier shaves," and similar proclamations. The whole apartment was appropriately decorated in this fashion before Paddy hit the scene.

The English, of course, had some Scotsmen in the command, and they had bagpipes. So we piped him aboard and took him up to his room, to his quarters. We set up a table with a buffet. Paddy was quite amazed. Finally, we got down to the point. When his orders came in, they said, "The Earl of Banning is promoted to Brigadier." He was a titled Irishman and we didn't know that. Consequently, we really rode him about this. "This is where his Honor, the Earl of Banning, sits ... sleeps, bathes, eats, etc."

I had a bottle of Scotch that I had transported over to India, and I'd never taken it out of my footlocker. It was Queen Anne—well, maybe it was, maybe not. But it was a 30-year-old Scotch, and I set that out with a big ribbon on it for His Honor, the Earl of Banning. When Paddy saw this, his eyes sparkled. He said, "Who brought this in?" Pinky said, "McCord had it in his foot locker." Paddy quipped, "You mean you've had this all the time we've been here and haven't laid it out?" He grabbed it and said, "This is mine. You blokes are not going to get any of it."

It was a great celebration. All of the command turned out and got into the spirit of the occasion. I had my houseboy[55] dress me in a dhoti, a Hindu loincloth, and wrap my head with the typical headdress like a Pakistani. In place of an emblem we used a wineglass, like a martini glass, set up there woven into the headdress.

I had a musette, a seven-note musette, which has an odd scale and was characteristic of that part of the world. It was a double-reed instrument with a short little fibered-type mouthpiece. It fingered like a flute and was made of ebony, like the oboe I had. It played some weird music. The whine, whine, whine high nasal tone type. I played the dancing girl theme when Paddy came in and one of the Englishmen was dressed up as a dancing girl. We had a real ball out of it.

---

[55] Dad said that houseboys in India had a "button allowance" to replace buttons lost when laundry was beat against the rocks. Dad also said that he would spend weekends with a high class Hindu family to learn Hindi. When he ordered his food in Hindi, they would bring exactly what he had said, whatever it was. He soon learned some Hindi.

Then we presented him with his promotion. Paddy acknowledged it, and by that time we all had had enough to drink that the speech was interesting, to say the least. He extolled the virtues of being in the military. He also then said he did not believe in passing title from father to son, title should be earned. Of course, this didn't make him very popular with some of the other titled Englishmen in the crowd.

The Rickshaw Walla Race

Once, when four of us went out to eat together, we decided that we would go to the Peking Café in Calcutta. This was back off The Maiden. (Aside, to me... *Do you remember Kipling's story about the big park in Calcutta, The Maiden?* I did. Dad had several years before suggested I would enjoy reading Kipling's <u>Kim</u>, and I found it fascinating.) *Along one side of it is Chalringi Road, peopled by nothing but rickshaws. We went down there and went in and told the manager of the Peking Café that we were inspecting it to see whether we'd take it on or off limits for the military. And he bowed and scraped and all, and said, "I will show you the entire place."*

He took us through the kitchen, and we checked it out thoroughly. When we came back from the tour, we said, "Well, we believe we'll give you a clean bill of health." He said, "I must show you what kind of food we have." So he sat us down, and we ate and ate and ate. He served several—well, maybe seven or eight—different dishes. It was all choice, very good. We got ready to pay him for it. "Oh no," he said, "I am simply demonstrating what we might be able to provide you when you come back." He wanted us to tell our friends and to come back.

When we left the Peking Café, all of us, including Jack Leather, the chap from Liverpool; Pinky Alden; Paddy Daniel and I, had made arrangements with the rickshaw wallahs, the men who pull the rickshaws. We had a bet that the rickshaw passenger that was the laggard and didn't win the race down to Chalringi Road would have to pull his wallah. He'd be the rickshaw wallah, and he'd have to pull his rickshaw wallah back up to the starting point. The three of us plotted and had an arrangement made that Paddy was going to have to be the loser. We ensured that, because as we were going down four abreast practically, on Chalringi Road, we got Paddy in the middle and the adjacent rider then reached over and turned his rickshaw over.

So Paddy lost. But he was a good sport. He pulled his rickshaw wallah back to the starting point, and we then paid the rickshaw wallahs about five rupees each. At that time a rupee would be a week's wages. It was a lot of fun, and it was a very interesting experience. I never will forget Paddy, the Earl of Banning.

Frequently on Saturdays during our off-time from the office, we'd go down to have dinner at the Peking Café. Really, I think that was the best Oriental food that I ever ate. The manager always managed to notice us come in, and we always had service that was out of this world.

I never will forget that race down Chalringi Road. We really had a lot of fun out of that. Of course, the Hindus, the natives in the area, thought, "Those crazy Americans." At that time the people who did the service jobs in that area, the taxi drivers, what taxis they had and operators of such services were all Pakistani. They were larger in stature than most Hindus and were soldier types. I've often thought about it since. How unusual the change in the relationships—the ethnic relationships—in India now. The Muslim-Hindu conflicts.[56]

When I returned to Washington during the early 1950s, Paddy came over to this country. We lunched together in the officer's mess at the Pentagon and reminisced over some of the things that had happened. We also had at our table, as my additional guest, Colonel Gabriel P. Dissoway, the officer who later in that period became the commanding general of the Tactical Air Command at Langley. He had been the commanding officer as a colonel at the Instruments Training School, the flight school at Bryan, Texas, where I got my instrument rating.

There is another side to the tour in India that my father never mentioned. It is told in Dad's medical records: "Dysentery, India, 1944. Hospitalized six wks. No complications. Dengue Fever, India, 1944. Hospitalized 10 days. No complications. Malaria, Rishra, India, 1944. Mild recurrence, 1949." That's a lot of illness for less than five months' duty.[57]

---

[56] It was while I was in India in 1977-78 that I read <u>Freedom at Midnight</u> by LaPierre and Collins, a gripping story of India's 1947 independence and the ensuing bloodbath between Hindu and Muslim. We had both Hindu and Muslim staff in our demonstration village projects and finding appropriate material for rituals was a challenge. The poetry of Rabindranath Tagore, a Bengali, was a stunning choice.

[57] I had amoebic dysentery twice during my year in India; it is the only time in my life I knew I was hallucinating. An Indian gynecologist and her husband, an

When Dad left the CBI command, "upon mutual concurrence of the commanding generals concerned," clearances and sign-offs were required with every officer: mess, finance, supply, billeting, personnel (Dad put in his own initials here), provost marshal, base laundry, etc. He also had to sign that he had received 35 copies of his orders.

WWII, October 1944 to September 1945

In October, 1944, the newly assigned assistant chief of staff personnel reporting to the 1250th AAF Base Unit, North African Division, Air Transport Command, had his work cut out for him. The year my father was assigned to Casablanca, October 1944 to September 1945, proved to be quite a year.

The fate of French North Africa had been decided several years before. When Paris fell to Hitler in 1940, the French government moved first to Bordeaux then to Vichy when the Germans designated it the capital of the unoccupied zone. The terms of the German armistice had left three-fifths of France under German occupation, kept more than 1.5 million French POWs under German control, and had set up the French government in an unoccupied zone so France could continue to administer their colonial empire in a manner to save some measure of face as well as ensure continued German superiority.

ENT physician, gave free medical care to our project staff. She curtained off part of her office and brought in a bed for me; her 10-patient ward was full. The geckos on the walls, normally adorable, appeared sinister and threatening in their distorted shadows; the buses roaring down the street just outside became huge orange monsters bearing down upon me like giant amoebas. A dehydrated body and weakened spirit can play strange tricks with a mind struggling to separate various realities.

237

The Allies had other plans for French North Africa. In November 1942, Operation Torch, the largest amphibious invasion force in the history of warfare to that time, had within 76 hours of their first landing secured 1300 miles of the African coast from Safi to Algiers. Gen. George Patton was on the beach leading the chaotic landing operation.

Tunis, however, was not in Allied hands until May 1943, forcing the Allies to ship supplies via the Cape of Good Hope. Rommel had been steadily pushed back as Hitler denied him the troops and materials he so desperately required. Rommel was ready to abandon the African theater of war in November 1942, but Hitler refused to even discuss it at the time.

By October 1944, the British had been at war with Germany for more than five years, the Russians for more than three years, and the Americans had been involved for nearly three years. That month, Germany stepped up its campaign of atrocities against so-called Enemies of the People. Among other delusional and unbelievable events, Rommel was presented with the option of a public trial or suicide. He had just suffered a brain concussion when his command car was shot up and driven into a ditch. The already ailing "Desert Fox" chose the cyanide offered by two German generals.

The strain of war was evident on all sides. Also that October General Dwight D. Eisenhower distributed a report by the Office of the U.S. Surgeon General on the hazards of war to all combat units in Europe. It said:

"The key to an understanding of the problem is the simple fact that the danger of being killed or maimed imposes a strain so great that it causes men to break down.

"One look at the shrunken, apathetic faces of psychiatric patients as they come stumbling into the medical station, sobbing, trembling, referring shudderingly to 'them shells' and to buddies mutilated or dead, is enough to convince most observers of this fact. A wound or injury is regarded not as a misfortune but a blessing.

"As one litter bearer put it, 'Something funny about the men you bring back wounded. They're always happy ... they're sure glad to be getting out of here.' Under these circumstances it is easy for a man to become sincerely convinced that he is sick or unable to go on. This in turn leads to the premature development of genuine psychiatric disability and to needless loss of manpower. It also leads to self-inflicted wounds and to misbehavior before the enemy."[58]

Everyone had had his or her fill. Even the U.S.O. entertainers wanted a respite from the rigors of a war-weary world.

The Fur-lined Fox Hole

In the midst of all these events my father's tasks as a personnel officer in Casablanca included morale. It was a 24x7 job and included

---

[58] Gilbert, Martin, The Second World War, A Complete History, ©1989 by Martin Gilbert, published by Henry Holt and Company, Inc., p. 599.

meals, housing, exercise, recreation, education and spirit, not to mention a lot of paperwork. He did it all and with style. With compassion, with regard for the local citizens and local customs. In the middle of a war. It was one of those rare periods in life where circumstances conspire to bring out the best of times in the midst of the worst of times.

In October 1944, I was requested for assignment to Casablanca under Brigadier General James S. Stowell. I had known General Stowell when I was at Randolph Field. In '44 when he needed a replacement for his assistant chief of staff personnel, I got the nod. In Casablanca we had in our area of supervision all of Africa and the Mediterranean area, and the airline that operated from Hirati west to Santa Maria in the Azores. It would prove to be another fascinating operation and a memorable experience.

Col. Francis "Frank" M. Williams, Lt. Col. Robert "Bob" E. Lee Turner and I were assigned a villa. The newspaper publisher in Casa was pro-Vichy and was not exactly in good repute. We just took over his station up in Nordland.

This exceptional villa comprised the better part of an acre and a half of land, was encircled by a high fence covered with bougainvillea and had a main entry gate. The Arabs didn't try to climb that fence. It was too much of a hazard. Like hedge rows, it was real thorny stuff, and sticky, sticky, sticky.

The two-and-a-half story building itself was quite fabulous. Each of the three of us had a private bedroom and bath—the baths were all marble. The place was an extremely high-priced operation and came

very well equipped. It had silver plates and silver knives and forks...
everything. It also had, among other things, a grand piano.

When General Stowell assigned those posh quarters to us, he said,
"I'm gonna let you guys have that villa, but you're going to have one
responsibility. Every now and then we get in celebrities that have to
be handled with kid gloves. I want you to take care of them, entertain
them and provide whatever's needed. I'm sure you can work out
whatever the details are going to be."

We could do that, and we had a lot of fun. Harold Ickes[59] was our
guest there one time for a week. He had been on one of the
presidential staffs back in the Roosevelt era and was representative of
the clientele that we had to take care of. It wasn't hard to do.

General Stowell liked to remind me that, as chief of personnel,
command morale was my area of responsibility. He primed the pump:
"We've got a fine USO troop due in here. I think they ought to put on
a show for us. See what you can arrange." Our guests included stars
like soprano Lily Pons, the opera singer, and Andre Kostelanez,[60] the
orchestra leader. They were part of the professional USO

---

[59] Harold LeClair Ickes, 1874-1952, a Chicago newspaper man who was active in Republican Party reform and then the Progressive Party from 1912 to 1916. He was also the U.S. Interior Secretary from 1933 until 1946.

[60] As Americans were gathering their resources following the attack on Pearl Harbor, Andre Kostelanez approached Aaron Copland, Virgil Thomson and Jerome Kern with the idea of a series of concerts that would prominently feature "a portrait gallery of great Americans." Thomson's subject was New York's Fiorello LaGuardia; Copland's first choice was Walt Whitman, but when Kern chose Mark Twain, Kostelanez suggested that Copland choose a statesman, rather than another literary figure. Abraham Lincoln seemed an inevitable choice. Sifting through the President's speeches and writings, Copland chose a few excerpts that were particularly relevant to America's situation in 1942. "Lincoln Portrait" was the result.

entertaining crew. They had a special request. "We've been traveling, traveling, traveling. We'd like a rest." So the "rest" was what I negotiated with them. We took care of them for a while, and it was a pleasure to have them as guests.

We worked out getting a theater in which they could perform and put on a production of "Madame Butterfly." Luther Leavengood was at that time head of the music department at Kansas State. I had him bundle up the full score of "Madame Butterfly," along with other music, and send them all to Washington. They were put on one of the Casablanca flights, and the music came in assigned to me. We received them eagerly. Some were particular favorites of mine, like the "Caucasian Sketches" by Rimsky-Korsakov.

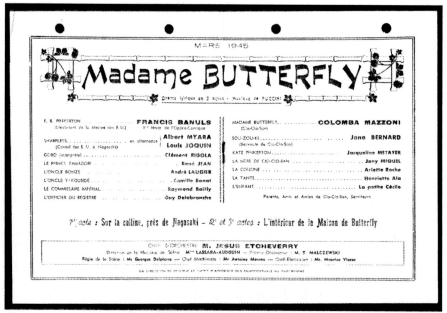

Program from Madame Butterfly

I promised Leavengood that I would take good care of all of those different orchestrations. The kids just loved it. The selections fit their category of good music, the full orchestration of "Madame Butterfly," "Overture to Pheadre" by Massenet and many other excellent scores. The stacks of music we had were about yea high.

Out of the command I then assembled about 30 musicians in a small salon group. We also put together a talented string quartet. One of the men had been the concertmaster for the Denver symphony. Another fellow was the chief cellist from the Philadelphia symphony. And, of course, Andre Kostelanez, director of one of the major symphonic orchestras. We really were in high clover.

Salon Musicians. Berj Vaughn, coordinator and author of thank-you letter is in front row, third from left.

Marilyn McCord

Quartet members were first violin, Walter Eisenberg, who had scholarships with Juilliard School of Music among others; second violin Sam Shamper, who had played on many well-known radio programs broadcast on major networks before entering the service; viola, Irving Becker, who appeared in a recital at Carnegie Hall at the age of 17 and was a member of the Pittsburgh Symphony; and cello, George Neikrug, who made a Town Hall debut at the age of 19 and

> *Handwritten by Dad on the back of a Casablanca String Quartet program:*
>
> **In a shell case for a vase,**
> **tea roses, carnations, hibiscus**
> **in a stern little chapel, the world's best music –**
> **Unpainted rough furniture, poor lights –**
> **Beautiful silk American Flag.**
> **Brick, stone and concrete altar.**

was first cellist of New Friends of Music Orchestra and on the Firestone Program.

From program notes put out by the String Quartet with one of their concerts:

"The purpose of these concerts is to foster enjoyment and appreciation of fine chamber music. We feel that concerts of this nature, particularly string quartet music, need not be relegated to the few who could heretofore afford the forbidding prices of the concert hall.

"The popular belief that to appreciate chamber music one must have acquired an extensive amount of study and knowledge is far from true. The comparative few who are undaunted by the barrier of the so-called cultural atmosphere of the concert hall are as enthusiastic in their appreciation as the most rabid addicts of good jazz. As a matter of fact, there are many points of similarity between the two.

"The finished performance of a work such as the Beethoven Quartet Opus 59, No. 1, involves many hours of patience and work to achieve the desired precision of rhythm, dynamics, ensemble and general teamwork which one so admires in a band such as Benny Goodman's.

"It is our aim to dispel the notion that this music is meant only for old men with beards and ear trumpets, instead of something fine, exciting and contemporary."

Stowell observed, "Well, you're getting a good crowd together. We can't have this wonderful group to ourselves without sharing them with the command. What do you need to accomplish that?" "Well," I said, "I want a C-46 set up so that we can move a grand piano for the pianist in this crowd and capability like a military air transport, a

MAT command." That meant a pilot, co-pilot, engineer, radio operator and that type of crew—where they could operate that Charlie-46 and send everybody wherever we wanted them to go and put on good music.

When we started sending the salon orchestra and string quartet out to different stations, they found a most appreciative crowd for good music. The theater commander, General Ben Giles, wanted them for his headquarters in Italy. So, we just re-scheduled that whole C-46 crowd to travel a circuit of different areas in the command, providing good entertainment. The musicians were excellent; this was a fine service to the troops. Everyone was very well received. Those kids just ate it up.

The musicians stayed together until we closed out the command and were shipping everybody home. I had to find out where these people wanted to go, and we sent them back to wherever they wanted. The concertmaster for the Denver symphony found out they wanted him back, and this was his decision. His assignment was to go back to Denver.

Several of the other musicians wanted to go there as well, and they were discharged at Lowry Air Base. We just ushered everyone out to wherever they wanted. Since the War, I have seen a couple of those people from this group. They were so pleased to be a part of this schedule, and they were pleased to get back home. I enjoyed meeting with them again. It was quite an adventure in good music, one of the events that was a highlight in what we were doing.

Casablanca

Sept. 18th.

Dear Col. McCord;

Now that our mission as the North African
Division Band and our association with you have come
to an end, 1 am taking this opportunity to tell you
how grateful we are for your sympathetic understanding
and guidance.

We all feel singularly fortunate in having
had# a CO who so intelligently comprehended our problems
musically and otherwise, and upon whom we could always
rely for the fullest possible cooperation. There is no
doubt in our minds, that we owed our very existence as
an organization to you and we all feel that thru your
efforts _that_ existence was a pleasurable experience. One
that we will always remember as the nicest thing that has
ever happened to us in our army career.

The best of luck on your new assignment. With
fondest regards from the boys and myself,

Respectfully yours,

Sgt Berj Vaughn

Thank you letter from Berj Vaughn, coordinator of salon orchestra

Then came an assignment to catalog POWs. We had about 8,000 to 9,000 Italian prisoners who had been troops of Mussolini. They had just been moved down and put in a stockade at Oran, Algeria. We were charged with determining their skills and experience levels. As personnel officer, I ordered eight Italian-speaking officers into our headquarters with the intention of having them interview the rest of the prisoners. They each took a crew with them and set up key selector cards. These were 5" x 8" cards that had punches around the edges so that you could take a prong—like an ice pick—and shake out of those pre-punched cards almost any category you wanted. This was really a preliminary-type computer.[61]

What I wanted first were people who had prior experience in maintaining high level administration of a good kitchen and dining room. We had a couple of chefs that had been in major hotels. One that I remember in particular had been in Milan. He was a real good kid. They probably weren't too unhappy with the duty either. It was a little bit different than the stockade.

I brought the kitchen staff in, and explained to them that there was a set of service quarters in this villa. "That's where you'll live. But, let me assure you, if you screw up, you will think that the stockade was a garden club. Don't, for any reason, cause any problems."

This was essentially what General Stowell had made plain to me: "Do what you like, but do not under any circumstances cause me any

---

[61] Exactly! When I taught junior high math in Aurora, Colorado in 1972-73, I had my students do something similar to this with a box of half-size Hollerith punch cards I got from IBM.

embarrassment." Another time he jokingly asked me, "Did I command all that?" And once, "Now, what did Stowell say this time?"

Each member of our service team received a special permit and ID card so they could go to the Post Exchange and get items such as cigarettes and candy. In return for this ticket, they had to run a first-class establishment. The chief of the kitchen, the maitre d', was a boy named Mario, who just loved running a fine show. Our head cook was a kid named Armundo Caneperi. Armundo loved to cook and he was a cook of fine capability. We had a good set-up. In wartime.

General Stowell's senior administrative staff, Dining in the Villa Nordland. Beginning at lower left front and going clockwise: Col. Robert E. Lee Turner, director of priorities and traffic; Col. Frederick C. Kelly; Col. Robert Smith; Maj. Art Sherry, staff member; Brig. Gen. James Stowell, commanding general; Col. Hal H. McCord, chief of staff personnel; Col. James Fred

McClendon, chief of staff; Maj. John W. Carroll; Maj. Gerald J. Linares,[62] intelligence officer. In the back are our houseboys, Armundo Caneperi (left) and Mario, two of the Italian POWs.

Later, when I had to make a trip to our force headquarters in Italy, Armundo asked me if I was going to be anywhere near Milan. "Probably, I will." "Well," he said, "here is where my folks live. I haven't been able to hear anything from my people. Please see if you can find them." "I'll see what I can find, but I may not have time to do this."

However, I did fly over that area and noted where he said his folks had lived. The English had done a Short Sunderland heavy bomber foray and had dropped a 12-ton bomb right in the area he had identified.

"Please show me," he pleaded. I hated to have to say it. "That block has been completely ... it's just a crater." He was afraid that had happened. Then he asked, "When you go back to the States, will you take me as your house boy? Just for being able to get there and live with your family, I will take over the household. I'll run it." He also wanted to get his education in the United States, I know. But there wasn't any way to get this done. The State Department attaché wouldn't approve it.

When we left and closed out that operation, the Villa Nordland, we granted the POWs exceptional returnee status and returned them to Italy. Of course, the Italians were then anti-Mussolini and anti-

---

[62] The town of Linares, Spain was named for his family. He was fluent in all languages of that area—a great intelligence resource.

anything that was attached to the Germans or "le Boche" as their slang term went. Armundo wanted to go to Naples so we brought him there. Apparently he had some relatives somewhere in that area. I don't know what happened to him after that.

You may have heard that the Air Force had a reputation for living high on the hog, the kind of thing we had going at Villa Nordland. Stowell's famous saying was, "Any poor son-of-a-bitch can be uncomfortable. And I don't believe in being uncomfortable." This was the way he influenced our operation. He wanted us to run a first-class show, and we did. It was an easy type of thing to operate by just using the communication system. We could invoke the general's rank for anything we wanted. "... by order of the commanding general." And bang, done. These people saluted, too.

We'd bring fresh fruits and vegetables like pineapple and mangos and all types of wonderful produce up from Dakar, Senegal. We had a network that included the Kellogg Weed & Seed family operations out of Wichita, Kansas. They had a big feed store operation.

Not that we needed seed and weed in our villa, but Bob Kellogg was a captain on staff at Dakar. He was a K-State graduate, so he was in the network. When there was a transport coming back empty, we asked Bob to load it up with the produce we wanted, and he did. We would bring it into Casablanca at Cazes Air Base.

Navy escort carriers came in and set up at Cazes because they were escorting transports—Merchant Marine types. They would come in with their reefers, as refrigerators were called, full of stateside beef. We'd trade with them fresh fruit and vegetables for beef and milk. This got us a fine exchange in produce, and we ran a very fine kitchen. The clincher was the Italians doing the cooking and having such a wonderful assortment of fine foods to do it with. We lived like ... well, everybody said we had a "fur-lined fox hole." And we did.

We had a good time maintaining that facility, and it was pleasant to entertain people there that enjoyed it. We had our own transportation, we had our own airplane. (The story of finding the B-25 in the desert appears later.) *There wasn't anything we lacked. And we had the authority, the General's authority, that gave us the right to say essentially, "Hey, it would be a good idea if we did this."*

Well, that was the same thing as writing an order. It made living quite, quite pleasant really. The war wasn't just exactly all a hairy conflict and an unfortunate situation. If you had the imagination and the authority, there wasn't anything you couldn't do. We were in this villa the better part of a year, a little more. We surely hated to break that crowd up when they closed the command. You know we did.

Initially, I found myself aghast at the extravagances in Casablanca, the contrast with my visions of men in the trenches. Later I remembered a scene from the 1966 novel <u>Tai-Pan,</u> by James Clavel that impressed me. When the Hong Kong economy was depressed, the powerful movers and shakers gave a ball, a smashingly outrageous ball. With a $100 prize, a lot for the mid-1800s time period. The community, instead of being downtrodden by the dire circumstances, focused on something fun, playful, anticipatory. Spirits lifted, times got better, perceptions changed, reality changed.

The mood was the opposite of hoarding, of being fearful, of closing up. There is something to be learned in this. Being expansive and creating spirit where despair had taken lodging. The "Little Brown Jugs" story coming up later in this section is about the same thing. Seeing the beauty in the underside of war not selfishly but doing it for everyone. At Casablanca the troops, the musicians, even the POWs participated. This typifies morale-building at its best.

There was an ATC Guest House at Payne Field, Cairo, that performed a similar function. An old clipping in Dad's files, undated and unidentified as to source, points out the importance of home comforts for traveling VIPs. "King Farouk, of Egypt, given a buffet supper there, was so crazy about [Sgt. Peter] George's hamburgers and soft drinks that he invited him to visit the palace, which George did.

"Lily Pons and Kostelanez sampled his apple pie and suggested that he come and see them in Connecticut when the war was over." The article's author, Mary Day Winn, discovered for herself that "the place was an oasis of comfort, hospitality, good food and American efficiency."

She goes on to say that, "Traveling these days ... is not always a bed of roses. Formerly good hotels have developed strange ailments: water that goes off and on at unexpected hours in Casablanca, Karachi and Delhi,[63] flies and native servants who'll steal the gold from your

---

[63] This was also true in Taipei, Taiwan when I lived there in 1974-77. You might just get lathered up good with shampoo and, oops—no more water for several hours.

teeth at the renowned Shepheard's in Cairo; heat that reaches 167° at Abadan, an airway station in Persia; lukewarm, chlorinated water, powdered milk and English cooking in India; primitive plumbing—to put it kindly—in China; and mosquitoes everywhere."

Providing accommodations such as the villa in Casablanca was part of getting the entertainers to come. Another important cornerstone of building morale.

A membership card for the *Royal Jupoopian Army* caught my curiosity and I asked about it. Dad giggled a little. *All of the officers were enlisted personnel in the Royal Jupoopian Army, and the enlisted personnel were the officers, just the reverse of the way it really was. It was mostly just the ID cards, but one of the morale type things, and we went along with it. My principal secretary was one of the organizers. I still have a letter opener to "1ˢᵗ Sgt. Hal McCord" from the Jupoopian personnel.*

The Sultan of Morocco

Mohammad Ali Bey[64] *was the Sultan of Morocco, a constitutional monarchy. We did several things for him during the war, and I got to know him quite well. He was an exceptionally interesting individual.*

---

[64] Mohammad V, 1911-1961, was proclaimed sultan of Morocco in 1927. Deposed by the French in 1953, nationalist agitation forced his return in 1955. On his death in 1961, his son Hassan became king, and maintained excellent relations with the West. Dad was instrumental in helping Hassan get into Harvard when the State Department attaché, according to Dad, was not very interested in getting Hassan admitted to a U. S. school. The Casablanca Airport is named Mohammed V. The first modern university in Morocco, University Mohammed V, bears testimony to Mohammad Ali Bey's enduring interest in education.

At Rabat, about 80 kilometers or so north of Casablanca off the coast toward Gibraltar, they had a water problem. The Atlas Mountains were back to the east of us. I had flown those; we all had. We pretty well knew that area. There was snow on those mountains, so water had to be there somewhere. We couldn't locate where it all went but we did recognize that it disappeared into a subterranean river someplace. Finding the point where that was identifiable, where the run-off was kind of absorbed into the terrain was easy enough.

We decided we'd try to find the subterranean river. Where did the water go? How could we trace it? We dropped some high intensity dye in that water then figured the approximate flow rate. Mounting a photographic mission out in the Atlantic, we discovered where the dye surfaced into the ocean. Next we located a line through the mountains about where we estimated this subterranean stream would go. Sure enough, we found it. We also figured that if we put a pump in there we could get water to the surface. Enough of a resource was available that engineers could develop a significant water supply.

Additionally, the land was very rich—high in nutrients. They could grow wheat that was shoulder high and would sport big heads on each stalk, if they only had water. Also, we knew wonderful oranges grew in the Sultan's grove. Red-orange meat in them like blood oranges. Good sized and as tasty as could be. These were the best. But only the Sultan had them. If Morocco could develop that land with water, we believed they could set up quite an operation.

We had our people check with the agricultural staff at Cornell University to determine whether the soil samples from this area in

255

Morocco would be adequate and nutritious enough to provide for good agricultural operations. Cornell came back with fantastic reports. They said, "Yes, it could be an absolutely superb farming venture." If we were able to get a program set up so the water could be supplied, the irrigation. Then probably from the ports there at Casa and at Rabat, Morocco could feed all of Western Europe as well as the channel ports from their potential produce. It was a very rich area.

Of course, Mohammad Ali Bey, the Sultan, was interested in seeing that this was done. Because Morocco was still a French protectorate and subjugated like mad, he couldn't get permission from the French to proceed with the water and agricultural ideas. That was a great loss for that area.

Mohammad V on gold throne

Market at Festival of Masacar

Later I was invited to participate in the Rabadan Festival at Masacar, a Muslim celebration to be held on the Atlantic coast of northwest Africa south of Casablanca. It was a rare privilege. I got permission from our command and from the State Department to represent the Army Air Corps at the festival of Masacar. This was in 1944 or, '45; I'm not sure about the time frame. I do have some pictures of the gold throne they set up for the Sultan. A cloth of gold was placed across a big chair and this is where he held court for that festival.

The French were very angry that we were working so closely with the Moroccan hierarchy including Mohammad Ali Bey. The Sultan left no question in anybody's mind they wanted to become a protectorate of the United States rather than a protectorate of the French. The French of course were not pleased about any potential change in political affiliations. They didn't like it one bit.

The Festival of Masacar provided some wonderful photo opportunities, and we took advantage of them. When we had finished taking pictures, we had sense enough to take the film and hide it, putting other film in the cameras. The French confiscated all the film in our cameras; they didn't take the cameras but they confiscated the film. We would laugh about it later because there wasn't anything on that film. I'm sure this didn't help cement relationships with the French and their crowd. Even having returned a French general's son didn't make any hay with DeGaulle. But that's another story.

Several other events were interesting. I had 135 to 140 individuals in my personnel operation. A philosophy that I kind of instilled into their heads was this: "When there's work to do, work like mad and get it done. When there's no work to do, let's play." [65]

One weekend everything was caught up to snuff. I got permission to take some personnel carriers—these were ton-and-a-half, six by sixes personnel carriers. [66] *We arranged with the chef in our mess to make a real big to-do for two meals, and we drove up into the Atlas*

---

[65] A 26 Feb. 46 organizational chart shows the staff under Lt. Col. McCord: 45 Officers, 53 Enlisted Men, 62 Civilians—a total of 160. My friend from days at Texas Instruments, Ruth Loyd says that you still hear this philosophy in the corporate world from old military personnel. "Unfortunately," she says, "there is always more work to do than can be done."

[66] From Dad's orders, 10 Feb. 1945: "Officers authorized for points within 100 miles radius for 12 Feb. for recreational purpose. Return same date. Transportation for 10."

Mountains into those areas where the Sultan had invited us. "Fine, be my guest." This was in the Sultan's preserve. Beautiful, beautiful country. We took the whole bunch, both men and women officers up there. Because it was flat ground, we could play softball. When it was time to eat, our mess crew served everybody. And we had a great big time.

We got back late that night. The outing was a tremendous morale builder. Those kids in my section—there wasn't anything that I couldn't ask 'em to do that they wouldn't do. It was a good philosophy to have that when there's work to do, do it, and when you've got time to go fishing, go fishing. This wasn't normal because many times commanders would manufacture work for their troops to do, to keep 'em busy. No real progress happens as a result of make-work type operations. I thoroughly enjoyed that crew. They were good people.

Knowing how much he enjoyed hunting, I asked Dad if he ever got to go hunting in Morocco. He did.

After we got out on the hunt, one of the Arab guides was telling me, "Through that valley, the first draw, there is a boar coming. Be ready." I had an M1 30.06 heavy duty with steel-jacketed bullets. That first bullet went through the boar without expanding; I saw it kick dirt up behind him. Two times. He kept coming.

I aimed at the eyes and hit his skull. The force of the shot peeled the hide back over him, blinded him. One of the Arabs was screaming for everyone to get in a tree. The boar passed 20 yards to my left and kept going. Didn't see us. He was blinded. After he passed by, we followed the blood-clotted trail down the mountain for about a half-mile and found him dead. We called a camel in, rolled that boar into a panier (basket), took him back along with several other boars, butchered them and ate fresh pork. Of course, the Arabs wouldn't eat pork.

The French were going to chastise Mohammad Ali Bey because he was too friendly with the Americans. They figured that he was fomenting a movement to have the Americans take over Morocco. They sent him to Madagascar, exiled him to Madagascar. Two things they hadn't counted on: His popularity with his people, who agitated until he was returned two years later; and the Sultan's replacement, Hussan the Second, currently the Sultan of Morocco.[67]

He went to school in the United States and was a Harvard graduate. He came home and took over the job of Sultan of Morocco, his present assignment of course. He is an outstanding political boss in Morocco. Hussan II was carefully indoctrinated not to antagonize. Since that time of course, the French have given up Morocco, and they've given up their other colonies, the same as England has done with its colonies. That colonial mentality no longer fits with our times, if it ever did.

Hussan has tried to bring some level of stability to Morocco and has tried to have the Sheik Alif at Marrakech join with him. He is

---

[67] We recorded these stories in 1996. In 1999, King Hassan II died after 38 years on the throne and his son, Prince Sidi Muhammad, was crowned King Muhammad VI. He has pledged to make the political system more open, support economic reform and advocated more rights for women—opposed by Islamic fundamentalists.

maintaining his prowess and base of power at Rabat, the capital, north of Casablanca. Marrakech is south and a little east of Casa, and the Sheik Alif is the religious head of the Muslim crowd. Hussan, of course, is the political head.

They have not agreed much on many of the policies. The Sheik Alif of Marrakech has wanted to maintain the old customs of the Muslims. Hussan has tried to introduce a new feeling and a new political base into Morocco, grounded particularly, I expect, on much of his experience in America when he was in school at Harvard.

The Sultan—Mohammad Ali Bey—his father, was a forward-thinking ruler and was very good with his people who appeared to love him. I don't know what Hussan's acceptance is in Morocco but apparently it must be pretty good because they haven't had an uprising or anything like that. Overthrowing the current head of state has been characteristic in much of that area. Algiers, for instance.

Salvaging a B-25 Out of the Desert

We were flying from Tripoli, Libya, back to Casa, over the Western Sahara, when we noticed a B-25 on the desert floor. Dropping down, we circled it to see what was going on. There wasn't anybody around. It looked as though the aircraft was practically undamaged. We came back later with a small aircraft and landed in that area to evaluate what had happened.

We discovered that a ferry flight had been delivering B-25s to the command on the eastern front at Abadan, Iran at the top of the

Persian Gulf. Apparently, this particular aircraft had run out of fuel. They landed it, ditched it, really. This was the nearest place they could get to, but then all there was was desert sand. In our evaluation, they had come in and had made a wheels-up landing. They did the belly landing rather than using the wheels on purpose to avoid the risk of flipping it over and having a major accident.

We found out that there wasn't too much wrong with it and that it was salvageable. The flaps and props were damaged. One of the activities at our station in Casablanca was the maintenance of aircraft. I enlisted our aircraft recovery unit, which included a big heavy-duty trailer. Finding a route that we could drive over there, we took a crew, picked it up, put it on the flat bed, and brought it back to Casablanca.

Here was a good B-25 that had been dropped from inventory because it had been undeliverable and had been dropped from the shipment because of an inability to get it delivered. I asked General Stowell, "What are we going to do with it?" He said, "It's yours. You went and got it. I don't want any responsibility for it." He just wanted somebody to go do this job. He got to be a general knowing what you have your colonels for.

We brought the plane back. We put it up on big jacks and requisitioned the necessary parts to fix it. When we checked the engines out, they were fine. No problems there. The only thing we needed to do was install new props and flaps. We removed the war paint and it became a silver-finish-aircraft, not an O-D finish aircraft. It may have stood out like a sore thumb among all the other aircraft, but then nobody could really identify it. We also took all of the hardware out of it, the military armament. In place of the bomb racks and the bomb bay capable of dropping bombs, we put in long-range, bulletproof tanks for extra fuel. For long-range navigation we added Loran equipment.

Then we decided it would be a good idea to put in a vertical and oblique camera. An oblique camera is one that shoots at angles rather than directly overhead. One that takes a shot and is controllable. These extras are all operated by compressed air. The inner-velometers on those instruments were all in place and undamaged. They had been used for other purposes, but we converted 'em real easy to the use of a Fairchild camera that reconnaissance people had managed to use in their operations.

We then had an aircraft that would take good air photography and also, with the long-range tanks, we could fill up the tanks with fuel and take off from Casablanca and fly it to Dakar non-stop. This was pretty good to have, and we could use it. Trips from Casa to Dakar had to fly over the Sahara or go via the ocean route, bypassing the Canaries that lie off the southern tip of Morocco. The Canary Islands were Spanish and Spain was neutral.

General Stowell had his pilot, Rosy, I forgot his last name but we called him Rosy, check us out. O'Brien (O.B.) was the other pilot who had flown with me previously. O.B. and I got into the B-25 and Rosy ran us through all the maneuvers he could think of. The '25 is a fine aircraft to fly. Rosy came back and told General Stowell, "These guys can fly that airplane, no problem." So Stowell called us in and said,

263

"I only ask one thing. We can't pick it up on inventory. It's already been dropped, so there's really no accountability for it. But, let me assure you guys, you won't live long enough to pay for it if you scratch it."

And he meant that. He said, "That would be a major embarrassment. So, you just take care of it. Whenever you need it for transport, use it. I don't have to pull off a separate transport aircraft or another crew to carry you guys wherever you've got to go."

His philosophy was that we couldn't sit at our desks and maintain the requirements that were necessary in the command. We had to have capable subordinates who would sit at the desk and do the deskwork. We, then, were to get out in the command and go where we needed to go and check everything out. If we needed to fix something, fix it right there. Just tell him about it. This was a great philosophy. I ended up going to every station in our command.

So, we could be our own bosses. And we were. Frank Williams was the chief of supply, Robert E. Lee Turner was the chief of air priorities. Chris Johansen, Col. Harry B. Johansen, the director of operations in the command at Casablanca, was the other member of our group.

Johansen came back after the War and ran the Johansen Plant Products in St. Joe (St. Joseph, Missouri) for Johansen Shoes. I don't know whether Chris is still in business or not. When he came back after World War II, he was one of the chief officers in the Missouri National Guard.

Frank Williams, Bob Turner and I teamed together on a lot of things, and we covered a lot of the operations. Williams was in what we call A-4 for the supply officers for the command. McCord was the personnel officer for the command, A-1. Between supply and personnel we had a pretty good procedure. We did get whatever we needed.

We took the '25 all over Africa. All over the Mediterranean. They wouldn't let me bring that B-25 home. I wanted to. Later I was mighty glad I couldn't because I could never have afforded the fuel and maintenance costs.

Events like these could never be repeated. Many of the things that happened and the things that we did, for instance, that Charlie-46 that we hotfooted with and put that music group on, you couldn't pull off. In addition to that, the Air Force would never have an appropriation for fuel that would support such a movement. It would take a major act of Congress to get it done. But in war time nobody kept track of where the fuel went. It was both good and bad. With a grade of colonel I could more or less write my own ticket.

After Dad said he ended up going to every station in that command, I looked up some of the locations in his 201 personnel file: Dakar, Senegal; Atar, Mauritania; Marrakech, French Morocco (F.M.); Oran, Algeria; Tunis, Tunisia; Cairo, Egypt; Accra, Gold Coast, now Ghana; Tripoli, Libya; Benghazi, Libya; Teheran, Iran; Abadan, Iran; Bahrain Island; Sharjah, Trucial Oman, now Saudi Arabia; Port Lyautey, F.M. And there were still other stations identified only by military ID number, not by name. The names may sound romantic but this was the desert. Some of the hottest places on earth. Lonely. Exceedingly far from home.

Howard Fast wrote about these places from personal experience in a 1945 Coronet magazine article, "Courage is a Quiet Thing." Fast was following some former bombers from units who, with the winding down of the War, were reassigned to remote ATC posts called "the milk run." Since ATC had no bombers, no comparable assignment was possible. Other men in those units were assigned to help in the tasks required to transport men home as commands were being dispersed. Fast observed that putting former top guns into isolated, faraway areas was a mistake in assignments if there ever was one.

He describes the posts.

"There is a classic description of going to bed in Abadan: you throw a bucket of water on your bed, soak your sheet in water, wrap it around you without wringing it out, and lie down on the wet mattress—and you wake up an hour later dry and gasping for breath. And it's not only the heat—it's the utter loneliness, the devastation, as if God had vented all His anger on this land.

"At Bahrein Island, the desert looked the same. The heat was a little—just a little—less intense than at Abadan and the drinking water was dirty green instead of crawling brown.

"Sharjah might have been hell, except that there were no real flames. ... White sand that is endless and sight-destroying, and heat like molten metal. And nothing anywhere, no place to go, no men, no women."

Reading Fast's poignant words on some of the forgotten spots of the war jerks me back to reality instantly. Dad was definitely encountering some of the best of the assignments, but also then remembering some of the best of experiences within an extremely harsh environment. Instead of seeing the half-empty glass, he celebrated in seeing it half full. The men in his charge in the stations he visited were in places remote, desolate, inhospitable and unheroic.

Morale had to be tough. It was Dad's job to care for them. And who cared for the caretaker?

Rescuing a French General's Son

One of the senior French generals, General Cornet, had a son who had been injured in the original German sortie in Africa. General Cornet was really crooked. Anyway, General Cornet made a request to our command to bring his son back to France from a hospital in Dakar. I had to go to Dakar on some other mission, and Stowell asked if we wouldn't pick up this young chap and bring him back. We said, "Yes, we would." So we radioed Dakar and said, "Have him ready," that we would transport him back and deliver him to France.

When we picked him up, he wanted to go to Nice. He had friends there. He also told his father, who as I said was one of the French senior officers, that he was going to come back. So we dropped back. We went first to Oran, then headed across the Mediterranean to Nice. We flew towards the French base at Nice on the northern coast of the Mediterranean and the south coast of France. As we approached and requested permission to land, they didn't have any English-speaking people in their operation section there. This young chap said, "Let me have that mike." And he told 'em who he was and what we were going to do. He said, "They're coming into land."

Well, here was a major French officer's son being brought back. Believe me, the place looked like somebody stuck a big firecracker in a beehive. Everything began to happen. They cleared the runway and gave us complete clearance to come in. We were delivering royalty as far as they were concerned. I never will forget O'Brien and I were both then offered the keys to the city by the mayor of Nice. We were very happy to deliver the son of the French general to Nice, but we didn't have time to stay there for all of the celebration that was going on—red carpets, bands and so on.

We went on to Orly airport, just south of Paris. When they found out what we'd done, the French officers there created a celebration, too. I never will forget the chief of the prefect of police for Paris and his expressions of gratitude to us. General Juin, another senior French officer, was a good friend of General Cornet and also wanted to meet us. He wanted to find out what was going on, how we'd done it and the whole works. He also presented us with the keys to the city of Paris.

This was great, but we didn't have time for all that protocol. We were happy though, that we were able to help cement relations that were a little touchy, particularly with the senior French. DeGaulle wasn't exactly one of the happy guys with the American forces or the American forces with DeGaulle. If you remember history, DeGaulle wasn't extremely well received. "Further, the deponent (one who gives evidence) *sayeth naught."*

The Case of the Missing Navy Refrigerators

We had a detachment at Manama, Bahrain Island, of about 40 people. It was a service area. Handled refueling and did some flight operations. The transport service that we had from Karachi ran to Casablanca, from Casablanca back to Karachi, then to China. The troops in Manama were active in helping maintain that network of support for planned shipments of supplies and equipment to General Vinegar Joe Stilwell's operation in the China Theater.

When I came through Bahrain, Lt. Col. George Norman was the unit commander. He was complaining bitterly that they needed a couple of refrigerators because everything they tried to keep would spoil without refrigeration. Particularly, they liked cold beer.

On one trip back, as we were flying back to Cairo from the stations we had at Abadan and Baghdad, we flew over the Navy base at Khorramshahr, a short distance northwest up the river from Abadan. There on the storage service area for that Navy base we saw a whole bunch of refrigerators.

We got into Cairo and turned around the C-46 we were using at that time. I said, "I'll just take this over, we'll go and do a service job." I figured we could provide some special services for Bahrain Island. We loaded up with good liquor, some booze—gin, bourbon and scotch, that type of thing. I had briefed my crew that we were going to pick up some refrigerators on the Navy base, but first we had to immobilize the guards on that supply section. We also took along a couple of Jeeps and one of those military-type four-by-fours. Refrigerators could be hauled on those in fine shape.

Fully "armed," we went back and landed at Khorramshahr. Our boys took the cases of good liquor over and promptly got the Navy boys, shore patrol guards, happy with their consignment of good drink. They got to the point where they didn't care a bit about the refrigerators. We proceeded to pick up probably four or five refrigerators, put 'em on that four-by-four, took 'em out to the Charlie-46 and just loaded 'em on. I gathered my crew back together, bid the Navy bon voyage, and we took off to Bahrain.

They weren't just ordinary kitchen-type refrigerators. These were big refrigerators, heavy-duty types. Military strength. To service a 40-man detachment. We distributed those refrigerators to several stations where they were badly needed. We didn't think the Navy needed 'em. Bahrain was provided with refrigeration for storable produce as well as good beer. They just never did get used to drinking hot beer like the English do.

I went back to Casablanca and I expect it was probably three days when the command got an inquiry. Did we know anything about refrigerators that were missing from the supply base at Khorramshahr? General Stowell said in our morning staff session, "The Navy's kind of upset about this. Do any of you guys know anything about these refrigerators?" None of us knew. Not a thing.

Gen. Stowell subsequently had a meeting at Karachi with someone from that branch of the CBI operation. Stowell came back through Bahrain and stopped to talk to the people and meet with the detachment there. He found out they not only had two refrigerators, but also extra supply for all of the needs of their operation, their 40-man detachment.

Following that, Stowell came back to Casablanca on that leg of the trip and commented, "You know, it's one of the funniest things. All of a sudden George Norman ended up with some very good refrigeration. That's the only station over there in Manama that has any refrigeration at all." The Arabs don't use refrigeration except whatever they might be able to devise with deep wells that they'd keep stuff in. And he said that it was a great find, that Norman was very pleased about this. "What do you know about this?" he asked the staff. Of course, we still didn't know anything about it. He laughed, and said, "Well, I've got a message here from the Navy headquarters at Caserta, Italy, (north of Naples)*. They are really, seriously trying to find where those refrigerators went because they're an accountable item." Still, none of us knew anything about it.*

Besides Norman's station, refrigerators went to John Payne Field in Cairo and the station at Bengazi, Libya. We had about four or five units and those would do at least three stations without any problem.

271

These were small detachment operations, but they were able to service whatever requirements the aircraft had in order to continue their trips to supply the China Theater with military items.

General Stowell knew what was happening because he had the report of the transportation use of the big Curtiss commandos, these Charlie-46s. And, of course, I had turned one of those around on the flat schedule, and it had to be filled in along the line while we diverted it for this operation. He kind of figured that he had charged me with the morale of the troops in his command, so we had a session on it.

He said, "Now, I think this is a fine thing to have. It's a fine morale builder. But let me tell you, staff, please don't do anything more that's going to embarrass me with my Navy counterpart. The admiral over at Caserta is very upset about this."

I don't know what happened to those Navy guards. I didn't really care. Some of those guys still may be looking, trying to find those refrigerators yet. It's amazing what can happen in theaters of war. Stuff gets what they call lost—lost, missing, found type stuff. Missing in the line of duty ...

It was a lot of fun. That was a morale builder for our station. And the Navy didn't need that many, anyway. They gave 'em up willingly. As a matter of fact, they were not in any position to argue. I don't think they could've hit the floor with their hat. You'd be surprised what a bottle of gin will do.

Chaplain E. J. Killion

When I was assigned to Casablanca, the adjutants in the command were responsible for placing people in their billets. We had taken over the Excelsior Hotel in Casablanca. The adjutant told me, "Hal, I only have one slot open. You'll have to bunk with the chaplain." I said, "Well, that doesn't bother me a bit. If the chaplain can put up with me, I know I can put up with him."

I checked in and found my room. When I met the chaplain, I introduced myself, "My name's McCord, and I'm going to be your roommate." He said, "Great! Do you play chess?" "Yes, I do." "Wonderful! We're going to have some good times." I found out that he was an accomplished and challenging chess player. If we kept score, he'd beat me as many times as I'd beat him. We'd sit up in the evening after dinner and play chess until 0200 or 0230, 0300. We certainly had a lot of fun out of it.

Father E. J. Killion was such a joy to be with. He was so different than what I had known in other clergymen. Very human. He was an excellent command chaplain, exceedingly good. An Irishman, educated in Nuremberg, he had been through 12 years of post-graduate school. Catholic, a Jesuit.

We had an Easter service coming up with, of course, a mixed crowd. He was the only chaplain around. I said, "Ed, you better make your peace with the Pope 'cause you're going to conduct Good Friday services for our entire command. There will be a lot of non-Catholic people there. Can you handle it?" He assured me, "Of course I can handle it." I countered, "Well, what's your protocol as far as working with your management level in the church?" He affirmed, "I'm in the military. I can do anything. And, well, I've got God on my side." This was a big help.

Later, when our forces were moving up the boot of Italy, we got into a warehouse that had some exceptionally fine wine, a cognac-type that the Germans had liberated and stored. We re-liberated the contents of that warehouse. One of the selections was a Napoleon five-star brandy that was absolutely out of this world. I got a couple of bottles of that, and I went back to my command, my roommate and the chess games.

Ed and I had an after-dinner drink, a small amount of this brandy. He saw the bottle and said, "Hal, where in the world did you get that?" I said, "I got it in Italy. The Germans had stashed it in one of the warehouses, and we found it. I ended up with a couple of bottles of it." He glowed, "You know, that's probably the best brandy that has ever been bottled." His eyes just sparkled.

I said, "How would you like to have a snifter of brandy?" "Now?" "Why not? You don't have anything coming up, do you?" He said, "No." So, we poured a goblet of brandy, a brandy snifter, and he was just as happy as could be about it. "That's the best. I know you got it in Italy, but, is there any more available?" I didn't know whether we could get any more or not.

Sometimes we'd get started singing. Father Killion had a beautiful Irish voice. One time we were entertaining and had a group for dinner. After our evening meal, some of the guys there knew that he did sing, and they asked him to sing "Home on the Range." It was beautiful—he just did an exquisite job with it. Of course, he sang with an Irish brogue. Then I requested "I'll Take You Home Again, Kathleen." He was outstanding. He did a lot of different Irish songs after that. That was where I learned "Have You Ever Heard the Story of How Ireland Got its Name?"

(Dad, singing with an Irish brogue.)

I'll tell ye so you'll understand from whence ol' Ireland came.
'Tis no wonder that we love that land so far across the sea,
Oh, here's the way me dear old Mither told this tale to me.
Sure, a little bit of heaven fell from out the sky one day,
And nestled in the ocean in a spot so far away.
And when the angels found it, sure it looks so sweet and fair,
Suppose we leave it there, it is so peaceful there.
And they dusted it with stardust just to make the shamrocks grow.
'Tis the only place you'll find them no matter where you go.
And they then decided that it would be so grand,
We will call that fine land Ireland.

He did that song and everybody loved it. Ed had an excellent repertoire, good music. He had the voice to do justice to the songs.

When I moved to Paris, I took Killion up there with me. He enjoyed Paris, too. That was where he was located when we were breaking up the command and needed to assign people of the

275

occupation forces. I asked Ed where he wanted to go. He said, "Well, I really would like to go to the Slavic area." I found out that he read, wrote and spoke all of the Slavic languages. He never ceased to amaze me. I asked the command if we could send him to Triest. Triest is so far to the northeast of Italy it's almost in Yugoslavia. But Ed belonged to Cardinal Spellman in the New York diocese, and Spellman wanted him back. No, he wouldn't approve it.

I had a trip to Rome coming up anyway. I asked for an audience with the Secretary to the Pope in the School of Cardinals, and I got it. I made an overture to them, told them that I had this extremely well-qualified clergyman who had been through that area, spoke all those languages and would be a terrific asset in that area under occupation forces. The Secretary said, "What's the problem?" I said, "Cardinal Spellman will not approve it." He looked kind of puzzled and said, "Spellman, Spellman. Do I know Spellman?"

I told him that he was in New York. He said, "I think maybe the Good Father will approve Father Killion's going to the Triest occupation forces. Give me half an hour." So, I came back and asked him what the situation was. He told me that The Holy Father decided that he was going to tell Cardinal Spellman that he had another assignment for Monsignor Killion and that he wouldn't be back to Spellman's diocese.

I came back and told Ed that I had made the trip and had permission from the Vatican to have him re-assigned to the occupation forces. He said, "How in the world did you get that done? Spellman wouldn't release me." I responded, "In this case, Spellman didn't have much choice. The Holy Father decided that you were needed." A little higher authority there. Just keep going up until you reach somebody above. The guy who has the final authority.

"Oh, and when I get through with this, do I have to go back to Spellman?" He was wishing I could do something more. Spellman wouldn't believe it, of course. He was quite upset. He accused Ed of having gone over his head. Ed chided me, "You really fixed me up." He ended up, the last I knew, in the Balkans. Father E. J. Killion was absolutely one great guy.

HEADQUARTERS

NORTH AFRICAN DIVISION

AIR TRANSPORT COMMAND

1250 TH AAF BASE UNIT

APO 396, N.Y., N.Y.

22 August 1945.

In reply
refer to

To Col. Hal McCord:

Dear Hal:

After four years of dreaming, praying and sighing that I might get into Europe somehow, I'm finally on the way - thanks to you. There are so many things I want to say to you that I thought the best way was by this little note instead of by word of mouth.

One says a lot of trite, insignificant things at a moment like this, such as: "It's been grand being with you"; "I certainly enjoyed working with you", etc, but none of them, even though raised to a superlative degree, can do justice to my feelings as I depart for the north country.

Hal, I've worked with and under a lot of officers in this man's army. They've all been my friends and the hand-clasp that denoted our final parting was always sincere. But of all the men I've been associated with there is one who reached a pinnacle in my esteem and his name was McCord. Your gentlemanliness, your grand traits of character, your splendid efficiency always combined with a gracious sense of humbleness will stick with me down thru the years till the time comes for "shuffling off this mortal coil". To say that I deeply regret leaving you and our fine association is the grossest understatement that was ever couched in human language. That it was inevitable sooner or later, doesn't soften the edge of that regret in the least. I only hope that in the few final months that remain to me in a GI uniform, I may meet up with bosses, or associates with a tenth of your qualities!

After getting mustered out I'll go back to my little monastery cell in Saratoga Springs, New York, where I'll indulge in hour-long reveries over the hectic period 1940 to 1946. Old familiar names and faces will flit over that screen of memory but yours will be the one most prominent and best respected. If you ever come that way, whether for the races in August or to quaff the healing waters of America's greatest Spa, look me up, and we'll toss off a drop of the craythur "for the sake of Auld Lang Syne".

Sincerely,

Ed Killion

Letter to Hal from Chaplain Ed Killion

278

Courts-Martial Boards

In addition to being authorized to handle TOP SECRET material, being on promotions boards, officer candidate school boards, boards to evaluate applicants for the counter intelligence corps, awards and decorations committees, and boards to consider rotation of war-weary pilots, being a personnel officer brought with it responsibilities to serve on boards for courts-martial. Dad was on such boards in both India and North Africa.

On June 21, 1944 Dad was the ranking officer and thereby president assigned to such a board meeting in Calcutta "or at such other places as might be necessary, at the call of the President thereof, for the trial of such persons as may be properly brought before it." The employment of an interpreter and an enlisted man as reporter was authorized.

On Sept. 4, Dad was appointed to another such board again as the ranking officer. In one incident coming before this board, a 1st Lt. Sherry of the CBI command, ATC, "with intent to deceive his Commanding Officer" made a local flight from Kunming, China in a C-46 with a reported time of 2 hours 30 minutes.

The actual time was approximately one hour and five minutes.

In Specification 2, Sherry similarly reported a flight from Kunming to Chanyi and back to be of 3 hours and 30 minutes duration. Actual flight time was one hour, and the charge was that he misappropriated military aircraft and didn't go to Chanyi. Specification 3 charges that Sherry reported a six-hour flight that was actually not made at all. There were six more similar charges. The decision of the board was guilty on all but two of the nine counts. Sentence was a fine of $1,200 to be paid to the United States.

November 12, 1944, Dad was assigned to another general court-martial board, again the ranking officer, this time meeting at the 1260th AAF Base Unit of the ATC in Tunis, Tunisia. PFC Bailey of the 1260th was charged with "wrongfully, without authority and with intent to use the same, have in his possession 95 counterfeit Army Exchange Service Ration Cards of the North African Theater of Operations of the United States Army."

Specification 2 charged that he did "wrongfully sell to ... a civilian three (3) Emerson yellow gold wristwatches, with leather straps; and one (1) Olma silver wristwatch, Number 4020, with strap; all articles purchased at retail from the 1260th AAF Base Unit ... Army Exchange."

Specification 3 was similar, but the merchandise resold included 12 cartons of cigarettes, toilet soap, shaving soap and chocolate candy.

Specification 4 charged that Bailey did "wrongfully have in his possession the sum of $78 in regular currency ..." It was forbidden to have regular U.S. currency in excess of $1. The currency used was a yellow seal currency specifically issued to prevent black-market operations.

This time the charges included a violation of the 96th Article of War. Bailey had had a local printing service print 200 counterfeit Army Exchange Service Ration Cards. He was found guilty on all counts, dishonorably discharged, had to forfeit all pay and was sentenced to be confined at hard labor for three years. The dishonorable discharge was suspended until he was released from confinement.

When Dad bought a watch in Casablanca, he paid $29 and had to sign forms that included a witness signature that the watch was for his own personal use.

Another incident from the same date as the one above carried two charges of violating the Articles of War, the 86th and the 96th. "In that Private Floyd Combs, 17th Depot Supply Squadron, AC, being on guard and posted as a sentinel, at El Aouina Air Base, Tunis, Tunisia, on or about 26 October 1944, was found drunk upon his post."

Along with that it was charged that he "did ... through carelessness, discharge a carbine in the area of El Aouina Air Base..." He was judged guilty on both counts. His sentence was to be dishonorably discharged, forfeit all pay and allowances due, and to be confined at hard labor ... for two years. One previous conviction was considered." Dad remarked that one of his so-called friends had apparently filled his canteen with wine the night he was found drunk.

Undiscovered Egyptian Ruins

I had gone to Cairo for a court-martial case. As a senior officer, the Judge Advocate General used me rather extensively as president of a general court. Some gang had been caught transporting industrial diamonds, and I was scheduled for supervising and producing a general court action in Cairo. The group was a joint French, German and American operation. They were selling industrial diamonds out of Africa in Europe and really making a big take on it.

I arrived in Cairo before they got everybody assembled, and it was a weekend. My birthday, in fact. The commander at John Payne Field had an AT-6. Well, this was like going-home week. I asked him if I could have his '6 for the weekend. He said, "Certainly!"

From Cairo I flew south along the Nile, down the river to the confluence of the White and Blue Nile south of Khartoum. This was at about 8,000 to 10,000 feet altitude. High enough that I could still see pretty well. The weather was excellent, and I didn't have any serious problems.

On the way back, it was late in the evening, and the western sun showed the desert floor pretty well to the west of the course I was flying. There appeared to be mounds there that were repetitive-type undulations in the desert floor surface. I became very interested. Circling around them. I determined, yes, it did look as though there was something there that was unusual. I marked it on the map.

When I came back, we turned this information over to the archaeologist people in Cairo. We had seen something down there that looked like perhaps some sort of man-made objects that the desert sand had covered. They thanked the command for having turned this information in and subsequently did go down to check it out. They found some ancient ruins that dated back to early times. I don't know what the site was called, I just knew that they did find it.

That was exciting from a historical standpoint, and I was fascinated to have a part in it. It was a new find at that time and tied into some of the other areas that they were interested in excavating and getting more information on.

A memorandum dated March 30, 1945, details another court, again with Dad as the ranking officer. It was scheduled to meet at 0900 hours April 2 at the ANFA Hotel in Casablanca. "Uniform will be Class 'A' and blouse will be worn."

An Unexpected Strafing

In the North Africa command, we were flying a freight line across the eastern end of the Mediterranean from Casablanca to Karachi. One of the fighter pilots newly assigned to this transport command nearly created an international incident.

His military transport plane, a C-46 Curtiss Commando, was customized so the radio operator could extend the antenna by dropping a heavy lead weight with a fishtail on the end. The antenna was still extended when the pilot decided to make a pass on a British transport column below, as if he were on a strafing mission. Further, the pilot neglected to tell the radio operator of his sudden change of plans and also forgot about getting the antenna reeled in.

Cutting through the cab <u>between</u> the two drivers in each truck, the fishtail went through all three trucks. The commanding general told this particular young pilot that he could leave his pilot's credentials on the desk and report to infantry. No court-martial, though.

A Pierced-Steel Plank Runway

One time I landed on a makeshift runway. A pierced-steel plank runway. This happened in Italy at Cappuccino. Cappu had a 2800-foot planking over an area that was not very stable ground. The noisiest runway I ever experienced. You couldn't bring an aircraft in on it without getting in real trouble.

Each plank was a section of steel plate that had holes in it. I don't remember exactly how big each piece was except that they were about 10 feet long and were chained together. Kind-a. This type of thing, (Dad put his hands together interleaving the fingers) *to make a runway. I expect it was 150 feet wide.*

I remember that I was flying the '25. I had come up to Italy for a meeting, and Phil Meyers, commander of the 12th Air Force at Florence, was going to meet me. Meyers had been director of operations when I was at Randolph Field, and he and General Twining, then commander of the 18th Air Force, had invited me to come visit in Florence. They just wanted to talk. I remember that, when the request came through official channels, General Stowell called me in. "McCord, front and center. Hal, are you unhappy with your assignment in this command?" "Most certainly not, sir." "Well, I have this request from General Twining for you to go up and be their guest at Florence ..."

I knew where the field was; they had it marked where we would land. I came in and got down on the deck to fly over the runway and see what it was like and what I had ahead of me. I would have to

284

make a short-field landing. I circled back, came back in and set that B-25 down. I hung it on its prop, full flaps (slants his hand, drops the fingers to simulate flaps down) *and put it down in the first ten feet of the planks. I was on the ground, and just as soon as the nose wheel touched down, I stepped on the brakes. I had less than 100 feet left at the end of the runway when I finally got stopped.*

Oh, did Phil bless me out! He jumped up and down and said, "Don't ever do that again! Put that aircraft away. You're going to ride with me from here out on this trip."

During a couple of trips to Italy, Dad would also meet up with his cousin, Hal Irwin. The other Hal was a lieutenant colonel in the Army and port commander at Naples. Dad remembers going out to dinner with him at the home of one of his employees, a special treat.

Inside the Blue Mosque

The Aqsunqur or Blue Mosque dating from 1346, is one of Cairo's most remarkable mosques. Blue-gray marble does grace the façade, but the name Blue Mosque comes from its interior walls. The inside of the mosque is quite ornate—stunning with marble panels and painted ceiling, and covered in isnik blue and turquoise tiles outlined with plant and flower designs.

These Ottoman tiles were imported from Istanbul and Damascus and added when the structure was restored and modified in 1652. It is cruciform in design with porticos originally covered by groined vaults instead of a wood ceiling and arches supported by square and octagonal pillars. Most unusual architecture. And very beautiful, with inlays of precious stones, polychrome marble and mosaics in soft plum, salmon, gray and green colors. I can see why my father would be interested enough to risk seeing it.

During another Cairo trip, I went out to see the Sphinx and the pyramids at Giza. While I was observing the amazing architectural details, an Arab approached me. He was about 40 years old, good looking and spoke excellent English. "Monsieur Le Colonel, may I give you some advice?" He told me how the Sphinx was put together. With the body of a lion and the head of a king or god, the paws alone are 50 feet long; it truly is a mysterious marvel.

I asked about other significant structures in Cairo. He suggested several places to visit and made the arrangements. On our itinerary was the Blue Mosque, and entry was forbidden to Westerners. This took some special planning. If we were found out, it would be our necks.

Ali, my Arab guide, dressed me in a burnoose—a hooded caftan of a beautiful light blue, fine heavy fabric. I have since wished I could have kept that garment. He also provided slippers and insisted I was not to speak. The desert sun had tanned my skin sufficiently to pass for Arab, but my voice would have been a dead give-away. Both of us were clean-shaven.

The arches of the mosque were beautiful, three-centered arches with lots of blue stone inlay. Inside the mosque classes were being conducted to teach youngsters the Koran. The instructor would read and the children would memorize, swinging their bodies in rhythm while they recited. All in Arabic, of course. Learning the Koran by rote. There were about eight in a group and they sat in a circle around their instructor on mats on the floor of an auditorium.

The Soothsayer

We also met up with a soothsayer near the Sphinx. He cast a circle and "read" the stones. He forecast that I would have an extended trip. He also told that I would have a family of five children. I laughed and told Ali, "I don't believe that guy knows what he's talking about." Within a couple of months, I would have orders to go to Washington then to Orlando to attend a Personnel Management Course, and I managed to meet Ivalee in Florida. I certainly didn't think there would ever be another couple of youngsters, but the fortune did come true.

Ali was educated at Oxford, had two wives. This was two less than the legal limit of four, but he said he couldn't take care of the two he had. They didn't get along. Ali was very familiar with Cairo, also the area of the pyramids. He was generous with his time, and the fees I paid him were insignificant for this rare opportunity. It was a very pleasant two-day encounter.

Dispersing the Command

With the cessation of hostilities in May 1945, boards on which Dad served began to take on a different character. There was an Officer's Separation Board ... On June 20, 1945, a board met to discuss "Plan, Policies and Procedure for Evaluation and Selective Classification of Officers for Manning the Postwar Air Force." The command at Casablanca was being dispersed. The Green Project, an effort to transport US soldiers back to the USA as soon as possible, involved a lot of reassignment of personnel, which in turn involved Dad as personnel officer. The plan was to ship over 50,000 men a month from the European and Mediterranean theatres back to the States without interrupting the regular air transport schedules. The ATC loaded C-46s and C-47s and slipped them in and out of Payne Field in Cairo. From May until September 1945, more than 7,000 C-54s transited through Santa Maria in the Azores, where newly completed facilities cut flying time from 70 to 40 hours for the trip from North Africa to the US. After a year or two overseas, the boys would be home in three days.

Promotion to Full Colonel

Gen. James S. Stowell wrote a letter of recommendation for Dad's promotion to full Colonel. It was dated 26 Dec 1945 even though the promotion was official on 22 May 1945. He cautioned Dad, "Son, this doubles your responsibility and cuts your margin of error in half." Stowell lists his reasons for the recommendation pointing out that Dad had "more than demonstrated his qualifications" and "that failure to promote this officer would be a direct violation" of the paragraph detailing requirements for such a promotion.

Stowell called Dad "an exceptionally well-qualified individual who has shown and is showing an unusual amount of initiative in the discharge of the responsibilities of his duty assignment as Assistant Chief of Staff, Personnel." He used phrases like "superior performance," "exceptional ability of leadership," and "has the tact necessary to handle and direct personnel under his jurisdiction, both military and civilian and, at the same time, establishing and maintaining their highest esteem." "He has performed his duties with the greatest efficiency and competence."

Flight to Caserta

As a part of my impending transfer to Paris I needed to go first to Paris, then to a briefing in Caserta. It was one of the best trips ever with the B-25. When I left Paris, I flew through Germany, crossing the Rhine at tree top level. I could see "mouse castles" below.[68] Over Brenner Pass at the top of Italy, just south of Innsbruck in Austria, bypassing the highest of the Alps. The vibrations of the plane started a small avalanche. It was a beautiful trip.

WWII, 1944-45

Operation Overlord, the D-Day landings in Normandy, opened the western front on June 6 1944. The drive for Paris began that August.

---

[68] A reference to the three luxurious castles in Bavaria built by mad King Ludwig II: Neuschwanstein, the castle used as a model for the castle at Disney World, Linderhof and Herrenchiemsee. I explored Linderhof with my sister and our husbands, but only saw Neuschwanstein castle from the outside. They truly are magnificent.

With Montgomery in the North, Bradley in the South, and spearheaded by Patton, the Allies drove the Germans back. By August 25 the Allies reached the Seine River in the North and the Loire River in the South, and Paris. Allied troops liberated more of France, then entered Belgium and Holland.

By mid-September, they reached the Siegfried Line, the West Wall of Germany's frontier. Allied air superiority was so overwhelming that by the end of August 1944, Britain's RAF's Bomber Command had begun to abandon night aerial bombing to attack Ruhr targets in daytime.

August 25, Paris. A day of snipers firing, captured Germans being attacked after they surrendered. One column was machine gunned as they were being marched around the Arc de Triomphe. By mid-afternoon, the German commander of Paris surrendered. An hour and a half later, DeGaulle reached Paris.

The day of triumph came at a cost; more than 500 Resistance fighters along with 127 civilians were killed during the liberation of the city. Many who had collaborated with the Germans were killed without trial or debate.

On August 26, General DeGaulle walked in triumph down the Champs Èlysée. Many French civilians were seized and executed by retreating German troops southeast of Paris. August 28 the allied forces entered Toulon and Marseilles in southern France and took 47,000 German POWs.

General Sir Bernard Law Montgomery proposed operation Market Garden to smash across the barrier of the Rhine River in the north and outflank the West Wall. "Market" was the code name for dropping British and American paratroopers into Holland behind the German lines to disrupt German defenses. "Garden" was the invasion of the Ruhr, which never came off. The movie "A Bridge Too Far" tells the story of "Market." The assault on Holland's bridges was launched September 17, 1944. Only 2,000 out of 9,000 Allied troops survived this operation.[69]

That same summer of 1944, fighting in the Pacific opened the way to the Philippines. Invasion was set for December 10, but was moved up two months. The greatest naval battle, the Battle for Leyte Gulf, occurred in late October. Japan put up a lot to try to keep its important fuel source and deny the Americans this victory.

Japanese kamikaze pilots made deliberate suicide attacks on the ships of the Seventh Fleet, a maneuver more destructive than decisive. Damage to ships and maiming of crews were intense.

In the CBI Theater, the tide began to turn in favor of the Allies; with sufficient supplies and men the Allies began regaining areas of Burma.

In Europe, the Battle of the Bulge had begun by Christmas 1944. The 101st Airborne Division in Bastogne, Belgium, was surrounded but refused to surrender. Fog grounded American bombers, interfered with supply drops and caused confusion. Eisenhower put Montgomery in charge in the north sector of the Bulge and Bradley in

---

[69] My sister Janice Winchell and her husband Bill make the pilgrimage to Arnhem in the Netherlands every September for the commemorative ceremonies of this event.

the south. Reserves were fed in from both directions as soon as possible. Patton reached Bastogne on Dec. 26. Despite the lesser numbers and some disorganization, the Americans held. The weather cleared, the Allied aircraft appeared and the Allies swiftly redeployed troops. The Germans were running out of steam and supplies.

Also that Christmas saw the first irradiated slugs of uranium in the US; a month later the first plutonium was ready for shipment.

By the end of January, the Allies had flattened the Bulge in the Ardennes and were preparing to drive into the Rhineland. By early '45, there were daily bombings on Berlin. Patton and Montgomery continued the race for the Rhine.

April 1945 was a momentous month. Roosevelt died and Mussolini was shot, killed by Italian partisans. On April 20, Hitler's 65th birthday, he was deep underground in Berlin and the American Seventh Army took Nuremberg. The end of April saw continued deterioration of German resistance and the ruins of the Third Reich. Hitler married Eva Braun on April 29; the same day Italy surrendered. The next day Hitler put a gun in his mouth and pulled the trigger. That same day, the Seventh Army reached Dachau. The GIs found it hard to believe what they saw there.

May 4, the German forces in Holland, Denmark and northwest Germany surrendered to Montgomery. The next day the German troops in the south surrendered to Gen. Jacob Loucks Devers' Sixth Army Group. V-E Day, Victory in Europe, was declared on May 8.

The next day the unconditional surrender was officially ratified in Berlin.

Meanwhile in the Pacific, kamikaze pilots sank 17 ships and damaged 50 more. The assault on Iwo Jima began Feb. 19, 1945. It was the toughest battle in the history of the Marines. Twenty-six days of fighting. On March 16 the island was declared secure, yet there was a final banzai charge 10 days later. Japanese dead: more than 21,000; Marines dead: more than 5,000. The battle for Okinawa came Easter Sunday.

August 6, the Enola Gay, piloted by Col. Paul W. Tibbets, Jr., dropped the first atomic bomb on Hiroshima.[70] Another bomb was dropped August 9 on Nagasaki. August 15, 1945, Hirohito sent his message of surrender, and the hostilities in the Pacific soon came to an official end.

But new conflicts were already beginning to appear as Ho Chi-minh moved in North Vietnam, and the cold war began to heat up. Punishment of the war guilty took precedence over the healing.

24 Sep 1945—29 Jan 1946: EURD-ATC

A radiogram from EURD (European Division) was received in Casablanca 13 Sept 1945.

---

[70] A friend gave Dad a large-print version of Bob Greene's story of Tibbets, the book, <u>Duty</u>. Dad enjoyed reading this book immensely and bought a copy for me.

From: **PARIS PRIORITY**

TO: CASA, CO NAFD ATC

FOR: NELSON PERSONALLY

JPING COLONEL HAL MCCORD RECOMMENDED FOR ASSIGNMENT AS DEPUTY CHIEF OF STAFF EUROPEAN DIVISION. PLEASE INFORM THIS HDQS IF HE IS IMMEDIATELY AVAILABLE NOW.

SIGNED

WEBSTER

By the fall of '44, things were moving toward a finale with the Germans in Europe. The command at Casablanca, all of Africa, was closed down in mid '45. Because of my familiarity with North Africa, I was moved to Paris for the staff there with Major General Robert M. Webster and given the job as Assistant Chief of Staff, Personnel.

The Legion of Merit

When I was transferred to Paris as assistant chief of staff, the chief of staff, Col. George C. Van Nostrand, was detailed to a meeting with the Russians in Vienna. I came in on a Thursday, and he had to leave on the following Monday. General Webster said, "Hal, I want you to take over. George has got to make this trip. There isn't any way I could put somebody else in his place because he's been working on this project for some time and there's nobody prepared to step in for him." He reassured me, "I know that you can take over. I'll have the Adjutant General publish your orders that you are acting chief of staff."

Well, things began to happen. I said, "General, I don't even know your people." He said, "That's all right; you'll learn." Hell, we had 35,000 people in that command. Before the end of that week, orders came in detailing Webster to Washington for a high-level conference in Washington. General Bryant "Bitsy" Boatner, vice commander, was then ordered to Vienna to meet with the Russians on trying to set up over-flight routes from Paris to Karachi across that portion of the Eastern Front controlled by the Russians. That left me, then, as senior officer in the command after I'd been there less than 10 days. I just transferred a cot over to the headquarters, moved in and lived there until we got things kind of stable. There was only one way to do it— that was the right way.

I did learn the names of the people on the staff quickly. Every morning at 1000 hours I had a staff meeting. It might be only 15 minutes, but for anything that came up we operated as a group not as individuals. It's particularly good management to do it this way when you're new in an area, don't know the people, and don't know all of the problems.

If they had a special problem, they threw it on the table for us to work on and make recommendations for that particular instance. It worked. Webster had said, "At the end of every day, just send me a brief message of what goes on. If you need any help, let me know what

I can do to help." He was a great manager, too. I liked Bob Webster immensely.

I remember one incident in which Webster had a special, sensitive mission come up. He asked me, "Please recommend two officers to me to do this work." I gave him a list of five that I thought were capable of doing what he wanted. Three of them were West Pointers; two of them were ROTC graduates and had come up through the ranks via that route. Webster himself was a West Pointer. I was amazed. He picked the two ROTC types.

I asked him about that. "General, why didn't you pick the West Point people?" He said, "Frankly, because the two ROTC boys are more innovative, and they'll get the job done better than my professional types from the Academy. I found that they do better. That's why you're here." I said, "Well, you amazed me." He responded, "I haven't any question that, as long as I'm going to be gone, you'll sit on top of the whole thing." I appreciated that advice and that confidence.

Paris was where Webster gave me the Legion of Merit. It's one of the top awards for administrative operation in the Air Force. In one picture I have, the top medal on my uniform, or the top ribbon, is the Legion of Merit. I was very pleased. He also gave me letters of performance approval—that's a green ribbon, and I've got one of those with two or three devices on it indicating that I've been awarded that two or three times. This represented a letter of appreciation or a letter of approval from a major general or higher.

Jackie Cochran in Paris

When I was later chief of staff in Paris, Jackie Cochran came over and had a letter of introduction from General Hap Arnold. That letter gave her the U.S. Air Force. Whatever she wanted she was going to get. She came in, and we put her up at the Ritz Hotel, right around the corner of the square from Chapparelli's, a high-class department store.

Jackie wanted to go over there and buy some clothes. She didn't have enough money with her to buy much, so she asked me, "Can you arrange for me to get a letter of credit?" I said, "I might be able to do better than that." Colonel Williams was my finance officer. I called him in and told him what Ms. Cochran wanted. He said, "I think this can be arranged. How much does she want?" So I asked Jackie, "How much money do you want?" She said, "I want $10,000." "OK, let's see what we can do."

Williams wired Washington, contacted the finance officer there and told him that Jacqueline Cochran wanted a—what did they call it—a stipend deposit, for $10,000. Could he arrange it? Faherty checked quickly with the people there in Washington and radioed right back within 30 minutes. "Yes. We'll make the money transfer. Where do you want it to come?" He said, "Well, send it to me as the finance officer for the command." And the transfer was made.

When Jackie came in, we told her everything had been arranged, and she could go to the finance officer to sign for the $10,000. She got the money, but it was different from the currency that you have now, which is a green seal currency, if you'll notice. The currency we had in Europe was a gold seal, so that it could not be used for black market operations. We gave her $10,000 in gold seal money. It wasn't good any place but in Europe.

I told her, "If you have some left over, bring it back to Col. Williams, and he'll replace it with a letter of credit that's cashable in the United States." She said, "I don't know that I'll have any left over." She bought a slug of clothes from Chapparelli's. I don't know where she'd ever use all of them, but I wouldn't question it. That was Jackie Cochran.

Her husband was Floyd Odlum, the one who took over TWA and brought them out of the doldrums. Odlum provided the management guidance to bring them out of approaching bankruptcy. At one time, I had a letter of invitation to be their guest at their California ranch. I never did exercise it. That was a level above and beyond my sphere of social life; it was a little too rich. But I enjoyed meeting her and talking with her and, of course, participating in getting what she wanted.

We were buddies in an airplane and a crew; wherever she wanted to go in Europe, we would take her. She was in Europe for exploration, familiarization with where her women pilots were flying, and how they performed. These women did a lot of ferrying of things and moved planes that the military needed to have in another location. They did not fly combat missions, but they did have to fly many different kinds of planes. The women did quite a job.

Jackie was the one who got the training set-up and put that program together. They replaced military-type, combat-capable personnel with women who did the ferrying jobs. They performed a fine service without due credit given. This was one of the sorry things. I don't know whether they ever got credit for what they had done. They didn't even get retirement. They came out with nothing. It was unfortunate, and I never did think they were treated correctly.

Ms. Cochran was a very strong-willed woman. She grew up in poverty in Florida. The "sawdust trail" they called it, and she made her own way out of it. She was a director—had a knack for being in charge. In 1939, she had written a letter to Mrs. Eleanor Roosevelt suggesting the need to plan for the use of female fliers in a national emergency. She also liked to have men on a string, and she could manipulate them. Like General Luke Smith. She knew how to use sex and did. Jackie had him on her string. So did she have Hap Arnold, and Hap at that time was the senior officer in the Army Air Corps.

Jackie also played a role in persuading General Eisenhower to run for president, talking Ike into going into the Republican fold. She and Floyd helped run his campaign. They knew that Ike would be elected if he just entered into the fray. And this was true.

M. and Mme. Guy Verdier

I had asked Dad about a small card in his files, from M. and Mme. Guy Verdier. He broke into a grin and began this story. *In Paris our quarters were at the Hotel Plaza Athenee.*[71] *I was in room 607. M. Verdier and his wife were wonderful people. Not everyone got to know them. They owned the Magazin de Verdier with stores both in Paris and San Francisco. Those were big department stores they needed to restock.*

However, the Hon. Sir Jefferson Caffrey of Louisiana, then the U.S. Ambassador to France, would not let them get a slot to go to the USA and restock. He was a pompous political type. I don't know how he got the title—he must have bought it. At any rate I got a military slot and was able to get M. Verdier back to the States. He was very grateful. That card was sent to my quarters at the Hotel Plaza Athenee.

The card is an invitation: M. and Mme. Guy Verdier request the pleasure of Colonel McCord's company for dinner at home the Friday 21st of December, 20:15. RSVP. There is another notecard included in the small envelope, and it says: "Dear Sir—Please will you send to Mrs. McCord these samples of the French nylon production. I hope she will like the color and that the size is the right one. With all my thanks for all you have so nicely done for me, Very sincerely, G. Verdier." The business card identifies Guy Verdier as "Directeur, des Etablissements Gaston Verdier" in Paris.

Although I had heard the story about Mr. Verdier before, I had never seen the accompanying cards until I took Dad's 201 military

---

[71] The Hotel is still there. Their website shows a fabulous picture and advertises, "In the heart of Paris on the famous Avenue Montaigne, the Plaza Anthenee offers a unique location with the best opportunity to enjoy the haute couture, entertainment and business life of the city."

file home with me in 1999. The file revealed several missing family puzzle pieces. I can imagine that Dad wanted to reciprocate on the stockings. His request to my mother to send some American nylons as a gift for the "wife of a friend" became, I now believe, one of the miscommunications between my parents.

The "How Ya Gonna Keep 'Em Down on the Farm (in Kansas) After They've Seen Paree" mentality of some of her friends raised questions. "Yes, and if you believe that 'wife of a friend business,' I have a bridge in Brooklyn I'd like to sell you ..." Another wedge driven, another source for misunderstanding and mistrust. Once such seeds are planted, it takes a lot of faith to keep them from growing. Separation and poor communication allow unresolved issues to mature and magnify. The unknown feeds fears; truth gets lost and forgotten as doubts begin to stack up. More casualties of war. As a result of a kindness performed.

People need to know they are valued. When I teach week-long computer classes in industry, there is one gripe I too regularly have: seeing carts of coffee and donuts plus possibly fresh fruit and other goodies, going down the hall to another classroom, one with outside (translate real) customers. The good employees, the most important asset of the company, are taken for granted and given no such special treatment.

There are exceptions, but in most cases I try to compensate a little for my students when their companies fail to come through. I always will at least spring for donuts on Friday morning, the last day of class.

It's a way of acknowledging that their efforts, lab work and attention during the week are appreciated.

My dad feels the same way. One Christmas at Orly he knew his men and women weren't going to get home. They would be separated from their families by several time zones, by an ocean, by circumstances and experiences vastly different. Sort of like cruel and unusual punishment but born of the necessity of the duty to which they were bound in holding the fort and keeping vigilance. This time the chief of staff personnel pulled some strings to deliver his equivalent of donuts for his people at Christmas.

Little Brown Jugs

I served as chief of staff in Paris at Christmas time. Both of my generals and the vice commander were off on special assignments which left me in charge. We had a bunch of kids who had enough points to come home, but somebody had to replace them in their jobs because the stations where they were located needed to be maintained. So we decided on a special plan as a good morale builder.

A C-46, a big Curtiss Dumbo, can carry five tons. We flew one down to Shannon, Ireland, and over to Edinburgh, Scotland. We loaded on one jug of Scotch and one jug of Old Bushmill for every individual in my command who had to spend Christmas in Europe. I set up a shift. We had each station identified and the number of people and had supplies allocated for each. We didn't have a big contingent on each station, but everyone got a jug of Scotch or Irish whiskey for Christmas.

When I radioed General Webster, who was back in Washington, and told him what I was going to do, he came back and said, "Save one for me."

They all worked hard, and Christmas wasn't going to be real happy away from home and family. Anyhow, it worked out quite well. Everybody had a jug—a little brown jug—and the morale factor improved.

The "Who's In Charge Here" Lesson

When Supreme Court Justice William O. Douglas and his party were being assigned to the Nuremberg trials, their first leg was to England on the Queen Mary. They then were transferred to an aircraft that supposedly was to move them to a station in Darmstadt, Germany. Nuremberg was where the trial was to be held, and they were scheduled to go from Darmstadt on to Nuremberg.

The transport taking Douglas and his party left from Bovington, England, to go to Germany. On that same plane was a Major General Royal B. Lord, one of Patton's neophytes. He wore high boots, had a pair of ivory-handled pistols on each side and a lace handkerchief in his pocket. That sort of thing.

Lord walked up to the front of the airplane to the pilot's compartment to ask the pilot where he was going. "I'm going to Nuremberg." Lord said, "No, I don't want to go to Nuremberg, I want to go to Orly in Paris." That's where John C. H. Lee, John "Courthouse" Lee we called him, was commander of the theater rear headquarters. Major General Lord was one of his deputies. "I want you to change course now."

The pilot was young and here was a major general giving him orders. Perhaps he didn't realize that he was the captain of the ship, and whatever decisions he made were final as far as any passenger was concerned. It didn't make a difference whether it was a major general or not. But being politically inexperienced, he changed course and headed to Orly.

Once he got to Paris, the weather closed in tighter than a tick. I mean even ducks were walking. Besides that, it was foggy and the fog was going to hold for quite a while. There was absolutely no way that Justice Douglas and his party could get to Nuremberg in time to meet with the French, British and Russians to set up the procedures for the trials.

Justice Douglas got on the Trans-Atlantic telephone to President Truman and told him what the situation was. Truman then immediately called General Marshall and told him how disappointed he was in this operation. The President said it was going to embarrass the United States terrifically and everyone concerned if there wasn't an immediate correction made to get Justice Douglas and his party into Nuremberg.

The Trans-Atlantic communication system really got all hot. I mean there was vitriolic comment expressing the displeasure of the President in the way this was handled and would our command please provide an immediate radiogram that described the characteristics of the situation and how it happened.

Just as soon as we got word that Douglas and his party were there in Orly instead of being in Nuremberg, my director of operations at that time, Col. Bill Arthur, had started the ball rolling to find out what had happened. He got hold of the crew of that aircraft and found out that Royal Lord, the major general, had diverted the plane. The young pilot was told exactly what his responsibilities were, that he was the man in charge, captain of the ship, and that he had full authority to do whatever he needed to.

We made a full report by radio almost immediately back to Washington. General Marshall then sent a directive over to have us make a detailed analysis of what had happened and name those responsible. There was only one responsible party: Major General Lord. Marshall sent a message back over to have Major General Lord placed under house arrest and have him returned to the United States on the next available west-bound airplane.

They apologized to the French, British and Russians for the delay in getting Justice Douglas and his people in position. When they got Major General Lord back to the United States, they demoted him. He was dropped from a major general to a lieutenant colonel and retired. And denied all pay allowances and privileges. His stars didn't mean a thing then.

The President sent a note of apology to the tribunal for the delay in our operations, and that he guaranteed it would never happen again. I'm pretty sure that this type of thing was not repeated. Justice

Douglas was, of course, irate. We had to put him on a special train to get him to Nuremberg because the weather was absolutely impossible to fly in. It wouldn't have been if he had gone directly to Germany from Bovington.

One of Douglas' assistants on that trial was an attorney from Houston, Texas. I had previously supervised the building of his house in Houston, and he was later involved in the investigations surrounding President Nixon and Watergate. I happened to meet him at Orly during this incident, and he recognized me. He was interested in the story and wanted to know how this all happened. I told him exactly what the sequence was. He said, "Well, I don't dare talk to Justice Douglas. He'll have that guy crucified, drawn, hung and quartered."

Douglas' party did get to Nuremberg, but they were a few hours late making their initial meeting. This was a hot topic around Orly, and perhaps other locations, for a couple of weeks. Our command was instructed to indoctrinate the pilots of our crews properly when they were handling special mission operations. A pilot was the god, judge, jury and hangman and had full authority to place a guy under arrest right there. If they had to use sidearms, do it. But never let that sort of thing happen again.

Retrieving Roger Crow's Career

We were establishing communication facilities in Greece to provide radio assistance to our troops flying from Europe to India.

This was an actual air base facility in Athens manned by the military. Since I was stationed at Orly, I needed someone else to be on site and supervise that job. While I was considering the options, I heard that Roger McKee Crow, a fellow K-State engineer during my undergraduate days, a Pi Kappa Alpha from Topeka and a fellow officer at Ellington Field in the early 1940s, was going to be retired due to disability. Roger's leg had been shattered in an accident at a flight school in northwest Texas.

He had detected fumes in the hangar, which he reported to the maintenance people. The investigating mechanic flipped open his cigarette lighter to explore the dark hangar better. There was a gas leak. The building blew up, and Roger was on the second floor at the time. He had been transferred to the hospital at San Antonio for reconstruction of the splintered leg.

"Under no circumstances will you retire him," I said. "Send him to me. I can use him." He immediately came to Paris. I set up a rehab program for Rog with my flight surgeon, Dr. Norman C. (Lt. Col.) Veale, who agreed with my plan. And it worked beautifully to restore circulation. Roger's leg mended. He went on to become commander at Vandenburg Air Force Base eventually and was later transferred to the Strategic Air Command (SAC). In that assignment he got star grade Major General, was assigned to the Joint Chiefs as the Air Force representative and stationed at the Headquarters Command at Bolling AFB. Roger married Dorothy Hacker; her father was a surgeon.

During the time I had the T-6, I once flew to Randolph, got Rog, and we went to Ellington to renew acquaintances. When I was later ordered back to duty in Washington, I stayed with the Crows at Bolling a week or 10 days. Roger and Dorothy were good friends. Roger was a hard worker, but it finally got him. One day he was found slumped over his desk as the result of a heart attack.

Dad, too, experienced stress from his wartime job. Especially in Paris. He confessed that he got to the point where he was chain-smoking three packs of cigarettes a day. I hadn't known he had ever smoked. Dr. Veale, his flight surgeon, was with him once when Dad started coughing. He said, "Let me get a sample of that." He cultured the sample from Dad's throat and reported back. "Within 30 months, I'll be cutting cancer out of your throat. I'll guarantee you that." Dad quit cigarettes cold turkey.

V.E. Day and Winding Down of Events

Many things happened during that job in Paris. VE Day occurred May 8, 1945 as I recall. I was in London on VE Day on a special assignment. When I went to 8th Air Force Headquarters, the celebration had begun. Bells were ringing all over London. (I also have childhood memories of all the church bells ringing in Manhattan, Kansas, on that day.)

We were blessed with the supervision of a lot of air traffic operations from Orly, so we had an excellent vantage point from which to observe all that was going on in that command. There were many events that occurred then pretty rapidly. General Patton had been in a car accident on the Frankfurt-Mannheim Road. It appeared to be minor. Patton's chief of staff Hap Gay and the drivers of both vehicles were only shaken. But General Patton was thrown forward from the back seat then hurled back again. His neck was broken. Though he was sitting up and fully conscious he was paralyzed from the neck down.

Mrs. Patton was to be sent over from the States to be with him. Her airplane was coming in. After it left Santa Maria in the Azores, the designated landing station was Orly in Paris. A thick fog moved in, and they couldn't land in Orly. The plane was diverted to Marseilles.

We had to make arrangements quickly to get Mrs. Patton into Germany to be with General Patton. Although he made initial improvement, a pulmonary embolism subsequently destroyed one lung, and he failed rapidly.

General Joseph T. McNarney, who was then Theater Commander of the forces in the Rhine, was stationed at Wiesbaden. We called and asked for the control of Mrs. Patton's travel on General McNarney's private train. "McCord, who in the hell are you?" "I'm chief of staff for Bob Webster." "Are they there?" "No, they're on a special mission." "You ARE in charge, then."

We were going to send to Marseilles to pick Mrs. Patton up and move her back into Germany. We asked to have the French clear the box. McNarney directed that the train would have priority rights over any other movement. He said, "I want a clear block on this train from

Marseilles to the destination in Germany." We had to make those arrangements pretty fast, and it worked. We got Mrs. Patton into Germany in adequate time to be with General Patton before he died at Heidelberg.

Everything was coming apart at that time. After VE Day, unnecessary personnel, those who had served their time were being repatriated back to the States. But we hadn't secured the Pacific yet, so it was necessary that we select certain units to be transferred to the Pacific Theater to continue the operations against the Japanese. We set up what was then called the Green Project. We had to supervise the selection of certain heavy bomb units out of the European Theatre and move them to Casablanca and Dakar, across to Belèm and then into the United States for transfer to the Pacific Theater.

In August 1945, we dropped the A-bomb on Japan. Twice. Japan capitulated; this ended the Pacific threat. The units set up for the Green Project were repatriated to the United States. I was the project officer out of Europe on that operation, moving those units to the United States; it was quite an undertaking. Those units that were being transferred on the Green Project got to the United States and were never sent into the Pacific. That terminated the Green Project.

I was scheduled to come back to the United States. Ford Fair, the chap who was to replace me, was on a familiarization tour through the units in the Mediterranean and en route from Caserta, Italy, back to Paris. His plane was lost in one of those terrific storms over the Tyrrhenian Sea. They never found hide, hair nor propeller of that aircraft. My return to the States was delayed, and that was not a happy situation. I had experienced dengue fever, two types of dysentery, malaria, yellow fever and now had hepatitis. It was time to go back.

When Dad contracted hepatitis and became the *color of a goldfish*, it became imperative to get him back to stateside medical help. His tour of Europe was over. His Separation Qualification Record notes that he "... served overseas in the India-China Division, North Africa Division and European Division of Air Transport Command for 20 months in India, China, Africa and Europe. Formulated policies and supervised execution of administrative procedures pertaining to personnel of the command (military and civilian). Planned for and supervised procurement, classification, reclassification, assignment, pay, demotion, transfer, retirement, discharge and replacement of military and civilian personnel. Was responsible for and supervised utilization and management of personnel. Was responsible for decorations and awards, leaves and furloughs, religious, recreational and welfare work. Was responsible for preparation of strength reports, casualties reports and pertinent personnel statistics. Supervised preparation of organizational requirements and developed studies to determine manpower requirements in the Army."

The Additional Information section gives the following remarks:

"Authorized American Defense Service Medal, Asiatic-Pacific Theater Ribbon and one Battle Star, European Theater Ribbon, American Theater Ribbon and World War II Victory

Medal. Has letter of Commendation and Ribbon, dated 23 January, 1946 from Major General R. M. Webster."[72]

---

[72] I wrote to the National Personnel Records Center to request copies of Dad's records. In addition to those records, I received a duplicate set of Dad's nine awards and decorations along with information on their proper placement. I intend to make a wall hanging of them.

HEADQUARTERS
EUROPEAN DIVISION, AIR TRANSPORT COMMAND
(1400th AAF BASE UNIT)
APO 741, c/o POSTMASTER
NEW YORK, N. Y.

23 January 1946

SUBJECT: Letter of Commendation.

TO: Colonel Hal H. McCord, O-302922
1400th AAF Base Unit - Paris, France
European Division, Air Transport Command
APO 741, U. S. Army

1. I commend you for the highly outstanding manner
in which you performed your duty as Chief of Staff of the
European Division, Air Transport Command.

2. Your assignment was made at a very critical time
in the history of this Command and your thorough application of well directed efforts maintained continued unity
throughout the staff and efficient operation.

3. The successful establishment of plans and policies necessary to insure organized redeployment and re-
trenchment within this Division, I attribute in a large
part to the conspicuous loyalty and devotion to duty displayed by you. It has been a true pleasure to have you serve
in my Command and I consider the results obtained, with
respect to assisting me, as being of inestimable value.

/S/ Robert M. Webster

/T/ ROBERT M. WEBSTER
Major General, U. S. Army
Commanding

A TRUE COPY

Bernard A. Mayer
Captain, Air Corps

Letter of commendation from Maj. Gen. Webster

Marilyn McCord

Endnotes:

Resources used for WWII History:

Farago, Ladislas, <u>Patton: Ordeal and Triumph</u>, Copyright © 1963 by Faracorn Ltd., published by Dell Publishing Co., Inc.

Gilbert, Martin, <u>The Second World War, A Complete History</u>, Copyright © 1989 by Martin Gilbert, published by Henry Holt and Company, Inc.

Jablonski, Edward, <u>A Pictorial History of the World War II Years</u>, Copyright © 1977 by Edward M. Jablonski, DoubleDay & Company, Inc.

National Geographic World War II Europe and North Africa map, December 1991.

National Geographic World War II Asia and the Pacific map, December 1991.

Shirer, William L., <u>The Rise and Fall of the Third Reich</u>, Copyright © 1959, 1960 by William L. Shirer, A Crest Book published by Simon & Schuster, Inc.

Marilyn McCord

Part Six: Life After the War
1946-2002

Coming Home

Shortly before returning to the States, I had gone from Orly to the Greek Islands to assist in establishing communication facilities as a part of the air travel between Europe and India. Apparently I was exposed to contaminated water there and picked up hepatitis. My doctor said, "You've got to go back to the States for treatment. We can't treat you here." He gave me a certificate saying that I had been taking Adequit, which turned my eyeballs and my skin yellow. "This will get you cleared through any medical people that might off-load you someplace and stick you in a local hospital, because they can't handle your treatment here."

They sent me home with a full clearance to the United States, to Bolling Field in Washington. From there, I was sent immediately to Walter Reed Hospital for treatment of the hepatitis. It took about four or five weeks for them to get that under control.

When Dad requested to return to the States, it became form city for a bit. His customs form is dated 25/1/46. There is a form certifying no infectious or parasitic diseases despite the hepatitis. A subterfuge to get him back quickly. A baggage declaration verified he was taking back only his personal effects. There is a record showing total accrued leave of 160 days, of which only 15 days were granted. Hence his actual separation date ends up being June 7, nearly five months later than the actual physical return.

The War Department wrote a letter of appreciation for Dad's service and his willingness to accept an appointment in the Officers' Reserve Corps, Army of the United States. His Military Record form gives a history, and finally there is his Report of Separation form.

On January 27, 1946, he reported to the 1400th AAF in Washington, D.C. and Walter Reed Hospital. On January 28, Dad was released from duty and attached unassigned to A8F Separation Center, Ft. Leavenworth, KS, to revert to inactive status. That same day he received the Army Commendation Ribbon; three days later was a memo authorizing him to wear that ribbon.

From March 1, 1946 to March 15, 1947, Dad worked for Milton Eisenhower at K-State. He was the engineer in charge of developing family and single units for the emergency housing program of Kansas State College.

Beginning March 15, 1947, he was a self-employed consulting engineer involved in the construction of private residential and apartment units and the development and construction of subdivisions in the Manhattan area.

In 1950, he went to work for a consulting firm in Topeka, Kansas, Servis and Van Doren, doing design work. He had just gotten started on a project to rehab family housing at Forbes Air Base in Topeka in 1951 when he was called back to Washington, D.C. and active military duty. Within the first year back in the Pentagon, he was assigned to do family housing for the U. S. Air Force, an assignment that ran to mid-1955. He finally returned to retired military status in 1966.

Working for Milton Eisenhower

I was returned to my discharge point in Kansas. Initially, I went into active reserves, going to work for a year as administrative assistant for Milton Eisenhower, brother of Dwight D. Eisenhower. Milton was president of Kansas State College, and he put me in charge of student housing. We negotiated with the Air Force to accept the gift of some temporary housing units from the advanced flying school at Coffeyville Air Base, Coffeyville, Kansas.

Randolph Gingrich was superintendent of the power plant at KSAC. He and I took a crew down to Coffeyville to assess the options. After a discussion with the campus maintenance supervisor, we decided to split those barracks down the center and cut them in thirds. Initially they were 30' wide by 100' long. Each was then cut into six units of 15' x 33'. We cut them with a dragline that was available at Coffeyville, a crane with a big bucket that we took off. Using a high boom, we set them on flatbed trailers, stacking one on top of the other. Approximately 20 barracks made up the 120 or so apartment units we then moved up to the campus.

A Salina firm named Busboom and Rau assembled the apartments, then they were rehabbed. Most of these housing units were placed just west of Nichols Gym where the tennis courts used to be, now a parking lot south of the Union. Some others were down in a playground area at the east campus. These sections provided temporary housing for married students on the campus, a stopgap measure until we could get the new housing program completed. They called it Splinter City. Altogether we provided 336 family units and 640 single units for that emergency housing program. Eisenhower thought he would surely get approval by the Kansas Legislature to build student housing on the campus. It took a while to get it through, but he did achieve it.

Meeting the Eisenhower Brothers

There were a couple of times I flew Milton Eisenhower different places in my T-6. Milton, as president of K-State, was on several occasions asked to deliver commencement address speeches, and I provided transportation. In addition, I once took him to Minnesota where the five Eisenhower brothers were getting together at their recreation camp. When Milton asked me if I'd fly him there, I assured him that this would be a great joy, I would certainly delight in making that trip. I flew him to their meeting place and met all of the brothers. This was the fall of 1946 or '47.

I got a chance to have a really good conversation with Ike. Milton was trying to exhort him to abandon any thought of getting in politics. Milton's concept was, "You've already made your mark in the world. Don't get into politics. It's a dirty game." And he knew it.

Jackie Cochran was one of the ones who helped talk Ike into it.
Herbert Brownell, Jr. also was one of the guys that talked him into
going into the Republican fold and assisted in running his campaign.
Brownell knew that Ike was so popular from commanding the
European Theater during the war that he would be elected if he just
entered the fray. This was true. Later, Brownell was awarded a
position on Ike's staff, that of Attorney General.

I compliment Colin Powell for not getting into politics and
running for President or Vice President.[73] *Ike was talked into it, and I*
believe it hurt him.

The story around Manhattan, Kansas, is that after Ike became
president, Milton had a desk near him and served as a trusted adviser.

There were a couple of other stories from Dad's time after he
returned to Kansas. I like this one because *getting even* was not the
objective with Dad. Here he was making a point with class and with
humor and saving face for those involved.

Buzzed by Navy Corsairs

In the late '40s I had flown the T-6 from Kansas down to San
Antonio to talk to the National Housing Authority. Coming back,
three Navy Corsairs decided I was their target. They came in and
buzzed me like mad. They didn't realize that this T-6 was not exactly
fair game. I got the tail numbers on two of the planes. Instead of

---

[73] This was recorded in 1996, prior to Powell's becoming Secretary of State in
George W. Bush's cabinet. Dad thinks Powell is doing a super job in that sensitive
position.

coming straight back home, I flew to the Navy station at Olathe, Kansas.

I landed and identified myself as "Colonel McCord, Air Force." I asked the line crew if I could talk to the commander. They said, "Sure." So, the boys at the line took me right up and introduced me. I talked to the commander and told him that I had a rather interesting experience with three of his Corsairs. He said, "Tell me about it."

I told him about their buzzing me, putting me in their backwash and really playing tag with me. I said, "Finally, I got down on the deck." Flying on the deck was flying as close to the ground as possible. There was a heavy south wind. I popped over a big wash, and they were afraid to get down there because I was too close to the ground for them to continue playing tag with me. They didn't notice that I had flown off to Olathe.

I gave him the numbers of the two airplanes that I had identified and, of course, he knew who the third one was. He said, "All right," and he got the names of the guys. "I want them to report to my office just as quickly as they land."

When they came in, they hadn't recognized the T-6 sitting there on the flight line, and they came in strutting, jaunty as three hens. The commander, the Navy captain, got them in his office and said, "I want to introduce you men to Colonel McCord, United States Air Force." They responded, "We're pleased to know you." He said, "I'm not sure you really want to know Colonel McCord. He has your three numbers as the Corsairs that buzzed a T-6."

Those guys were fit to be tied. They didn't know what was going to happen to them. They didn't realize that they had buzzed an Air Force colonel. Their commander continued, "OK, now you've met Col. McCord." Turning to me, "Colonel, what do you think would be a fair punishment for this escapade?" I replied, "Well, let me think about that a little while." "Yes, do that."

I thought, then said, "I'll leave it up to you; these men are not in my command. I think they ought to know better than to take a civilian aircraft that doesn't have military markings on it and give it a hard time." He said, "I think you're right. I'll figure out something for them."

He decided to let the three sweat out what was going to happen. "OK, you guys report to me for a hearing tomorrow at 1000 hours." He asked me if I could come back to Olathe. I said, "Sure, I can come back if you want me to." He said, "I'll take care of you. Next time you're out over the area, call in and come back in. I'll welcome you, and I'll take you to lunch here at the station. I'm gonna give these guys something to think about." He planned to have the three pilots there for lunch, also.

The next morning, he told the boys, "All right, I think one thing you need to do is to provide the Colonel and myself with a fine lunch. And you'll pay for it." When I came back later, we all went to lunch and the Commander said, "Whatever you want, Colonel, just order." I don't remember exactly what I ordered, but it was probably a steak, I'm sure. They had a good mess; the Navy ate well.

We had a lot of fun out of that. These guys, I know, spent 24 hours trying to figure out what in the world was going to happen to them. Sweating it out. And, he asked his men after we got through with lunch, if they were going to buzz another civilian aircraft. They decided that maybe that wasn't a very good thing to do. Especially if they didn't know who was in the plane.

"McCord's Folly"

I had vague memories of Dad having something to do with Lake Elbo northeast of Manhattan, so I asked him about that. He chuckled and said that the project had been locally labeled "McCord's Folly." The landowner who owned that area had tried several times to create a lake there, but it kept draining away. Dad took up the challenge.

He had core drillings done every 50 feet to determine the composition of the underlying layers. There was a lot of porosity. Dad put in a retaining wall of interlocking sheet pilings and sealed off the leakage. The runoff from the creek formed Lake Elbo. Initially, the water supply of the folks downstream dried up, so they had to install a device to allow water to flow through when the lake reached a certain level. The original housing was all on the west side. I drove out there in January 2002 to check it out after nearly 54 years. The sign says "Lake Elbo, est. 1948." It is a membership community with around two dozen houses plus the lake recreational facilities.

Another contribution to the Manhattan area was Dad's pursuing a building code change so houses could be spaced no closer than the width of a fire truck. He said he knew all the city fathers in the late 1940s. He designed houses for Blake Wareham and Fritz Moore and others. In a recent conversation with Gary Dierking, the museum curator for the First Territorial Capital of Kansas, Gary queried, "You don't mean <u>Hal</u> McCord, do you?" "I do." I could hear the pleasure in Gary's voice as he remembered, "I have a photo he gave me of three AT-6 airplanes! And Hal was the architect on my mother's house at Alta Vista. Remind him that it's the one by the city water tower."

Meanwhile, Back on the Home Front ... Continued

When Dad returned from Europe, the family was living at 1413 Laramie in Manhattan. It was a two-story house with a basement. The living room was long and took up the entire west side; the east side contained a dining room and a smallish kitchen on the south at the back. The front door opened to a hall and stairs up to the four bedrooms and single bath on the second floor.

Grandmother Hedge was just down Laramie Street at the red brick Wareham Apartments. That was our homebase from 1945 to 1954, the year Don went off to college at Phillips University in Enid, Oklahoma. Not Kansas State and engineering as he had previously anticipated. A call to the ministry required a school that could award a bachelor's of divinity.

There are plenty of good memories. Dad first got a radio operator's license in 1937 (W9MWT) and had learned how to operate shortwave radios. Don remembers being crouched over Dad's old

325

ham radio system in the southwest corner of the living room. Different units could be plugged in to give access to different radio frequencies over the whole world. Don said they especially worked at times when Janice or I might be busy practicing the piano, the piano that Dad transported to Manhattan from Texas in the belly of a plane. *Probably a B-17 or a C-46, I don't remember for sure.* Mother later gave that piano to my daughter.

Don and Dad started a train layout in the basement, HO gauge. They had a 4'x8' board with the track laid out in double ovals, a figure-8 crossover. Dad did most of the wiring to begin with, then one of Don's friends, Tom Obermeier, who played clarinet with him in band and orchestra, helped out. Don told me:

"Tom knew more than we did about electricity, hook-ups, relays, etc., for the switching units. He might be called a nerd in present days. We built an elevated switching yard that went on an extension overlay to the 4x8 board. I added most of the rolling stock, building from kits. There was a switch engine for the yards, passenger and freight locomotives, a diesel and a 2-8-2 Mikado, i.e., two wheels in front, eight main drive wheels, two following wheels. The board and most of the rolling stock were later stolen from the storage area over our Grandmother Hedge's garage when she lived on Poyntz Avenue."

That house was kitty-corner and a house east from the junior high school. When we left Manhattan for our three years in Nebraska in 1954, we stored several things there. The house and garage have since been torn down for a bank drive-through, but the location was perfect for having an occasional lunch with Grandmother when I was in junior high school.

Dad got to resurrect his own childhood experiences with spark coils. Don told about a spark coil contraption that Dad rigged to dissuade the dog from getting up on the couch. It had a wire frame that provided a shock of 12 volts, certainly enough to get the dog's attention. After a couple of exercises in applying that device, we no longer had a problem with dogs on the couch.

Don also had and still has an army blanket with a collection of military patches. Dad obtained the blanket and the initial patches for him, and Mother sewed them on. Don added to the collection as he saw soldiers around Manhattan and just brazenly asked them for a patch if he saw one he didn't have. It was another blue ribbon winner at the Manhattan Pet & Hobby show. Stolen at one point but recovered. Found recently in a drawer and still pretty much as it was in his youth.

Dad fixed up Don's bike. He either made or got a special frame on it to hold the newspaper sacks for his paper route. The bike was later stolen from in front of First Christian Church, teaching Don that just being in front of the church was not a guarantee of safety or security from harm or theft.

One April Fool's Day I switched the sugar and the salt. Dad usually put sugar on his oatmeal and salt on his grapefruit. I watched him eat breakfast with rapt attention that morning, but he never let on that anything was out of the ordinary. No hint from Dad, no triumph for me.

I also remember going with Dad out to the Kimball property to get daisies, then just northwest of Manhattan but now a part of town. We transplanted them to my small rock garden in the back yard between the apricot tree and the sandbox. Daisies are still my favorite flower.

Growing up, we always had a dog. Our favorite was Skipper, a reddish cocker spaniel with a freckled nose. Dad had taught him to sit-up. All of us were saddened when a hurrying college student could not stop his car in time to avoid the small dog crossing Laramie Street to meet his masters. We had other dogs, but Dad never involved himself with them as he had with Skipper.

Mother began teaching kindergarten at Roosevelt Elementary School. Janice remembers that one of the kindergarten students, a little girl, had been absent for several days. Mother made a visit to the home to find out why. When she discovered that the reason was the unseasonably cold winter weather and the lack of a warm coat, she immediately went home, found one of Janice's coats that would fit, and returned to the little girl's home with the coat.

Janice transferred to Roosevelt from Eugene Field during her fourth grade year and remembers, "The teacher at Eugene Field was horrible. My classmate, Bobby Ballard, got whacked on the hands with a ruler. Eventually the teacher was fired."

Mother, though still teaching kindergarten, picked up the parenting role and was a sponsor for Janice's fourth grade class skating party out at K-Hill Roller Rink. Good sport that Mother was, she ended up on the end of the line during a session of crack-the-whip, fell and cracked her tailbone. We still remember her taking the little foam donut cushion to church with her. Embarrassed for sure but not to the point where she would miss church over it. Church attendance was a given. Every Sunday. Although illness might damage our attendance records at school, the church made allowances for that. Attendance unless you were ill was the goal. We all had perfect attendance pins with extra year bars hanging below.

Getting three young children ready for church all at the same time to meet the starting bell is a challenge for many families. Even my daughter admits to using the in-the-car-spit-bath method occasionally resorted to when a mother finally gets a close look at all of her contained children. One Palm or Easter Sunday, Don said his hair really needed to be cut. Dad knew the barber personally, in Aggieville of course, and called him at home. He took Don over to the barbershop on Sunday morning to make him presentable for church.

As with Don's bike left at the church, just being at home was no guarantee of safety either. To make some extra money after Dad left, Mother took in roomers—college students. Some of them were great, like Van who played the piano and entertained us with wonderful renditions of "Dark Town Strutters' Ball" and other showy numbers. But one international student tried to fondle the little girls. The minute

Mother knew what had happened, he was evicted. There were many things she had to handle on her own.

In 1950, Janice and I took the Union Pacific from the depot in Manhattan to Topeka. Dad was working there, living there during the week and only home weekends. He had arranged through a friend a photo op for Janice. She was to be the little sister in a big sister/little sister magazine fashion ad. The big sister was a model in her early twenties. A bright-eyed, pigtailed Janice looks up adoringly in the photo. They both are dressed in stunning red plaid jumpers. Janice's pigtails were her trademark during elementary school, and when she finally decided to cut her hair, she cut off the braids and saved them.

Drifting -> Estrangement -> Divorce

By the late 1940s Dad began to drift away from the family and immerse himself in his work. He had been gone so much before that his absence was not as obvious to us as it should have been. What transpired during these next few years is an anomaly in my father's life. He was not the person he was before and not the person he was afterwards.

Stress causes us to do things we would not do otherwise, especially if it seems related to our survival. This is true of amazing feats of strength as well as what appears to be temporary abandonment of our usual good judgment. If we feel threatened, we use whatever weapons we can muster and do whatever makes the most sense to us at the time.

The relationship between my parents tumbled downhill rapidly. I cannot imagine the father I experienced then as the same father I know now—the images simply are not the same.

What causes someone to lose his bearings so badly? Would the diseases of India and the hepatitis from Greece have taken too great a toll at some point? Would the stress of so much continual responsibility and the demands of always having to come up with a bit more than maybe you were prepared to give have brought on an exhaustion that caused him to shy away from tackling new and different responsibilities at home? Might there have been actions that required forgiveness and yet remained unforgiven and unforgotten? Did my grandmother's criticism become a self-fulfilling prophecy and allow her to voice "I told you so" to my mother, perhaps even in front of my father? Any of these would have been difficult to live with.

As I said before, the reasons themselves no longer matter. For whatever reasons, he stumbled. And we could not catch him.

I am reminded of when I ended my marriage of 20 years. When everyone else in my family outside of my children was shocked, Dad said, *Well, I'm not surprised.* Divorce, much as I dreaded it, had become in my mind a matter of my own survival.

I will never forget coming home one evening, looking for my second son, a middle child, like me, and finding him sitting on the floor of the darkened coat closet beside my sewing machine, staring vacantly, voicelessly.

He desperately wanted to live with <u>both</u> his mother and his father but that would no longer be an option. And he was helpless to prevent the family separation. He simply did not know what to do, how to be. It broke my heart. At that moment, I was both parent and child. My own childhood pain surfaced and coalesced with the pain a parent feels on behalf of a child.

My father and I share the same dark piece of a quilt, and I have seen it from both sides. But I have taken the melancholy of its blackness and since embroidered those sad memories with tenderness. We do the best we know how, yet we are imperfect parents.

This observation came from Don, who was older, perhaps more aware of the developing friction and certainly one who saw himself as Mother's protector. "Dad must have been good as a Sunday School teacher. The Homemakers' Class gave him a great one-volume commentary on the Bible, which came into my possession. I remember sometimes thinking it the highest level of hypocrisy for the man I sometimes used to label home-breaker to be gifted and honored by the Homemakers. I'm okay with all of that now. In a conversation we finally got to have in Pittsburg, in the house he built and shared with so much love and vitality and creativity with Noni, I remember one of the slogans over his desk that translated into English from the French something like 'Faint Heart Ne'er Won Fair Lady'."

One of Mother's long-time friends, Agnes Chartier, still vital and beautiful at age 94, mentioned that Don often had to wear coats with the sleeves too short. It was her impression that Dad did not provide sufficient support, and she admired Ivalee for what she did. She also said that Ivalee was for a while part-time secretary at First Christian

Church to earn extra money. Sometimes Agnes would go down to the church office just to be with her.

Agnes said that Mother had come to her wild eyed during the 1951 summer flood in Manhattan, desperate to get to a working telephone. My father had returned to Washington, D.C. with an office at the Pentagon in June 1951, ahead of the big flood. Apparently Mother had received a letter from Dad with ominous indications the current separation was going to become permanent. They found a phone at a filling station.

The next summer Mother, Janice and I rode by bus to Ithaca, New York. Don stayed home and played summer baseball, leaving nearly every dish from the cupboard dirty on the counter by the time of our return, which he explained occurred sooner than expected and caught him by surprise.

Mother's brother-in-law drove us down to Washington, D. C., where Mom made a last-ditch attempt to achieve some sort of reconciliation. Her efforts to salvage the marriage were doomed to failure—it was already much too late. She finally became convinced, quit trying and proceeded to get on with her life. And ours.

In addition to the damaged self-image from a crushed marriage, Mother faced other problems. She emerged from these disasters with amazing strength and courage. We children knew that Mother was trying to pay off some debts in addition to trying to maintain the family budget. She had co-signed notes and felt responsible. She made payments every month until the banker finally told her, "You have paid enough. I'll just write these off at the bank as bad debts."[74]

Since long-range career goals necessitated better academic qualifications, Mother worked on her master of science degree. We remember her putting in long hours on the typewriter doing her own thesis. With four carbons, and no errors allowed. The heavy old black desk, surplus from someone's previous inventory, was in the northeast corner of the dining room. A built-in typewriter recessed into the center when you didn't need it. Mother earned her master's degree in 1951. It later became clear that she would also need to get some experience outside of Manhattan in order to break into college teaching. So when Don entered college in 1954, the remaining three women of the family relocated to Wayne, Nebraska, for Mother's home economics teaching position at Wayne State Teachers College.

I think that men measure success from glowing reports on their work. Dad had plenty of those and deserved them all. Wondrously written letters of commendation and thank-you letters galore. Women, on the other hand, gauge success from glowing reports on their children, and grandchildren and great-grandchildren. My mother had plenty of those.

Attending the celebration my brother's church put on for the combined occasion of his 15 years there, 40 years in the ministry and his 65th birthday all in August of 2001, would have made her

---

[74] Janice and I still find ourselves affected with feelings of financial insecurity. When Janice and Bill were closing on their first home, Janice adamantly refused to co-sign the note. Bill took her out in the hall and explained, "No sign, no house." She signed and of course, everything worked out fine.

absolutely radiant had she still been alive and able to attend. There were accolades in three languages. Choirs from black, Korean and other congregations. French nuns in pointy hats telling how much Don had contributed to the Chicago community's poor. On and on. Such events as these were my mother's letters of recommendation.

The above perception is a generalization, but not an uncommon one. I said before that parenting is the hardest job I know of. Wars, separations and in-laws can complicate the equations. I can understand someone gravitating to situations where they get praise instead of criticisms as a plant bends toward the sun. Still it was hard. Hard on everyone. Sometimes the only gift we have to give is presence, and yet we cannot give even that.

Asking my father about these years was, without a doubt, the most difficult of all of the questions I asked him. A sad, faraway look settled in his eyes. *After the war, it was a strange world to come back to. Ivalee and I had been separated, yes, but everything was different. A complete change of all I was used to. My mother-in-law had moved into my place ... did not like the military, did not like my work, did not like me. The war cost me that family. I lost myself in my work. I existed. I don't know how that happened, how I let that happen.*

His remorse was real and deep. As with the subsequent deaths of two wives, this was another sort of death for which Dad feels responsible and guilty. Who among us does not have incidents in the past for which we feel remorse? And I hasten to emphasize again— for all of us—that former failings are best relegated to the past. We learn from our yesterdays, we remember them, but we do not let them

335

define our todays. I am so pleased that as I left childhood I resolved to re-establish a relationship with my father. The father I came to know and love is today cherished by so many, including me.

Family Housing Programs

After my work with Milton Eisenhower and some self-employed construction work in Manhattan, I went to work with Servis and Van Doren Consultants in Topeka June 1, 1950. Good jobs were still not that plentiful, and the company really wanted me in this job doing design. It paid $104.50 per month. Things were deteriorating at home. The job offered me an out.

After I had been there almost a year, Servis and Van Doren got a contract for supervising the rehabilitation of base housing at Topeka's Forbes Air Base. The Korean conflict was just beginning to develop, and we had to have some additional utilization of bases. The Second Air Force was to move into Forbes.

Before I had really gotten started on my part of this, I received a call from Cal Phillips, chief of the colonel's group in Washington to wrap up the work at Forbes. Cal admonished me, "Get your house in order because you're going to be moved to Washington." I said, "I've got this engineering job, rehabilitating Forbes Air Base, and I've only just begun." He insisted, "Find somebody else to take that job because I'll give you just 30 days to report to Washington to the air staff."

While Dad was working in Topeka, he met Thelma Holuba again, a high school classmate. She had been a lieutenant commander in the Navy, had cryptographic skills, and was in charge of the coding for messages to stations in this country and ships at sea during WWII. Her degree from Kansas State was in industrial journalism.

Unlike Mother's family and friends, she appreciated Dad's military career and contacts. This was in sharp contrast especially to the feelings of Dad's mother-in-law, my Grandmother Hedge, who had wanted him to be a banker and leave the construction business. Thelma joined him in Washington, D.C., working as a writer. Dad and Thelma's later marriage would last nearly three decades until her death in 1983. The final seven years of their life together were spent fighting Thelma's losing battle with cancer.

The text of the telegram to Col. Hal H. McCord, 1710 Lindenwood, Topeka KS, dated April 5, 1951:

FROM AFPMP-A 32645 IN PREVIOUS CORRESPONDENCE TO THIS HQ YOU HAVE INDICATED THAT YOU WOULD VOLUNTEER FOR RETURN TO ACTIVE DUTY PD THIS HQ HAS NEED FOR YOUR SERVICES AS DEPUTY CHIEF POLICY DIVISION DIRECTORATE OF PERSONNEL PLANNING DEPUTY CHIEF OF STAFF PERSONNEL PD SINCE YOU ARE A MEMBER OF THE VOLUNTEER AIR RESERVE PLEASE ADVISE WHETHER YOU WOULD VOLUNTEER FOR ACTIVE DUTY PD THIS REPLY

SHOULD BE DIRECTED TO THIS HQ ATTN: COLONEL
W C PHILLIPS CHIEF COLONELS BRANCH PMP-A
ROOM 43-236 THE PENTAGON WASHINGTON DC.

I turned the job at Forbes AFB over to Hap Mathias. He was a Kappa Sig fraternity brother, an engineer and a fine clarinet player. He was in the K-State band with me. He took over the job of rehabbing the base housing at Forbes, and I went to Washington. That was my entry into Washington for that particular stint. I didn't leave there until the summer of 1955.

For the first eight or nine months, I was working in what they called the personnel planning group with General Parks in charge. One of the boys in that group found out that I had considerable high rank and that I was a structural engineer with housing experience.

Ted Timberlake in the air staff had to have somebody on whom he could depend for the development of the Air Force Family Housing Program. He called General Parks and said, "I'm gonna take McCord. I need him." Parks called me in and said, "You didn't tell me that you were an engineer and have had housing experience." I said, "No Sir, you didn't ask me." He said, "Well, I'm going to have to turn you over to Timberlake. You'd better go up and talk to him." That's how I got in the job of family housing for the United States Air Force.

My General was Lee Washburn, a Corps of Engineers type who had transferred to the Air Force. Not Army Air Force but the Air Force. In 1947, the US Air Force was created as a separate service.

Washburn told me, *"Colonel, I don't know a thing about housing. I don't <u>want</u> to know anything about housing. And I want you to go up and talk with General Twining because you're going to work directly for the chief."* [75]

Washington in the mid-1950s was quite a tour. I was working at that time for General Twining, United States Air Force chief of staff, and Air Force Secretary Hal Talbot. They were in charge of the housing program worldwide. It was an interesting assignment because I had unlimited travel authority, my own set of orders, my own method of transportation.

Doing the DEW Line

The Distant Early Warning (DEW) Line, a network of radar facilities in the high Arctic, began in 1954 when President Eisenhower signed the bill approving its construction. [76] *This system through Alaska, Northern Canada and Greenland was our primary line of air defense warning of an over-the-pole invasion of the North American continent during the Cold War years. Many tons of supplies and equipment were moved to the outer ring by air, sea and river barge. I was involved in the design and delivery of housing for this project.*

---

[75] Gen. Nathan F. Twining was the first Air Force general to head the Joint Chiefs of Staff. Dad still treasures his personally signed thank you photos of both Gen. Twining and Sec. Hal Talbot on the wall in his office.

[76] In 1961-63, I included the DEW Line as part of my general science curriculum at John Marshall Jr. High in Wichita, Kansas, not knowing at that time that my own father had been involved in this project.

It was a detailed assignment. For each of those stations there were five units covering the key personnel who operated the radar sites. We'd pick out the site and prepare the foundation. The fabricator, who built refrigerated cars for the railroad in Chicago, said they could build us a unit that would be pre-fabricated but in sections that could be set in place and then locked together.

We got a fantastic price from them on very good units. This outfit would deliver them to the rail site in sections, then the Air Force would pick these things up from the rail site by helicopter and set them on the foundations.

The economics involved were fascinating. We were spending an average cost of some $800,000 on technicians for three years of their four-year enlistment to give them training.

If they didn't like where they were or their housing situation was such they couldn't live with their family, they'd quit at the end of their enlistment. The Air Force would lose that investment and have to start all over again. We decided that it was certainly economical to provide the radar technicians adequate quarters. We would buy the women off to retain the men for at least another enlistment period and try to take advantage of their training.

We built good houses on those sites, super houses, and the families were happy with the housing situation. We even set up, in some cases, a capability for the children to be transported to school at government expense. This solidified the men's enlistment and provided for a continuation of that experience operating those radar sites—at tremendous savings. Satisfaction of our personnel became one of the linchpins in getting approval for that program, and we created some outstanding housing under difficult requirements.

A lot of these areas were in permafrost or really fairly inaccessible places. We even had stations at Barrow, Alaska. They had to be situated so that their orientation, stability and siting and this type of thing had to be permanent. We tried to provide a stable base, and we hoped that it didn't thaw out. We wanted to take advantage of as much passive solar heating as possible. After we put down a foundation, the rest was flown in by chopper and assembled in two days. It took an enormous expenditure, and we had joint American-Canadian assistance on that project.

One of the more southerly sites that I remember particularly was just east of Eureka, California. I flew in by helicopter to get there. That location was up in the mountain area, where they had a complete visual control by radar of that section of the Pacific. We were particularly concerned about preventing a Japanese infiltration. The Japanese and the Russians both were suspect peoples at that point in time.

I've wondered many times about those fine houses that were put into those places. What condition they are in now? How they were finally used? If they were used at all? I don't know how many radar sites are still being run. I do know the DEW Line remained in operation for around 30 years before beginning its eventual upgrading and down-staffing.

This change happened in 1985 with the signing of the North American Air Defense Modernization agreement between Canada's

Prime Minister Mulroney and President Reagan. Then the DEW Line became the North Warning System (NWS). The Air Force indicated the Alaska stations weren't expected to disappear for several decades because the Federal Aviation Administration also used them to follow civilian air traffic.

Congressional Interrogations

I really worked very hard for General Twining and the Air Force staff. We had a lot of difficulty getting the housing program accepted and in getting approval of the legislation that permitted the building of the family housing program. I was the Air Force representative to the United States Congress, both in the House of Representatives and in the Senate. Sometimes I would have to go to speak on behalf of the programs. I appeared as the Air Force witness to several different committees in the Congress, three in the House and three in the Senate. It was a rather interesting assignment but one that scared me to death.

When I went in before the Senate Appropriations Committee, Senator Patrick A. McCarren, who was then the Senator from Nevada, took the time to point out all of the errors that the Air Force had executed in connection with the stations in Nevada. He really took my hide off. Well, here he was a senator and I was just a colonel. And I couldn't say a word—I just stood there and took it.

When that session was over, Senator Styles Bridges of New Hampshire said, "Colonel, I'm sorry, but I want you to stop by my office. I need to talk with you." So I went by his office, and he said, "Please sit down." He reached in his drawer and pulled out a bottle of good bourbon and said, "You need a drink. So do I. I want to apologize for that hiding you took. Tomorrow when you come back for the continuation of this testimony, bring some help."

I went back to the Pentagon and asked Gen. Twining to send somebody with me. He got on the telephone and called Lt. Gen. Partridge, who was then in the Plans and Operations Division of the Air Staff. "McCord needs some help in his testimony before the Senate Appropriations Committee. Do you have time to go?" He said, "Certainly, I'd love to."

I went back then with Lt. Gen. Partridge. When we came in, Senator McCarren looked over his glasses and said, "Well, Colonel, I see you've brought some reinforcement. Welcome, General Partridge, I'm glad to see you." And that was the last word he said. Such was life in the fast lane.

The first housing legislation program that supported the military housing business was the Wherry Act. Kenneth S. Wherry was a Republican senator from Nebraska. When this authority ran out, we got what we wanted with the Capeheart legislation that continued the authority to do the family housing program. Dick Talley, from Silver Springs, Maryland, and Fred Close from Denver were both outstanding attorneys on my staff. Those two and I met with the people from New York Life and from Traveler's Insurance. Together we wrote that legislation. We had their blessing and underwriting on the housing program that we were directing and trying to get through.

This program was one of the mouthpieces of Senator Homer E. Capeheart, Indiana. He needed some real backing to maintain his bid to be re-elected. In order to be sure that the proper authorities were granted and to obtain the proper backing, we gave the credit for the legislation to Capeheart. It didn't make any difference. We weren't looking for a political office or anything of this sort, but we did want the legislative program approved. And it was.

So, we wrote the legislation. I never will forget the Traveler's representative in their real estate section. He said, "I will guarantee you, Air Force, if you get this legislation through I will make available to you $100,000,000 to finance your program." This was pretty good backing.

We had his blessing on it, and he had helped edit what we were writing as a legislative program. We presented this to the House Banking and Currency Committee, where appropriations all originated, chaired by Mike Monroney. We explained to him the backing and guarantee of financing we had. It made it real easy to get that legislation through.

It was interesting that the financing was provided outside of the Congress. None of it was provided as a tax-supported program; it was all a private program. It was tailored so that officers and E-4s, -5s, -6s and -7s in the noncommissioned ranks all had the housing allowance granted.

We'd build the houses as one-, not very many ones but two-, three- and four-bedroom units for the families of the military. They would get a facility to live in on the base and give up their housing *allowance so that they could get a three or four bedroom house for $94 a month. They couldn't have done this out in the ordinary market. Land on base was made available on a long-term lease to the people who supported that program. They did the construction, and bid on it within that housing allowance for the income that would support their program. It worked fine.*

The construction was all done under our supervision. I had a graduate architect from the University of Pennsylvania and two lawyers whom I had inherited with the position and later replaced when they didn't do the work I asked them to do. We were able, because of difficulties with the Corps of Engineers, to get the program transferred directly for supervision by Air Force rather than by Corps of Engineers.

Difficulties with the Army Corp of Engineers

The Corps would spend an appropriation as for the Distant Early Warning line housing program. We had $384,000 allocated just for design. I kept checking on it and checking on it, and the Corps kept saying yes. We'll have this out so-and-so, and it never did get out.

I asked the Bureau of the Budget people to check on that appropriation. What was its status? They came back and said, "The appropriation's been used by the Corps." I said, "Where is it?" "Well," they said, "it was used to design your housing program." I said, "We don't have any design for housing programs. Please do check. Where is it?"

This is when we took it to the Secretary of Defense, Charlie Wilson, who had been the chairman of General Motors before he went on Eisenhower's staff.[77] We pointed out to him that the Corps wasn't doing its job. They had used up their appropriations, and we didn't have anything to show for it. Nothing to work with, and they had used up everything.

We said, "We believe we can do this less expensively and get results if we supervise it rather than have the Corps do it. On all of these appropriations for Corps-supported projects, 38 percent goes to the Corps for overhead."

We presented all of these factors. Immediately Wilson said, "All right, Air Force, you have the responsibility. You do your job the way you want to do it." We got control of the Air Force housing program. My brother Max, also an engineer, was the special assistant to the chief of the Corps of Engineers.

Hal McCord in Air Force had taken that job away from the Corps and they blamed Max McCord for it. Because we were brothers, the Corps thought that Max had fed me inside information on their whole program. It stopped one of his assignments because they felt he was too cozy with the Air Force. It was too bad. He didn't have anything to do with it, and yet they blamed him for it. We had taken that responsibility away from the Corps and had taken from the Corps their income of 38 percent of whatever programs were allocated. It was a mess.

---

[77] *"What's-good-for-General-Motors-is-good-for-the-country Charles E. Wilson,"* Secretary of Defense 1953-1957.

SAC Housing

We also did some housing for the Strategic Air Command, SAC. General Curtis LeMay wanted to set up the 42nd Division at Loring AFB, Limestone, Maine. However, he was not going to activate the 42nd unless they had housing available for their people. In January, I assured him we could have housing for 100 by August. LeMay cocked his cigar, leaned over the desk and said to me, "Son, you better be right, or your career is over."

Instead of letting that contract for bid, we had authorization from the congressional delegation headed by Senator Margaret Chase Smith, Republican from Maine, to award the contract to Clinton Murchison.[78] Murchison's company was Tecon, short for Texas Construction. This maneuver to avoid the bidding process bought us the time we needed to meet the deadlines. The House controlled appropriations for the housing legislation.

Major General Bert Harrison was then commander at Loring. He and his wife Mildred invited me to be a guest in their home on several occasions. The B-36s were moved from a base in Puerto Rico to Loring since the Maine location would be the closest possibility for getting from the US to Russia in those Cold War days. But the B-36, a six-engine bomber, never saw combat. I did walk through one of the wings when the planes were being tested.

One of the things that I enjoyed in the housing operation during that period was that I was written up for two columns in the

---

[78] The same Clint Murchison who later owned the Dallas Cowboys NFL team.

Congressional Record. Maybe about '53, that was, or '54. I was written up because of my accomplishments in housing. I never did get a copy of that, and I've sometimes thought that I would like to have one. I'm sure the Congressional Record is filed in the Library of Congress.

When I finally got all through with that housing operation, General Twining sent me to the Second Air Force as a civil engineer. The commander at that time was Major General Richard Montgomery (the same person to whom Dad wrote regarding his request for Service Pilot Status). *Dick was a West Point grad, class of '36. I had known him when we were setting up the air bases in the States. I was able, as personnel officer under General Hubert Harmon, to send Dick to Coffeyville, Kansas Air Base to be commander of the advanced flying school there.*

There were other policy changes I helped instantiate as well. Sometimes military intelligence is an oxymoron. Personnel were then sent to Ft. Francis E. Warren in Wyoming, for example, to be processed for assignment to Washington, D.C. (Dad himself was sent there in 1951 for a medical exam authorized on his recall to active duty in Washington, D.C.)

Lots of unnecessary air travel and wasted time going out of the way one direction and then back across the country the other direction. And when permanent changes of station occurred between September and May, that disrupted the school year for families with children. To make sure that didn't happen we recommended to Brig. Gen. James McCormack, USAF personnel in the Pentagon that a change be adopted to prevent this disruption, and it was. It wasn't hard to be smart about taking care of people.

Flying Max to Oakland

During that active duty period Dad had the opportunity to fly his brother across the country in a B-25. Max, at that time, was Dad's official next-of-kin on records. This trip was a good opportunity for two busy brothers to spend some time together. Dad was a colonel in the Air Force and his brother Max was a colonel in the Army. Max joined the Army just before WWII, serving first in the artillery and later in the Army Corps of Engineers. Max was on General Douglas MacArthur's staff in WWII and was on the first US plane to arrive in Tokyo to take possession after Japan's surrender. His assignments included, among other tasks, battalion commander of an engineer combat unit in the Far East.

Brothers Max (left) and Hal McCord, Oakland, in front of B-25, 1953

In this 1953 photograph my brother Max who was with the Army Corps of Engineers, and I are standing in front of my B-25 in Oakland, California. The plane actually belonged to Colonel Stoyte Ross of Bolling Air Force Base, D.C. Stoyte and I had been very good friends; he was one fine guy. Whenever I needed an airplane to go somewhere, he'd let me take his B-25.

I had picked Max up in Selma, Alabama, and we flew to the Navy Departure Station at Oakland, California. We really got first class treatment there. When we radioed Oakland for landing instructions, I identified myself as pilot, McCord. They asked, "Please identify the highest rank aboard." "0-6." That indicated colonel. The tower had me go around one more time, and by the time we landed they had a red carpet out. Max was impressed. No honors were expected, but they'd have had a band and everything else if they had been given the time to put that together.

Max was headed to Korea to take command of the 10th Combat Engineers Unit, and Oakland was his point of embarkation. I remember one of his stories from Korea. The North Koreans were shooting at the engineers from across the river at the 38th parallel. Max lined up all the bulldozers with their blades turned up and brought the troops in behind that array of blades, providing them a metal shield. It was a very clever maneuver.

Investigated by the FBI

During the time when I was in the Pentagon, Eisenhower was elected President. Fred Seaton was his Secretary of the Interior. Fred and I had been in high school at the same time and at Kansas State together. We had jointly chaired the Inter-Fraternity Council and had both participated in other similar activities. Both of us had also worked for Fred's dad, who had the local Manhattan Mercury-Chronicle newspaper, writing advertising and articles. We were happy to work together again in Washington, D.C., but we had a bit of a problem with one of the presidential appointments in construction work.

A tractor dealer from Iowa, Franklin Floete, was appointed to one of the assistant positions for construction by the Secretary of Defense. He was no more qualified for that job than anybody else, but he'd made a sizable contribution to the Republican party and the Republicans practically forced Eisenhower's hand to appoint him to something. So, he was appointed to this job for which he was not qualified.

Jim Douglas, no relationship to Justice Douglas, had been a major general in World War II, and I had gotten acquainted with him there. By the time he was appointed one of the assistants to the Secretary of Air Force, I knew him quite well. Since we were having trouble getting projects through and approved, especially ones that were critical in time, I went to Mr. Douglas. I told him that we were having difficulty with Mr. Floete and was there something he could do

351

about it. He said, "Yes, I certainly can. Give me about a week." During that week he went to President Eisenhower and arranged to have Mr. Floete re-assigned to another job. Douglas then took over Floete's responsibilities himself and worked with us. This made an excellent working relationship, and we were able then to get programs pushed through.

However, Fred Seaton and I were curtailed in our contact with the Executive Branch. We had to go through a major general, the congressional liaison with the staff, who was the type who wanted to assume all credit and responsibility for everything. He became a barrier, and we had to figure out a way around him.

Fred would call and leave a message for me and say that he wasn't going to be available that evening because he was going to have to go to dinner some place. Usually dinner was somewhere over on 14th Street in D.C. as there were a number of good places to eat in that area; two or three were choice places. Napoleon's was one, excellent French cuisine. Nappy's was also a very good place to meet. Fred might say, "I'm going to be over at Nappy's tonight."

We'd go over for dinner, and maybe we'd meet with several different people. Every time we met with the Secretary of the Interior and his wife, the FBI hound dogs would write us up. A clandestine meeting. They wanted to know what we were doing. If the phone line was bugged, and some of them were—mine frequently—we were afraid that our conversations on a bugged line would get back to the congressional liaison. He would then find out that we were going over his head to talk to one of the staff members of the President's cabinet.

I managed to be wherever Fred and his wife were, Nappy's or the Shoreham or wherever they were going, and we'd have dinner together. We enjoyed the social contact. Not because they were political but because they were from our hometown, Manhattan, Kansas. Because we had gone to school together and had both worked for his dad back then. If we wanted something, that information got to the President. Fred was the source. We could explain to Fred what we thought was valid and necessary, and he'd take it up with Ike, and it happened. Particularly if it were valid. I mean, we didn't ask for any small items but something that was really essential, and we got it put through.

This caused some concern. Someone assigned a couple of Secret Service agents to check out our movements. I was under investigation by the FBI and Secret Service both for more than two years. They had a file on me about yea thick of everyone I contacted, talked to or anything else. They thought I was making special deals with the contractors who were doing our housing program because we were getting so much of it approved and so much of it done.

The Navy had even complained that we were illegally handling the way we were administrating the job, and they pretty well forced the FBI's hand to send somebody to check us out. Even within our own military establishment one group watches over another. For several months, our home phone was bugged, my office phone was bugged, the whole works. I knew about it while it was happening.

It was worse than the CIA, I'll tell you, but we always had a great time out of it. Fred and I always kind of laughed about it because it didn't make any difference to us. We were just enjoying each other and the operations that we were in. If it happened that part of our conversation was on some political point or some desire that the Air Force had in the way of authority to do certain things, it happened. The Navy just raised as sure as hell about the fact that I was too efficient, that I wasn't going through the slow channels. If you want to get to the top, go to the top.

Another Fred, Fred Irwin, my dear first cousin, was in the Secret Service. Fred would suggest that we investigate the Smithsonian, so we'd go to the Smithsonian and have lunch at their counter. He would bring me up-to-date on what he knew. Just like the movies where you meet in these museums or just happen to sit down on the same park bench. It was that way.

I remember one day at lunch he said, "Hal, what in the world have you been into?" I said, "Why?" He continued, "Well, you've got two Secret Service types that are following you everywhere you go." I agreed. "I noticed a couple of guys who always show up some places." And he gave me their names.

Beau Cornett, a very good friend of mine, was then the Commander of the 28th Reconnaissance Squadron out of Tacoma. I had served with Beau on the staff at Randolph early in the game, and we'd always get together if we could. One evening we had dinner at the Occidental Hotel, at the Occidental Restaurant in Washington on 14th Street. We went there frequently, and we knew the head honcho there. He'd seat us at a table, usually it was a table for four, but whatever was available, we got the table.

One day we went in there and noticed a guy named Carroll and his buddy in the Secret Service who had followed us in. Beau and I sat down and these guys didn't have any place to go. I called the maitre'd over and said, "Bring those two guys over and ask them to join us. Seat them with us. We'd enjoy having lunch with them."

I introduced Carroll to Beau. Carroll said, "How did you know?" I said, "Well, I know who's following me." He commented, "You're one of the most unusual individuals we've ever had to track." I offered, "If you'd like to check our complete file, I'll give you the combination of our three secret safes up in the office. You can look through those at your leisure." Carroll said, "We're sure wasting our time with you." I continued, "I mean it. Come by the office if you want to check the file, because every conversation we have is made as a matter of record and goes into the file. Usually it is authenticated by one of my two attorneys."

Every conversation I had went into the file. For instance, there was a contractor from Oregon who had the job to build the air base unit at Hill Field at Ogden, Utah. He was under indictment by the Federal Housing Authority, but he still had this contract to perform. Even under that indictment, he was being checked pretty carefully.

I remember one conversation in which he wanted some special consideration on the specifications, and I wouldn't give them to him. We had an old Edison-type tape recorder that was tied into my phone system. I had 17 cylinders of conversations with this chap on our working out the details and our control on his operations at Hill Field.

355

Hill Field had been one of those points of complaint. "Mr. Carroll, those are available to you, and they've been transcripted into a file. It's available, but also the tapes are available." (Aside to me, *Without nine minute gaps!*[79]) *He laughed. I said, "You can have access to this whole works."* So, he got the stuff, and they went through our files. He finally came back to whomever he was working for in the bureau and said, "There isn't anything here. There's no smoking gun; we're wasting our time." After three months of this they discontinued it and pulled out. They took their bugs out of our telephones and said, "Hey, this guy's clean." So, we got a clean bill of health.

But that one lunch with Cornett, and these two guys who were having a hard time, and bringing them in to sit down with us and my introducing them to Beau Cornett, it really blew Carroll's mind. He didn't know what to think or what to say or anything else. I'm sure he didn't enjoy his lunch.

These things are not figments of my imagination. This happened. And it was a lot of fun to have Fred Irwin tell me what was going on. Fred had said, "Well, I better keep you informed. If there's something that I really think you need to know, we'll get together and I'll bring you up to date." I'm sure he was violating some of the Secret Service operations. Here they were with McCord under surveillance, and he was keeping up on it and telling me what was going on. There was absolutely no fear in my mind because I knew that there wasn't

---

[79] A reference to the Nixon tapes, an event that happened decades later than this.

anything that I was guilty of doing. Except trying to do the best I could for the Air Force.

A Belly Full of Politics

I had to testify for different legislation that the Air Force was supporting and trying to get processed through the Congress. Those committees in Congress would ask you all sorts of questions about the necessity for this, or why you were doing that or something of this sort. I really got my fill of politics. So much of it was truly political.

I had decided early in the game that, were I recommended for star grade, no, I wouldn't want it. Because, as I said, you lose your identity really, as an Air Force officer. You become a political animal. If they want you to testify for a particular program, they'll dictate what you will say, practically, and you have to follow what the politics might be. You've got to become a party man, a corporate party person. Loyalty to the cause, whether or not the cause is right.

There were two or three in the political arena that I really loved and trusted. Margaret Chase Smith, senator from Maine, was a jewel to work with. And the senator from Washington state, Warren Magnuson. We'd have dinner with him at the Shoreham Hotel frequently. In order to avoid having to be cleared through protocol, he'd call and say, "Hal, I'm going to have to have dinner over at the Shoreham tonight. Maybe I'll see you." Well, this was an invitation, and we'd get together. He was a perfect gentleman. Senator Magnuson was a former commissioner of the Virgin Islands and came up through that arena first, then worked into the diplomatic side. Believe me, he was one I could count on 100 percent.

There was one congressman from South Carolina who was also extremely good to work with. He didn't believe in following the party line. What he wanted was whatever was right, and he usually did a pretty good job of determining what was right. I wish we had more of those folks these days. There are not very many, unfortunately.

Senator Robert S. Kerr of Oklahoma was another one. He was independent, and he was independently wealthy. He couldn't be bought. Kerr owed nothing to anyone.

I never will forget him coming into the office one day when I was in having a conference with General Lee Washburn. Lee looked up, and Kerr said, "General, are you the man? Or as John the Baptist said, Must I seek another?" Lee said, "Sir, I am your man." This is typical Kerr. He was given to this type of an approach many times. You could count on him, and he was excellent support if we needed something.

Senator Spessard L. Holland of Florida was another one that was unusual because he, too, could not be bought. Many in Congress could be bought, and I fear that's still the situation today. I particularly remember early in the game when Dole[80] was talking about getting into the race. He made a statement that he would guarantee that the Social Security trust fund would never be raided.

---

[80] Senator Robert Dole, from Russell, Kansas, received the Republican nomination for President but lost to Bill Clinton in 1996.

Dole was like Diogenes[81] with his lamp. He would get inside the beltway to try to find the object of his search. His lamp would run out of oil, and he would starve to death. I still believe that. Too many people don't know how to be their own person. That's why we have the problems we have today, because of the yes-man mentality. That and greed.

The LA Crowd

In the early 1950s, we did the housing for Edwards Air Force Base northeast of Los Angeles in the Mojave Desert. The Air Force needed to expand their capacity for testing mach 2 aircraft—ones that fly twice the speed of sound. A lot more support facility had to be added. Not only did we have a requirement to build the housing units but we had to build a complete town including a school, shopping center, visiting celebrity office facility and so on. Maj. Gen. J. Stanley Holtoner was the commanding officer; Chuck Yeager was one of the test pilots. It was another Cold War operation.

At the time Gen. Holtoner assumed command of the Air Force Flight Test Center, little more than the desolate remnants of the World War II base that had been built in 1940 remained. By the time he had completed his tour, new facilities completed included a concrete runway 16,800 feet long, 3,000 feet wide, and 19 inches thick; 14

---

[81] Diogenes of Sinope, who died around 320 BC, was a Greek philosopher and noted cynic. He is said to have gone about Athens with a lantern in the daytime claiming to be looking for an honest man but never finding one.

enormous hangars; telemetering stations; computation laboratories and technical facilities worth $150 million constructed and in place.

There were modern barracks for the airmen, 1,500 family homes, two churches, an officer's club, an airmen's club, an NCO club and a civilian club and all the accoutrements of a modern technical center. It even boasted one of the sportiest green-grass golf courses in that section of California.

Having a movie star for an opening was customary. Dorothy Malone is doing the ribbon-cutting honors for Edwards AFB housing in early 1950s. Hal Hayes is on the right, younger brother Ray Hayes on left. Photograph by Peter Gowland.

Los Angeles house designed by Hal McCord for Hal Hayes, early 1950s

One of my contractors on the Edwards project was a fellow named Hal Hayes. In addition to the official work at the base, I also served as engineer on a house that he built for himself. This house was off Sunset Strip in Los Angeles, back off west of one of the canyons that ran back from the strip. It was a most unusual house due both to the setting and to Hal's personal requests. To avoid potential mudslides, we anchored the building with cables back into the

361

hillside. I ended up running some steel channels out to the edge of a cliff to provide a place to park a car. The swimming pool was a beauty—like swimming in a lagoon.

Deciding to Retire

We had a tremendous program. When I was asked to stay an extra year in Washington, General Twining said, "I'll make a deal with you. You take the extra year. At the end of the year, whatever you want to do, I'll sign the orders." Before the year was out, I was scheduled to go to Stavanger, Norway, to build a U-2 base. I had a choice of either returning to active reserves or going to Stavanger. I was burned out at that point. Besides, I would have had to travel with non-congruent travel. That is, no family. There were no facilities for families. I couldn't see going to Norway. I couldn't speak Norwegian and I was pretty tired. I said, "No, please, return me to inactive status." This was 1955. It was at SAC that I finally went to retired status in 1966.

The Separation Record gives active duty dates on this segment of service as 7 June 1951 to 23 June 1955—4 years and 15 days. The *most significant duty* section entry states: "Chief Family Housing Div Dir Facilities Support Hq USAF Washington, D.C."

Post-Active Duty

Col. Hal H. McCord, USAF—McCoy AFB, Orlando, Florida, 1960

The Orlando Years

From Washington and a house in Arlington, Virginia, Dad took his family, Thelma and the two children, Marc and Marcia, to Orlando, Florida. That was the fall of 1955. Marc and Marcia were ages 2 and 1. Activities with these children probably alleviated the agony over missed opportunities with his first family.

Some experiences, though, I am sure he would rather have missed. Like the typical sibling rivalry drama in three acts. In Orlando, Marc at age 3 fell from the seat of his tricycle and split his chin, requiring stitches. Shortly thereafter Marcia brained him with a two-foot length of log chain in act two. Marc immediately followed that with act three in which he split Marcia's foot open with a stone axe, requiring four stitches.

Dad umpired Little League games. He did a lot of fishing and hunting, both rifle and bow and arrow. I met up with one of his hunting buddies, Phil Steinmetz, in autumn 2000 when I taught some classes in Orlando and on two subsequent teaching trips to that city.

Phil obviously adored Dad and the family and talked animatedly about their adventures. How they inadvertently locked their keys in the car during a hunting trip. About a P08 Luger with ivory handles Dad gave him. Phil still wants to know the history on that. [82] Phil

---

[82] From the unofficial Luger website: "Without a doubt, the Luger semi-automatic pistol is one of the most famous firearms of the 20th century. Its distinctive toggle lock and sleek lines make it very recognizable, as does the fact that it was a standard sidearm of the German, Swiss and other armies for a period spanning nearly a half-century, and produced in large quantities. It is well known even to many people who know or care nothing about historic firearms."

admitted, "I was so fascinated with it that finally Hal sold it to me." Phil showed me photos, reminisced and helped paint a friend's picture of Dad's family during those years when my contact was so minimal.

Three Outings in Florida
(as told by Phil Steinmetz)
1. Bow Hunt - Inverness, Florida

"I fondly recall a bow hunt Hal and I had in the Citrus County Hunting Preserve. We drove there on a Friday afternoon and set up our camp, sleeping in our sleeping bags on a ground cloth. We had a great fire and cooked some steaks; it was a fine meal.

"Hal dug a hole in the ground and put some of the coals from the fire in the bottom of the hole. He then put a large iron pot filled with chunks of stew beef, vegetables and potatoes on top of the hot coals and covered the pot with more coals then filled the remainder of the hole with dirt. He told me this was Hunter's Stew, and we would have it for supper the next day after our deer hunt.

"The next morning Hal and I got to our hunting spots. I was on top of a small hill, and he was at the bottom of the hill in some brush overlooking an open spot that had a lot of deer sign we had seen the day before.

"I observed during the morning hours several deer in the area, but all but one were out of range of our bows. There was one deer, a doe—for which we had tags—that walked within approximately 30 yards of Hal, but he did not shoot and I wondered why. He told me later that he had fallen asleep.

"While on our way back to camp, we noticed a large doe walking down the hill ahead of us. We also went down the hill, parallel to the deer, until there was an opening through the trees for a decent shot. Hal took the shot, and the deer was hit. We blood-trailed her for about 300 or 400 yards and found her dead. Hal had used an 80-lb. pull bow, a recurve, and we measured the distance. It was over 80 yards. The arrow went through the heart and exited the deer, breaking in half when it hit a rock. The best shot I have ever seen on any deer. We checked the deer in at the ranger station, and they agreed that it was the best shot they had ever seen as well.

"When we got back to our camp, we uncovered the Hunter's Stew pot. I will never forget what a wonderful meal it was, and I have never to this day had a meal I enjoyed any more.

"We spent our last night of the hunt and got up early Sunday morning. After a nice breakfast of coffee, bacon and eggs, we hunted until early afternoon. We did not get another opportunity for a shot but saw several deer that day also. I shall never forget this hunt, and the good times Hal and I had hunting and fishing together."

2. Rifle Hunt—Ocala National Forest, Ocala, FL

"I recall a rifle hunt Hal and I had in the Ocala National Forest. I had hunted in the forest before, but I felt there were too many hunters there and did not feel safe. Hal had studied topographical maps of the area and told me not to worry about other hunters in the area. It was far too remote.

"The area was beautiful, rolling with lots of mature long-needle pine trees. We were there for only that day, and we did a lot of walking, slip hunting. I don't remember seeing any deer, but there were lots of sign. We enjoyed a nice lunch in the woods. Thelma, Hal's wife, had packed us a picnic lunch; her food was always tops. Thelma made the best potato salad I have ever eaten.

"When we returned to the car, we found Hal had locked the keys inside. We broke one of the small wing windows to get to the keys. The area where we parked the car had a large stand of huge pine trees. I brought home a dozen or so of the large pine cones that I spray painted and decorated for Christmas. I still use them each Christmas and remember that day."

3. Hunting and Fishing—Ocala National Forest

"During the summer months, Hal, Thelma, Marc, Marcia and I would take trips to Alexander Springs in the Ocala National Forest. Hal and I each had leased a lot on the Spring Run from the state of Florida. We would put our canoe in at the Spring and fish down the run to our lots. We then would have a great picnic lunch there. The couple that ran the Spring liked us and would tell us where good fishing spots were. They even told us where to look for some albino catfish; the white catfish were 8 to 9 pounds each, and it was quite a thrill to see them.

"During the winter months Hal, Thelma and I would go without the children. Hal and I would hunt deer and Thelma would fish—she was quite the fisherwoman. She would fish for hours and always had a string of fish when the day was done. What great fun we all had."

After Eight Years, a Father-Daughter Reunion

I happened to be at Ft. Benning, Georgia, the summer of 1960 while my husband was doing part of his six-month active duty obligation. I took the opportunity to contact my father. We had not had contact nor seen each other for eight years. He immediately flew up to Columbus, Georgia to meet me. We spent a subsequent weekend at Cedar Key on the Florida Gulf Coast to get acquainted.

I met his second family—my new brother and sister along with Thelma—and tried my hand at surf fishing. I caught a stingray about the size of a dinner plate.

Four years later my husband, six-month old son and I joined them at Sanibel Island, Florida, for a delightful few days in August 1964. Previously when Dad and his family had gone shelling at Sanibel, they met R. Tucker Abbot, then with the Smithsonian and founder of the Bailey-Matthew Shell Museum. They spent an unforgettable day with Dr. Abbot shelling on the Sanibel beaches. Sanibel Island, the only American barrier island perpendicular to the mainland, is full of natural wonders. It was fun to hear my family share the knowledge they had gained from Dr. Abbot. I still have shells gathered from our walks along those beaches. These two trips began the relationship I established with my father as an adult.

A Gun Collector

On one of my visits Dad showed me some of the guns in his collection. He lovingly pulled each one out and told about it. Marc later expanded on some of these guns, and I found the details and Marc's knowledge of them fascinating.[83] Although Marc was not present when Dad showed me these guns, I have interspersed Marc's comments and explanations with Dad's story. Marc, since I have known him, has always referred to his dad as "Hal." Even as a child.

The first .45 that I had I used to qualify with a pistol team in Washington, D.C. I shot with the Secret Service pistol team. I remember there was some fussing because this was a noisy operation. The rounds we were using were a little louder than the 9-mm type. These shells here are an armor-piercing type. Lethal. They make very sophisticated shells now.

Remington-Rand made this Colt on contract with Colt. (I must have winced, and Dad noticed. I don't really like guns.) *That's okay. It's loaded but on safety. Ten or 12 years back I was doing some shooting at a meet in Columbia, Missouri. One of the Colt representatives asked if I would object if he took this gun and modified it. I said, "What do you want to do?"*

---

[83] Marc and Beverly McCord have a business called *McCord Custom*. They create custom leather goods, do gunsmithing, rent guns and set up special effects for movies. Beverly has twice been the national champion in the International Defensive Pistol Association, IDPA.

He wanted to put a revised trigger on it and modify it so that it had a safety release, either right or left hand. I said, "Fine." So, at the Colt factory, they added this right-hand side so it could be used either way and sent it back to me. I have, of course, learned to like it; it's an excellent safety piece. This is a Pachmayr clip. Instead of carrying seven rounds it carries eight. It's one of the few of those, I guess, in existence today.[84]

This Colt still has United States Property with an assigned serial number stamped on it. I had a shipping ticket signed by my general at the time that actually gave it to me permanently. Otherwise, I would have had to turn it in. I carried this all the time. Everywhere. The last time I fired it was five or six years ago at a firing range. Pull this back, and it's ready to go. Here's how the safety works. You push down, then you cock it, and it's ready. It's not as heavy as it looks. The last time I qualified with this on the range, I shot a 97.6, which is certainly creditable.

This is the stock, this cover on the handle. I have a set of those that were made for me in Burma out of Burmese ivory. I was always afraid something would happen to them so I haven't put them on. I can any time I want to, and they're made to fit precisely, like this. All I have to do is take these screws out and put those stocks on, and I have a highly collectible piece of equipment. I have a pretty warm spot in my heart for this gun because it was the difference between my

---

[84] Marc says the Pachmayr clip was an oddity then but is now commonplace.

ending up there in the Himalayas and being able to come home. Now those hill bandits would probably all have guns instead of machetes.

Marc's comments on two Colts Dad owned:

"The 1911A1 .45ACP (ACP for automatic Colt pistol[85]) service pistol Hal showed you was manufactured by several different companies under license from Colt for the war effort. His was made by Remington-Rand, the typewriter company. These pistols were not designed to be match-grade firearms, yet Hal could literally hit anything he could see at almost any distance. He got the ivory grip panels while he was stationed in India. The elephant has his trunk up, signifying good luck. The Army Air Corps star signifies Hal's branch of service. Bill Laughridge, one of the premier pistolsmiths in the nation, did the trigger and safety work in 1978.

"The other Colt pistol Hal had was a Colt Model 1903 in caliber .32ACP. This was also a military issue pistol, given to general officers and their staff members. At war's end, most of these pistols were turned in and then dumped into the Atlantic Ocean. As Hal's .45 was sold to him, so was the .32."

---

[85] Colt added the ACP designation to the .45 cartridge to segregate it from the .45 used in the single action army, the cowboy revolver Colt brought out in 1873. The two cartridges were supposed to be ballistically the same; to avoid confusion and possible misapplication, the revolver cartridge became known as the .45 Colt and the semi-automatic pistol cartridge designed for the 1911 model was designated as the .45ACP.

Dad continued, picking up a rifle. *I went through Camp Snelling in Minnesota with the K-State rifle team when I was in senior ROTC. We competed in intercollegiate rifle contests conducted by the ROTC staff. What they called telegraphic meets. As we fired our courses, whatever the score was would be sent in to compete with the other schools in the system. They used a specially made .22 long rifle. I always wanted to buy one of those, but they were difficult to acquire. Those were the ones used in the Olympics. Highly precise.*

I have an extra barrel for this. The barrel comes apart, and it all disassembles. One of the qualification trials was that I had to disassemble and assemble against the clock. I don't know whether I could disassemble this now or not. I don't have strength enough in my hands and arms to do it.

Marc's comments:

"Hal's most prized firearm from this period was a rifle. It was a Model 1903 Springfield military service rifle, caliber .30 government issue. A more common name for this is 30.06. This rifle had a star gauge or match-grade barrel and had been customized or sporterized for him by his friend Oliver W. Broberg. Hal said many times that Broberg was the finest gunsmith he had ever known. He was particularly attached to this rifle."

I do have a .380 Browning that is automatic and uses .38 caliber ammunition. It has a clip that carries 14 rounds. Maybe it's illegal today under the current laws because it has the autoloading capability. It will fire every time you pull the trigger. (Dad laid the gun down and pointed his finger.) *Bang, bang, bang, bang, bang.*

Dad picked up the Browning .380 pistol. *Browning made some fine guns. This one was made in Italy. It's light, too. Has a nice feel to it. And pretty potent. I had Noni shoot this a few times. I wanted her to get familiar with it. I haven't taken time to upgrade her. Now this is a close operation type item; when you need one, you don't need it 200 yards away. One hit anywhere is probably going to stop somebody. You wore it inside your belt, and this clips over your belt. A little lighter to handle than that .45.*

Marc's comments:

"The Browning .380 semi-automatic pistol you saw was purchased at a gun show from Dean Smith in 1979. At that time, these pistols came with a 13-round magazine. This pistol is actually a Beretta, being manufactured for Browning to allow Browning to expand their market into handguns. This would still be a legal firearm to own. The proscription on high-capacity magazines disallows the manufacture of new *hi-caps* while grandfathering in the old ones."

Marc also remembers Hal's having a couple of Winchester firearms when he (Marc) was young.

"Hal had a Winchester Model 12 pump-action shotgun, 12 gauge, 30-inch barrel full choke with a solid factory rib. It had been his father's. Besides being the first shotgun Hal duck-hunted with, it also was the first shotgun I hunted with.

"Another Winchester was a Model 70 bolt-action centerfire rifle in .243 caliber. It had a Weaver 4X riflescope as a sight. This was the first large rifle I ever shot. The occasion was the famous Bay Tree expedition when Hal and Phil Steinmetz went into the woods to dig up and bring home a bay tree for transplant.

"Hal loved bay leaves as a 'spice' for soups, stews and chili. If you remind Phil of this, I'm sure he will remember. Hal set up a paper cup at 90 yards and showed me how to get into a stable prone shooting position. I was so excited. I didn't dare miss. Phil was watching. I hit the cup just below center to the right, and made Hal very proud. I was eight years old.

"There are many more firearms Hal owned. Some we acquired together. We embarked on a collecting expedition in 1976, acquiring about 40 rifles, shotguns, pistols and revolvers over the next eight years. Sadly, all of these firearms were sold off at auction in about 1991 after a crime wave began making the rounds in Hickory and surrounding counties. Noni did not like having the guns in the house and was able to convince Hal to sell them. He took a rather severe loss on his investment and has regrets, I'm sure."

I agree. Dad handled each item as a special treasure that day. I know that there is some distress about no longer having any of these treasures, another loss in his life. In moving to the retirement center, there were a lot of things that had to find new homes. Having to give up material goods and pleasures and move on seems to be one of the inescapable and painful aspects of getting older.

Construction, Education, Computers

Again, Dad's construction work took him away from his second family a great deal of the time. He built houses. He built post offices up and down the eastern seaboard.[86] Dad said, *These post offices were owned by private firms who owned the property and leased it to the government. It was a guaranteed financing situation. Several attorneys were the primary financiers... some of the Michigan State Teachers retirement funds, even Vatican funds were invested.*

But the business was not doing as well as expected and it was hard to make ends meet. Thelma helped support the family with revenues from her antique shop. In 1966, Dad retired from the Air Force Reserves and also decided to try other income-producing options. He took a job at Eastern New Mexico University in Portales, New Mexico, teaching structural engineering and architectural design. ENMU had a four-semester course, 72 hours, for an Associates Degree. *Kids could get a salable skill in that program.* After a two-

---

[86] Dad also supervised the building of a post office in Lawrence, Kansas, around 1968 or '69, but said *it was a standard design and had no significant identifying characteristics.*

and-a-half month sabbatical at the University of Arkansas in the summer of 1968, the family moved into a larger, nicer house in the new good part of Portales. The dust and blowing sand in the Portales desert area caused problems for Thelma's lungs and finally necessitated another move.

In 1972, Dad accepted a position with the University of Missouri at their campus in Rolla, Missouri. This allowed him to work while continuing his own education in computer science. Thelma's health improved temporarily. In 1974, he took over the statistics services for MEMIS, the Missouri Extension Management Information Services. He worked first in St. Louis, then a year later in Columbia, Missouri.

Marc said "The moves were always unusual, and we learned to expect surprises. Our first night in the Clayton Road house in Ballwin, a suburb of St. Louis, there was a terrific auto accident right in front of our house. One car was left upside down, the other married to a tree. This at 1 a.m. Happily, no one was seriously injured. We didn't sleep the rest of the night, though.

"Then, the night we moved into the Anthony Street house in Columbia, Missouri, about 10:30 p.m. or so the house across the street caught fire. We found ourselves with front-row seats to a Columbia Fire Department exercise."

Dad gained a certain facility with the computer, especially with statistical software packages. He became a fixture of some note in the department. And he particularly delighted in wearing his K-State purple jacket on Missouri game days when everyone else was in Mizzou U. Tiger black and orange.

Once when I visited him on campus, his secretary Jane said she could always tell if the coffee she had made was strong enough for Dad. If a spoon would stand up in it, then it was okay. Dad never did like *brown water*.

Retirement in the Ozarks

In the fall of 1982, Dad left the academic campus scene and moved to the Ozarks and a lovely rural setting on Lake Pomme de Terre in southwestern Missouri. Pittsburg, Missouri was the official postal address. He renovated and built an addition to their house. They watched deer, wild turkeys and red fox. They planted flowers. They fished. Thelma was the better fisherman, though in fairness to Dad when they took the boat out the captain of the ship had other responsibilities. He cared for his dying wife. Thelma's cancer of the lymph glands had spread. Treatments were few, none considered routine, and she did not wish to be experimented on.

By March 14, 1983, she weighed barely 80 pounds; she told Hal, "It's time to go." The ambulance took her to Whiteman AFB with Dad following in the car. On the way, a concrete truck ran into the side of his car and wrecked it, no doubt symbolic of the way he felt about life at that point.

When Thelma died that spring I was afraid he might be gone within six months as well. I wasn't the only one concerned. The large house, so lovingly altered to fit their tastes, filled with fine antiques she had collected over the years, was not a good environment for him alone. He blamed himself for Thelma's death, for not being more forceful in pressing her to accept experimental treatments. After several visits, Marc moved in with him in May 1983, staying for six months until Hal's depression turned and he again became involved with life.

A Real Life Fairy Tale

Hal was much more a survivor than we figured him for, but additional help did come from unexpected quarters. A most attractive neighbor, walking distance away, lost her husband later that fall and Dad started courting Winona "Noni" Tatro. He was like a kid once more. Noni had not planned to marry again and made him work for a yes. Courting is such a sweet time—I perfectly understand any woman who would try to prolong that time period in her life, though Noni did have concerns about her faltering eyesight.

When Noni visited her son in California, Dad sent a May basket of flowers. It was a custom I had grown up with, making colorful baskets out of old oatmeal boxes, cottage cheese cartons, boxes and bits of paper, ribbon and lace. You fill them with spring flowers— lilacs, tulips, spirea—whatever you can find blooming on the first of May, add a bit of candy or cookies and leave them on doorsteps as a surprise. Sometimes with a note. For friends both old and young and perhaps even thinking about a hoped-for romance. Dad's 1915 May basket with pony Popo was definitely not the norm.

Well, Noni had told her son of the custom, and he did not believe her. "Mother, no one <u>really</u> does that." When they returned home from lunch, there on his doorstep was a huge basket of flowers. Craig said, "Oh, someone has sent me flowers!" Noni sweetly corrected him, "That card is for me." And rightly so, the flowers were for her. From Dad.

Skip a couple of years to June 1986 and fill in with boat trips on Lake Pomme de Terre, dining out, meeting family and other courting activities. Dad and Noni were having supper in Kansas City with Noni's sister and brother-in-law. Her son Craig was also there.

In the middle of the dessert course, Noni turned her pixie face to Dad, twinkled her eyes and said, "Hal, is there a question you've been wanting to ask me?" He broke into a broad grin and replied, "There most certainly is! Will you marry me?" "I most certainly will!" She delighted in all the jaw dropping.

While the rest of the family nearly choked on what was left of dessert, Dad immediately went to the phone to call Dr. Christy at the Little Brown Church in the Vale in Nashua, Iowa. He also phoned his children including me. In that gleeful, little-kid voice he has, he blurted, *I want your permission to get married.*

He asked Marc to be his best man. Marc said it was and remains the highlight of his life with his dad. Hal and Noni were married July 27, 1986. Dad was 74, Noni 66. They put together a photo album for the family and titled it "A Real Life Fairy Tale."

Wedding of Hal and Noni, Nashua, Iowa, July 27, 1986. Back row, from left: Sherri Hodnefield, Noni's granddaughter; Ben and Fay Spurgeon, Noni's brother and his wife; Marcia McCord. Front: Craig Tatro, Noni's son; Twila Phillips, Noni's sister; Winona and Hal McCord, Marc McCord and Bill Phillips.

Noni was the light and the love of Dad's life. With his and her houses only a few rural doors apart, they designed and built an ours halfway between the other two. By the spring of 1987, they moved into their new red brick castle in the sky. Living quarters were on the second floor, and a second-story deck surrounded three sides. They lived up high with the oak canopy, the birds and the squirrels.

Every spring they planted 89 flats of impatiens and bulbs, some 3000 to 4000 bulbs altogether. Dad even fashioned a drill auger to dig bulb holes. Together they could plant around 100 bulbs an hour. He would go around drilling the holes, and Noni would follow him, dropping in the bulbs and replacing the dirt.

They had two colors of dogwood, wisteria on a trellis arch, lilacs, daffodils, tulips, day lilies, roses, peonies and, most important, more than 100 different species of iris of all colors. Pots of petunias brought color to the deck. Sitting there you were surrounded by beauty near and far. They made for themselves a lovely garden setting for the lovely pair they were. Going to visit them always provided me with new inspiration and new hope in the enduring qualities of life and love. Both were gourmet cooks, and they enjoyed entertaining, especially family. I'm not sure I have ever been anyplace where I felt more appreciated, more valued.

They went square dancing, an activity Noni adored. Despite his bum knee, Dad danced. It wasn't the pain that stopped him. After two knee replacements, one was a disaster. He could no longer support his weight on that knee due to a damaged nerve. With great regret they hung up the square dance outfits.

Noni was an exquisite seamstress. She made her own square dancing outfits and many costumes for the both of them. One Halloween they were dressed as black and white cats; the next year they were clowns. They had several other matching color-coordinated outfits. In addition there were suits and dresses Noni had sewed for herself. If Noni admired a certain fabric, Dad might buy the whole bolt. And if she liked an outfit in a catalog, it was hers. She always looked as if she had just stepped off the cover of a fashion magazine.

Several months before Noni died, she gave me a partly finished quilt. A blue and white cathedral windows pattern. She knew she would never finish it. I'm trying to improve my hand-quilting skills before I complete her quilt. That will be a treasure and reminder of her continuing presence in my life. She also gave me a cross-stitch she had created of a girl with a guitar, a piece I had long admired and identified with.

Brief Encounters, Deep Wounds

Hal and Ivalee would meet three times in these later years at family events: an open house following my daughter's high school graduation, my daughter's wedding cleverly planned for outdoors at the rose garden in Manhattan's City Park so no seating arrangements would be required, and my second son's graduation from Logan Chiropractic College in the St. Louis area. I could see Mother's discomfort each time. Even though she had remarried and Dad was now married to Noni, a most gracious and loving lady who certainly posed no threat past or present, I think the former wounds were just too deep ever to heal.

Still an Active Engineer

In the late 1980s, Dad served as supervising engineer for the building of the Hickory County Jail in Hermitage, Missouri. He was a stickler for detail and for following the specifications in the blueprints. No sloppy workmanship was allowed. There were a number of incidents of correcting the work to bring it up to code or up to specs.

When the concrete block mason was not filling the voids with mortar as the specifications required, Dad insisted he do it right, even when that meant taking the concrete blocks out and resetting them. The stone mason quipped, "McCord, I hope <u>never</u> to have to work with you again." Hickory County, however, had nothing but compliments for Dad's efforts. There is a plaque on the jail wall that includes "Hal H. McCord, Supervising Engineer."

Once after working on a sewer project at Hermitage, Dad came home in the afternoon to find Noni dressed in only a fur stole. An obviously delightful memory. *She was ornery!* He picked her up and carried her off to the bedroom.

Dad told me that as a young man, *Sex scared the hell out of me. I never touched another woman before Ivalee, and not her the first week we were married.* I firmly believe our playful selves are our most healthy and happy selves.

The Fairy Tale Ends

In October 1999, Dad's beloved Noni succumbed to cancer. I was late getting to Dad's, due to finishing up a class in the Chicago area, but took the watch over from Marcia and her husband, John Kelly, when I arrived. Dad and I sat mostly unspeaking during Noni's final hours. What was to be said? Neither of us will ever forget the moment she looked up at us wearily from her bed, reached for the harness delivering her oxygen and removed it from her face. We knew she was exhausted and she was telling us that she was ready to go. We looked at each other and nodded in silent recognition. It was not long before the telling death rattle began, and her breathing ceased.

Because I had been through all of this before, both as a hospice volunteer and during the death of my own husband in 1992, I could provide a small portion of the support Dad needed during those hours. At the memorial service, I held a vase of flowers and suggested they were a symbol of both the beauty and the fragility of life. We invited friends to share their memories. Initial hesitancy turned into a gentle stream of loving tributes. With each remembrance I took a flower from the vase and placed it in the speaker's hand.

Dad took some of his favorite photos of Noni and had enlargements beautifully framed and hung around him. As before with Thelma, Dad blames himself for not being able to save her. Probably a typical but unrealistic response for someone used to being in charge. The flame in his spirit has been extinguished, and I think he will never recover fully from this gaping hole. Grief will be so close to the surface that any respite from it will be temporary.

Surviving

> Desire Is Dead[87]
> Desire may be dead
> and still a man can be

---

[87] *D. H. Lawrence, Complete Poems*, Penguin Books, © Angelo Ravagui and C. M. Weekley, executors of the estate of Frieda Lawrence Ravagli, 1964, p. 504.

a meeting place for sun and rain,

wonder outwaiting pain

as in a wintry tree.

Yet, in spite of all, Dad <u>is</u> a survivor. Sometime when I phone and ask how he is doing, he might simply say, *Well, I'm still here,* or *I'm surviving.* Other days he might say, *I'm feeling pretty good. What's your weather there?* His bad knee makes walking difficult, yet he still wants to hold open the door for me, always the gentleman. Though I am now in my 60s, the oldest of his three daughters, I will always be his little girl and he will always worry about his children.

Dad spends his time now doing several things. He is organizing photos, labeling them and putting them into albums. Especially the many catalog-quality photos he and Noni took of their beloved iris blooms. He listens to CDs, watches some videos and TV, especially if Kansas State happens to be playing any sporting event. He keeps up with the news and weather. He still has his pilot's eye on the clouds and what weather they promise. He does e-mail and sometimes still types notes on his old IBM Selectric typewriter. He does his own laundry except for bed linens. He does his own shopping and sometimes cooks his own meals, doing an especially fine job with soups and bread puddings. He makes his decanter of Gevalia coffee every morning.

Since he lives in a retirement community and meals are provided, he usually goes downstairs for breakfast and lunch. Sometimes supper, too, depending on who's cooking and what the menu is.

However, he has not been a bit happy with the food their kitchen has put out recently and has no hesitation in telling you so. He's even written letters to the retirement center headquarters, pointing out that it will be difficult to resolve their vacancy issues until they fix the dining room problem. I've eaten there at Dad's table many times and he is not wrong about this.

Besides, he knows from the CCCs and other military experiences that putting out good meals for large groups can be done and for a reasonable price. He has had to oversee such operations many times in his past. First, he offered to pay for cooking lessons for Wendy, the head cook. Wendy was less than impressed with the offer. So he ordered the book *Food for Fifty, 11th edition*, by Mary Molt, Assistant Professor of Hotel, Restaurant and Institution Management and Dietetics at Kansas State University. It contains many recipes, presentation illustrations and super ideas for groups.

I bought it thinking that maybe Wendy would like it. I sent it to her without any ID so hopefully she would not know who sent it to her. She would not accept it. She does not think that she can learn anything new about cooking. Obviously she could learn if she wanted to.

According to Dad, Wendy put the book out on a table for everyone to see but otherwise ignored it in irritation. Several weeks later, one night after midnight when no one else was up, Dad went down from his third floor apartment and retrieved the book. He then sent it to me for any possible use I might have for it with the remark

above adding, *Please do not say anything to anyone here about this.*
Dad, my lips are sealed.

Hal with four children and spouses in his Springfield, Missouri apartment.
Back, from left: Bill Winchell, Janice's husband; Don Anderson, Marilyn's
friend and companion; Hal McCord, Don McCord, John Kelly, Marcia's
husband. Seated: Ann McCord, Don's wife; Janice McCord Winchell, Marcia
McCord, Marilyn McCord.

Photo by Gerry Averett, Mignard Photography, Springfield, Missouri, August
2000.

In August 2000, four of Dad's five children and spouses gathered
at his apartment for a celebration of family.[88] Marcia ordered

---

[88] Marc and Dad had not seen one another for a decade, and Marc did not attend
this event. Marc came for a visit when Dad was hospitalized in February 2002 and
began their reunion.

MacCord Clan[89] T-shirts for everyone, in a lovely K-State purple with the McCord clan tartan and on the front the clan symbol, a navigator holding up a heart, "One way, one heart." Marcia insists it really means "my way or the highway."

Janice quips "As navigators, we're always happy to tell people where to go." There are family stories and jokes on this aspect of the McCord family. My brother's daughter Erika on a trip from the Kansas City airport to Manhattan, with me driving and my siblings definitely over-navigating to my barely reined-in disgust, remarked that she wished her husband were there, then maybe he'd understand this aspect of our family.

We had a professional photographer come in to take a group photo. We reserved the dining room for our large group for breakfast, went out for a lunch and planned a special dinner. We shared photographs and memories and reveled in being family. Some had come earlier than others had, and we left at different times so not everyone would leave at once.

I was still there when the others had left, and a phone call came to Hal from Anna Marie Owensby McCord that Dad's brother Max had

---

[89] McCord is an anglicized word for a Gaelic name meaning Son of the Navigator. McCords were navigators for hire in southwest Scotland who did not affiliate with any clan. Marcia says "That area of Scotland was pretty combative, known for rough characters, wide tides, bad weather, logging, cattle, muggings, murders and general danger to English travelers or anyone who was remotely civilized." There are many spelling variants of the family name: McCord, MacCord, MacCoard, MacCourt, etc. Sometimes changes in spellings even occurred from father to son. Some of the first North American McCord migrants included Robert, our ancestor, who arrived in America with his father John in the 1720-1740 time frame. The McCords spent the previous century in Ireland after leaving their home in the Wigtownshire, Galloway, Scotland vicinity.

just died. It is my belief that any loss triggers memories of all the losses you have ever had. Dad wept for all his losses. It was a bittersweet ending to our family celebration.

Dad says that *People are the one important thing in life; people represent the only real values in this world today.* It's too easy to lose track of what we know to be true, but Dad is definitely following this philosophy. People gravitate to him like I can't believe. They come from many sectors of his life, even out of the woodwork, I think, to appreciate him in response to his obvious concern for each of them. Their warmth and affection are a testimonial of mutual affection and respect.

When I was there recently for his 90th birthday, friends called, came by, took him out to lunch, sent e-mails and wished him well. Staff at Shoney's restaurant, staff from various doctor's offices, the lady who used to cut Noni's hair, the lady from the pharmacy at Wal-Mart in Boliver, friends from the dealership where he has his car serviced, friends from his Columbia days. After breakfast that morning, he greeted his housekeeper Patsy, who also serves at mealtimes, with a kiss. One of the other ladies clowned from her table, "Gracious! Right here in the dining room in plain sight." My father is obviously a people person. I am amazed and yet not amazed at the vast number of people who keep in touch and who care about him.

And when he entered the hospital recently with a leg infection, I notified family but had not yet contacted friends when his personal network took over. I must add that even though Winona's son Craig is not a McCord, he has been a true son to my father and is included as part of the family notification system.

Within a day, Dad's friends were visiting and calling. Friends from Cambridge, his retirement community; Noni's sister and her husband; friends from years back, friends from his contacts with the local PBS station, square-dancing friends, his lawyer, others. One of his nurses was so taken with him that she asked, "Can I adopt you?" That is not an unusual response.

Dress Blues

Col. Hal H. McCord, USAF (ret)
Photo by Stephens Photography, Bolivar, Missouri, 1994

My favorite recent photo is one taken in his dress blues—a uniform bought at Whiteman AFB, Missouri, in the eightieth decade of Dad's life. Who would go out and spend the money for a dress uniform at his age? My father would. That uniform is a symbol of military honor, responsibilities and accomplishments, a code of living important to the end. He wears it well.

When Marcia McCord and John P. Kelly married on June 27, 1977, Dad and Noni flew from Springfield via Denver to Oakland, California for the wedding. Dad decided to wear his dress blues. The airline pilot discovered they had a colonel aboard and invited Dad up front to the cockpit prior to takeoff. What a thrill it was for him to stand there in uniform as an honored and respected guest in front of the instrument panel of the Boeing 757.

Marcia said, "He looked so handsome when he got off the plane." On the return trip after the wedding, Dad didn't wear his uniform, but he did wear his colonel's wings and again was accorded royal treatment by the crew.

My father witnessed and participated in an amazing period of aviation history... from an Alexander Eagle Rock at age 16 to a Boeing 757 at age 85.

Thank you, Col. Hal H. McCord, for sharing with me the stories of your life and for allowing me the pleasure of knowing you, my father, in this very special way.

Marilyn McCord

Appendix 1: Chronology

1912: Jan 25, birth of Hal H. McCord, Manhattan, Kansas

1924: Summer move from 601 Thurston to 1504 Houston

1929: Graduation, Manhattan High School

1933: Coast Artillery Corps (CAC) summer camp

1933-34: Assistant to Riley County engineer

1934: Graduation, Kansas State College, BS in Architectural Engineering

1934: Jul 7 marriage to Ivalee Hedge

1934: Apr 1—Jan 1, 1935: Asst. supt. of construction, Winfield State Hospital

1935: Jan 1—Sep 1, Kansas State Highway Commission, Topeka, bridge department engineer

1935: Jul 1—15 ORC, Ft. Sheridan, Illinois; Range section chief and instructor (CAC)

CCC Camps:

1935: 1 Sep—8 Feb 1936: Salem, Missouri

1936: 8 Feb—1 Jun: Bardley, MO, Company Commander

1936: 1 Jun—1 Jul 1937: Ft. Leavenworth, Kansas, Company Commander, Headquarters

1937: 1 Jul—1 Feb 1938: Seneca, Kansas, Company Commander

1938: 1 Feb—1 Jun: Union, Missouri, Company Commander

1938: Jun 1—Oct 4, 1940: construction projects in or near Houston, Texas

1940: 1 Jul—15 Jul: ORC, Ft. Sheridan, Illinois, military training and executive officer (CAC)

Oct 4, 1940—March 1, 1946: Active military duty, U.S. Army

1940: 4 Oct—14 Mar 1941: Headquarters. 7th Corps Area, Omaha, Nebraska; morale and welfare, statistics

1941: 14 Mar—14 Apr 1942: Ellington Field, Texas; adjutant, administrative inspection

1942: 14 Apr—10 May 1944: Randolph Field, Texas; assistant chief of personnel, assistant chief of staff

1944: 20 May—2 Jun: Headquarters, ATC, Washington, D.C.

1944: 12 Jun—28 Jul: Headquarters ICWATC, Rishra, India; assistant chief of staff

1944: 25 Oct—24 Sep 1945: 1250th AAFBU, NAFD ATC, Casablanca; personnel

1945: 24 Sep—29 Jan 1946: 1400 AAF BU EURD ATC, Paris; chief of staff

1946: 29 Jan—501st AAFBU, Washington, D.C., awaiting separation

1946: 7 Jun: official separation date; entry into Air Force Reserves

1946: Mar 1—Mar 15, 1947: emergency housing program at KSAC

1947: Mar 15 - 1951: development/construction of subdivisions, Manhattan, Kansas area

1951: Forbes AFB housing rehab

1951 - 1955: Recalled to active duty, Washington, D.C., Air Force family housing

1952: Marriage to Thelma Holuba

1955: Return to inactive status; move to Orlando, Florida and post office construction projects

1966: Move to Portales, New Mexico; faculty member at Eastern NM University Retirement from Air Force Reserves; MBA degree from ENMU

1968: Two-month sabbatical at University of Arkansas

1972: Move to Rolla, Missouri; teacher at University of Missouri

1973: Master's degree in engineering management, Rolla, Missouri

1974: Move to St. Louis area; UM Extension statistics position

1975: Move to Columbia, Missouri; continuation of extension statistics position

1982: Retirement and move to Pittsburg, Missouri

1986: Marriage to Winona Spurgeon Tatro

1999: Move to Cambridge Retirement Center, Springfield, Missouri

2002: Move to Vallejo, CA

Military Promotions:

1 Jun 1933: commissioned second lieutenant, Coast Artillery Corps

16 Jun 1936: to first lieutenant, CAC

27 Nov 1941: to captain, USAAF

1 Feb 1942: to major, USAAF

23 Jul 1942: to lieutenant colonel, USAAF

22 May 1945: to colonel, USAAF

Appendix 2

PARTIAL[90] DESCENDANCY CHART FOR
HENRY JACKSON MCCORD

NAME	BIRTH-DEATH	BIRTHPLACE
1—Henry Jackson MCCORD	(1827-1917)	Erie Co, OH
sp- Rachel Elizabeth HOWELL	(1850-1905)	Salem, IN
2—William Bogart MCCORD	(1871-1947)	Blackhawk Co, IA
sp- Elleanor Jane HAYNES	(1881-1966)	Pottawatomie Co, KS
3–Henry Landon "Mick" MCCORD	(1902-1929)	Manhattan, KS
sp- Ella Martine ELLIS	(1907-????)	Bristol, TN
3—Wilma Irene "Beanie" MCCORD	(1906-1938)	Manhattan, KS
sp- James T. "Ted" HASLIP	(1904-1963)	Roswell, NM
sp- David M. ACKERMAN	(1908-1981)	Lamy, NM
3—Eleanor Mary MCCORD	(1914-1996)	Manhattan, KS
sp- Edwin J. WHITNEY	(1910-1989)	Riley Co, KS
4—William Edwin WHITNEY	(1938-)	Manhattan, KS
4—Alice Irene WHITNEY	(1939-)	Manhattan, KS
4—Mary Ellen WHITNEY	(1946-)	Manhattan, KS
4—Rachel Elizabeth WHITNEY	(1948-)	Manhattan, KS
2—Fred Vandercook MCCORD	(1874-1892)	Blackhawk Co, IA
2—Mary Amelia "Mayme" MCCORD	(1876-1964)	Blackhawk Co, IA
sp- William H. IRWIN	(1863-1957)	Grey Co, Ontario,Can
3—Agnes IRWIN	(1897-1980)	Manhattan, KS
sp- William Hobart BURCH	(1896-1937) (killed by lightning)	
sp- Earl Mile ELLSON	(1888-1946)	Muscata, KS
3—Fred Alexander IRWIN	(1898-1991)	Iola, KS
sp- Thelma Phyllis WILLIAMS	(1906-1994)	Plato, MO
4—Phyllis Ann IRWIN	(1929-)	Manhattan, KS
3—Lora IRWIN	(1900-2000)	Iola, KS
3—Henry Francis "Hal" IRWIN	(1902-1978)	Iola, KS
sp- Martha KNOX	(1903-????)	
3—William Wesley IRWIN	(1905-1994)	Manhattan, KS
sp- Martha Wilma FOWLER	(1912-1997)	Jefferson Co, MO
3—Alice IRWIN	(1909-1996?)	Manhattan, KS
sp- William R. DALLAS		

---

[90] Complete through third generation except for spousal information. I didn't go beyond fourth generation, and there are many omissions in this. I tried to include names relevant to the book.

NAME	BIRTH-DEATH	BIRTHPLACE
3—Patricia Devereaux IRWIN	(1912-)	Manhattan, KS
sp- James Madsen TOWNER		
2—George Lewis MCCORD	(1879-1960)	Riley Co, KS
sp- Olive Mae WORREL	(1878-1962)	Zeandale, KS
3—Georgie Ruth MCCORD	(1904-1995)	Zeandale, KS
sp- Glen O. "Weidy" WEIDENBACH	(1902-1972)	Danville, KS
3—Ray E. MCCORD	(1906-19??)	St. George, KS
sp- Ernestine HOBBS	(-1991)	Lebanon, KS
3—Dick B. MCCORD	(1910-1990)	Riley Co, KS
sp- Miriam HEALZER	(1915-1990)	Great Bend, KS
2—Carrie Melissa MCCORD	(1882-1977)	Riley Co, KS
sp- William Bryham "B" ROPER	(1880-1958)	Morganville, KS
3—Pauline Robb ROPER	(1904-1984)	Manhattan, KS
sp- David Austen ROSS	d. ca. 1980	
3—Richard McHenry ROPER	(1906-1992)	Manhattan, KS
sp- Blanche Ann MILLER	(1903-1993)	Hayes, KS
3—Rachael Anna "Pep" ROPER	(1907-1997)	Manhattan, KS
sp- Merton G. MATHEWS	d. ca. 1993	
3—Marian Velma "Trot" ROPER	(1909-1990)	Manhattan, KS
sp- Harry T. MCCLURE	(1908-1986)	Highland Park, IL
3—Maxine Gan ROPER	(1911-2002)	Manhattan, KS
sp- Elmo Erville YOUNG	(1909-1989)	Shelbina, MO
4—Richard Gan YOUNG	(1936-)	Hutchinson, KS
3—Katherine B. "Kay" ROPER	(1913-)	Manhattan, KS
sp- Robert W. FLICK	(1911-1994)	Manhattan, KS
3—Jean Louise ROPER	(1915-)	Manhattan, KS
sp- Eugene P. FARRELL	(1911-1999)	Wamego, KS
3—Sylvia Francis ROPER	(1920-)	Manhattan, KS
sp- Robert B. AUSTIN	(1922-)	Honolulu, HI
2—Henry Howell Hiram "Hal" MCCORD	(1884-1937)	Riley Co, KS
sp- Oma Alvaretta WORREL	(1893-1977)	Zeandale, KS
3—Hal H. MCCORD	**(1912-)**	**Manhattan, KS**
sp- Ivalee Beryl HEDGE	(1911-2001)	Norton, KS
4—Donald Hal MCCORD	(1936-)	Manhattan, KS
4—Marilyn MCCORD	(1940-)	Houston, TX
4—Janice Ivalee MCCORD	(1943-)	San Antonio, TX
sp- Thelma Franz HOLUBA	(1912-1983)	St. George, KS
4—Marc MCCORD	(1953-)	Washington, D.C.
4—Marcia MCCORD	(1954-)	Arlington Co, VA
sp- Winona "Noni" SPURGEON TATRO	(1920-1999)	Centerville, IA
3—Max Worrel MCCORD	(1914-2000)	Manhattan, KS
sp- Anna Marie OWENSBY	(1916-)	Pittsburg, KS

NAME	BIRTH-DEATH	BIRTHPLACE
4—Max Worrel MCCORD, Jr.	(1939-)	Manhattan, KS
4—Mary Margaret MCCORD	(1941-1999)	Phoebus, VA
4—Michael Owensby MCCORD	(1945-)	Ft. Riley, KS
4—Melissa Jane MCCORD	(1946-)	Manhattan, KS

Appendix 3: Additional Notes on Aircraft
(In the order of their appearance in the book)

Laird-Swallow: The Laird Swallow Manufacturing Company was formed in Wichita, Kansas, and the first Swallow was built and flown in 1920. Their photo ad gave the specs:

Spread: 36 ft.

Weight: 1075 lbs.

Speed: 86 mph

Climb: 4000 ft in 10 minutes with two passengers.

The photo I have with Dad also shows the word *Swallow* on the tail. In the late 1920s, they produced a three-seater known as the Swallow New Swallow and in the 1930s a Swallow Sport.

Boeing/Stearman Kaydet: This biplane was fairly common as more than 10,000 of them were built from the early 1930s through WWII and used by both the Navy and Army Air Corps for training. The Kaydet features normally staggered wings of almost equal length, unbraced heavy landing gear and "N" struts without an aileron connector.

Alexander Eagle Rock: This aircraft was manufactured by Alexander Aircraft Industries of Denver, Colorado. It was an open-cockpit, single-engine biplane with a 90-hp Curtiss OX-5 engine. There is a 1920s model in the Wings Over the Rockies Aviation and

Space Museum, a WWII hangar located at the former Lowry AFB in Denver.

Eleanor "Nellie" Zabel Willhite of Box Elder, South Dakota, was the first deaf female pilot to earn a license. When she caught the flying bug, she traded her typewriter for a cockpit. Her father bought her a plane, an Alexander Eagle Rock OX-5. "Even though I could barely hear the engine roar, I could tell right away if anything was wrong, just from the vibrations."

Once she applied for an air show job. The manager told her to get lost and hired a man who presented a mediocre act. Nellie climbed into her Alexander Eagle Rock and executed sensational stunts: rolls, spins, loops, crossovers and dives—the crowd was enthralled.

After she landed, the manager rushed up with, "Why didn't you tell me you could do that?" She left him speechless when she replied, "I did that just to limber up. Wait until you see my act." After barnstorming she worked as a commercial pilot until 1952. She founded the South Dakota chapter of the Ninety-Nines. Amelia Earhart was their president. Her plane is on display at the Southern Museum of Flight in Birmingham, Alabama.

"Vega Vultee": This was for a long time my mystery plane. I could not get a match on what Dad was describing and what I could find in the books. I even tried to check what aircraft were at Randolph during that time period and got a nice reply but no solid candidate.

We finally tracked down Beau Cornett, who made the described trip with Dad. Beau checked his Flight Document book and reported back in a letter:

"A **B-34**, two-engine bomber made by Lockheed, **Vega Ventura**. It was a great performer. We made the flight 27 Dec. 1942 on a round trip to Big Springs, and it took us a total of 3:20 flying time to go there and back. Our headquarters had a Navigation School at Hondo west of Randolph Field. There were a number of these B-34s for training."

Most of the Lockheed Vegas were single-engine planes with Wiley Post as their most famous pilot.

P-51 Mustang: The P-51 was developed by North American in 1940 to meet a British specification for a long-range fighter escort for British bombers that could operate over Europe from bases in England. Early models had remarkable performance at low altitudes, but performance declined above 12,000 feet. Therefore that particular Mustang was of little use for combat or interception roles in Europe. It was, however, well suited for tactical reconnaissance and had an obliquely mounted camera. Length: 32' 3"; wingspan: 37'; cruising speed: 390 mph. Standard armament was four 12.7-mm and four 7.62-mm machine-guns, so there was potential for ground attack.

Later models improved performance to a max speed of 441 mph at 29,800'. The book *100 Planes 100 Years*,[91] which features a plane for each year of the last century, selected the Mustang to represent 1943. "No other World War II plane better demonstrated America's ability

---

[91] 100 Planes 100 Years: The First Century of Aviation, by Winkowski and Sullivan. See endnotes.

to produce the right machine at the right time." In December 1943, Mustangs began escorting the heavy bombers by daylight. In addition, these agile beauties flew ground attack and interception. More than 15,000 were produced and they appeared in every theater of the war.

The Mustang has a long slim nose with a massive propeller spinner. The radiator air intake for the liquid-cooled engine is set well back under the cockpit. The unusual tail has the tail planes set very high and well forward to clear the full-length rudder on the tail fin. Most common is a bubble canopy for good vision to the rear (P-51D). Piper Aircraft acquired the design and continued to develop the aircraft as the Enforcer until 1984. The Mustang remained in US service post-war in SAC until 1949 and several more years in the US Air Reserves and Air National Guard. Now it is rare, most often seen at air shows.

J-3F50: This popular constant-chord (width) high wing, tandem-seat, two-person Piper cub trainer introduced nearly 75 percent of WWII aviators to flying. It was a little monoplane with a Franklin 50-horse engine, fabric-covered, very light. Length: 22'4"; wingspan: 35'3; cruising speed: 80-mph. Some 5,000 were built before WWII, then more than 5,000 for WWII observation-liaison duty.

AT-6: Called the Texan, the T-6 was almost certainly the most extensively used trainer of all time. Many future jet-jockeys were taught a bit of humility. With a military requirement for a basic combat trainer, North American ended up building over 17,000 of these. The SNJ is the Navy version; the Harvard is Britain's name for it. But T-6 Texan is the most familiar. It was in military service from 1941 through the Korean conflict.

There were other names used in previous versions, but when the AT-6 became an advanced trainer, the new role brought new designations. This plane is a fairly common relic of WWII, still a popular sport plane for veteran pilots. It has a long greenhouse canopy over tandem dual controls. The tail fin is markedly triangular. The wing shape is typical of pre-WWII design: a nearly straight trailing edge and a tapered leading edge. There is a rounded bump where the leading edge of the wing meets the fuselage. This is a fairing to hold the retracted main gear wheels. Length: 29' 6", wingspan 42'; cruising speed: 218 mph.

B-18: The Douglas B-18 Bolo was a response to the USAAC's requirement in early 1934 for a bomber with virtually double the bomb load and range capability of the Martin B-10, the standard bomber at that time. Douglas had the DC-2 commercial transport ready for its first flight and drew on that experience and design technology for the B-18. It was ordered into production in January 1936. Length: 57' 10"; wingspan: 89'; cruising speed: 167 mph; range: 1,200 miles. Accommodating a crew of six, the B-18 carried three 7.62-mm machine-guns in nose, ventral and dorsal positions plus a capacity for up to 6,500 lbs. of bombs. Most of the USAAC's bomber squadrons had B-18s or B-18As in 1940. A majority of those of the 5th and 11th Bomb Groups, based in Hawaii, were destroyed in the Pearl Harbor attack.

B-23: The B-18 was not in the same league as Boeing's B-17 Flying Fortress although they had the same specifications, so modifications were made to produce the Douglas B-23 Dragon. Wingspan was increased to 92'. The fuselage was given a much more aerodynamic form, and the tail had higher vertical fin and rudder. First flown in July 1939, it was delivered to the US Army Air Corps that year. Early evaluations showed performance and flight characteristics to be disappointing, and the chances were low for improving the model to something better than the bomber aircraft already in service. Consequently, the B-23 saw limited service in a patrol capacity along the US Pacific coastline and was then relegated to training duties. Many were subsequently acquired for conversion to corporate aircraft.

Beech Model 17: Jackie Cochran's plane was a Beech Model 17 Staggerwing. Walter Beech, Clive Cessna and Lloyd Stearman, in the midst of the razzle-dazzle barnstorming days of the 1920s, joined together to form the Travel Air Manufacturing Company to design and manufacture aircraft suitable for the man in the street (or woman, I might add) when he decided to take to the air.

The 1924 joint venture was acquired by the Curtiss-Wright Corp. six years later, and Beech formed his own company in 1932.

The Staggerwing was a four or five seat, high-performance airplane, required an experienced pilot and was unsuitable for the wider market sought. The backward stagger of its biplane wings provided a good field of view for the pilot and a good combination of speed and stability. Length: 26' 9"; wingspan: 32'; cruising speed:

185 mph. The USAAF expansion in 1941-42 resulted in a procurement of 207 Beech Model 17s under the designation UC-43, and an additional 118 civilian Model 17s were impressed for military service. The US Navy wartime procurement totaled 342, of which 105 were supplied to Britain under lend-lease. The Brits named the plane Traveler.

BT series: These single-engine, two-seater planes with fixed tricycle land gear were initially converted by Douglas from O-2Ks and O-32As for the US Army and National Guard units. Dual controls were installed and armament was deleted. Additional aircraft were built from scratch. The BT-2B variant was the first basic trainer ordered as such by the USAAC. With their excellent flight characteristics, they were then used for many years in basic training units. Length: 31' 2"; wingspan: 40'; cruising speed: 117mph; range: 320 miles.

P-26: Although Boeing's Model 266 (P-26) diminutive single-seat fighter had been retired from front-line service by the time the US entered WWII, P-26s were among the aircraft ranged against the Japanese at Pearl Harbor and in action in the Philippine Army Air Force's 6th Pursuit Squadron.

The P-26 was the first all-metal production fighter and the first monoplane to serve with the USAAC in the pursuit role. It had an open cockpit, fixed landing gear and externally braced wings despite Boeing's experience with retractable gear and cantilevered wings. These deficiencies were remedied in subsequent models. The P-26A included a revised wing structure and the addition of flotation gear and radio. Later aircraft also had higher headrests to protect the pilot in a rollover crash.

The need to reduce landing speed led to trailing edge flaps, retrofitted to aircraft already in service and designed into those currently being produced. Length: 23' 7 ¼"; wingspan: 27'; cruising speed: 200 mph. Armament included two fixed forward-firing 12.7-mm or one 12.7-mm and one 7.62-mm machine-guns plus bombs.

B-25: The Mitchell B-25 combines a high mid-wing with double tail fins. Unlike the Constellation, the tail plane does not extend through. Length: 52' 11"; wingspan: 67' 7"; cruising speed: 250 mph. Designed prior to WWII, more than 10,000 B-25s were built. Heavy losses during WWII kept the inventory to about 2600 maximum. The B-25 was produced with and without the glass bombardier's nose; a few have passenger windows. The book *100 Planes 100 Years* calls it "a lethal weapon with nothing hidden." Easy to maintain, easy to fly, now rare.

The B-25 was used for Jimmy Doolittle's raid on Tokyo in April 1942. From *100 Planes 100 Years*: "...only the B-25 was small, powerful and long-ranged enough to fly from the deck of a carrier and bomb Tokyo, 700 miles away. Sixteen planes launched from the USS Hornet the morning of April 18; all hit targets in and around Tokyo; all but one eventually crashed in China. But the raid was a success: although damage on the ground was slight, the Japanese now had to devote serious resources to air defense. Back at home the boost to U.S. morale was incalculable."

Waco: There were many Wacos, perhaps more than 100 different models of variations on the open cockpit biplane and the cabin biplane. The Army Air Corps bought hundreds of them for use as wartime trainers, fighters and bombers. The name comes from the initials of Weaver Aircraft Co. Pronounce it WAH-ko.

C-97: The Boeing Model 367 (C/KC-97) is the transport version of their B-29. In early 1942, Boeing's proposal was submitted to the USAAF for consideration and approved as a much-needed, long-range transport. The maiden flight was Nov. 15, 1944.

The KC-97A was equipped with additional tankage and a flight-refueling boom, the first plane to do in-flight refueling. Initially, the flight-refueling equipment had to be removed for full transport capability, but the later KC-97G had full tanker or full transport capability without any on-unit equipment change.

The fuselage looked like a double bubble that was basically the old B-29 fuselage attached to the new and larger upper bubble. The C-97A could carry 134 troops or a 53,000-lb. payload. The commercial version was called the Stratocruiser, and Pan Am was the biggest user. Length: 110' 4"; wingspan: 141' 3"; cruising speed: 300 mph; range: 4,300 miles; maximum take-off weight: 175,000 lbs. It was like the B-29 with the same wing, engine layout and same tail.

A-26/B-26: The Douglas A-26/B-26 Invader was first known as A-26 (for attack bomber) but redesignated as the B-26 after the war. The USAAF issued a requirement for an attack aircraft in 1940, before it had information on WWII combat operations in Europe. This led to three prototypes in different configurations. Initial deliveries of

1355 of the A-26B were made in April 1944. Length: 53' 10";
wingspan: 70'; cruising speed: 325 mph. Used in both Europe and the
Pacific theaters, it remained in service well into the '70s.

B-26 Marauder: Martin designed the B-26 to meet a demanding
US Army Air Corps 1939 specification for a high-speed medium
bomber. Martin's Model 179 proposal was considered to be so far in
advance of competing submissions that the company was awarded an
off-the-drawing-board contract for 201 aircraft, an action
unprecedented in USAAC history. It was first flown Nov. 25, 1940.
Note that this is a different aircraft than the Douglas A-26/B-26
above; the USAAF apparently used the B-26 designation for two
similar aircraft, but at different times.

The Marauder was a cantilever shoulder-wing monoplane,
accommodated a crew of five (later seven), had retractable tricycle
gear and was powered by two 1850 hp Pratt & Whitney R-2800
Double Wasp radial piston engines. It more than met the
specification, but at the cost of compromising good low-speed
handling characteristics. There were many training accidents.

After modifications were made, the Marauder went on to record
the lowest attrition rate of any aircraft operated by the US 9th Air
Force in Europe. It provided ground support to forces in Corsica,
Italy, Sardinia, Sicily and southern France. Length: 56' 1"; wingspan:
71'; max speed: 283 mph at 19,800'; range: 1,100 miles. It had eleven
12.7-mm machine-guns in fixed forward firing, trainable nose and
waist mounts, and power-operated dorsal and tail turrets plus carried

up to 4,000 lbs. of bombs. With the sleek aerodynamics, slender wing and powerful engines, it had outstanding performance.

B-10: The Martin B-10 is an odd looking aircraft with separate enclosed canopies for the pilot's cockpit (forward) and the gunner and radio operator's cockpit (aft), accommodating a three-man crew. Design began in the early 1930s. Its superior speed brought it into production and service by 1934. Length: 44' 9"; span: 70' 6"; max speed: 213 mph; armament: three machine guns in nose, rear turret and ventral positions plus up to 2260 lbs. bombs.

P-61: Northrop's Black Widow was the first US aircraft to be designed as a radar-equipped night-fighter. It had three-seats, twin-engines, twin-booms.

In 1944, they entered service with fighter groups in the South Pacific as well as Europe. Length: 49' 7"; span: 66'; max speed: 366 mph; max range: 1,350 miles; armament: four 20-mm cannon in lower forward fuselage and four 17.7-mm machine-guns in dorsal barbette, plus up to 6,400 lbs. on four underwing hardpoints.

C-152: The Cessna 152 is a single-engine, high wing, fixed gear, two-seater. When production stopped in 1986, 7,482 model 152s had been produced. Length: 24' 1"; wingspan: 32' 8 ½"; max speed at sea level: 125 mph. **C-172:** Cessna's ubiquitous four-seater version. Length: 27' 2"; wingspan: 36' 1"; cruising speed: 140 mph.

P-38: The Lockheed P-38 Lightning single-seat fighter had an unusual configuration to meet a USAAC requirement of 1937 for high-performance. It demanded a maximum speed, rate of climb and range that could not be met with the conventional single engine layout of that time. Twin booms extended from the extremities of the mid-wing center section, mounting two engines forward and twin fins and rudders aft, the booms linked by the tailplane/elevator assembly. Length: 37' 10"; span: 52'; max speed: 414 mph; armament: four 12.7-mm machine-guns and one 20-mm cannon plus up to 3,200 lbs. of bombs. The first regular combat operations began in North Africa Nov. 19, 1942. The Lightning was used in every theater of action. They destroyed more Japanese planes in the Pacific than any other fighter in USAAF service.

AT-11: Beech's AT-11 Kansan was the standard WWII bombing trainer with about 90 percent of the more than 45,000 AAF bombardiers training in AT-11s. It was a military version of the Beechcraft Model 18 commercial transport, like the C-45 transport and the AT-7 navigation trainer, with two Pratt & Whitney 450 hp. Engines. Except the Kansan had a transparent nose, a bomb bay, internal bomb racks and provisions for flexible guns for gunnery training. Length: 34' 1 7/8"; wingspan: 47' 7 ¾"; cruising speed: 150 mph; range 745 miles. Student bombardiers normally dropped 100-lb. sand-filled practice bombs. Proficiency standards specified 22 percent hits on target for trainees. Combat training missions were flown taking continuous evasive action within a 10-mile radius of the target, and final target approaches had to be straight and level and take no longer than 60 seconds.

C-46: The Curtiss C-46 Commando was a plane with no nose, greenhouse cockpit windows, wings like the DC-3 and T-6, strongly tapered on the leading edge and straight on the trailing edge, with

fully retractable landing gear. Length: 76' 4"; wingspan: 108";
cruising speed: 235 mph. Developed as a 36-passenger airliner in
1940 to compete with the DC-3, it was then built only as a military
transport. It was larger and bulkier than its counterpart and is a much
rarer survivor.

DC-3: The Douglas DC-3/C-47/Dakota was first built in 1935. A
tail-dragger that sits nose-up on the flight line, it has a very short-nose
look in the air due to the wings being set far forward. It seated 36 in
unpressurized discomfort, as many as 50 in its troop-carrying
configuration. Length: 64' 5"; span: 95'; cruising speed: 194 mph. By
1939, up to 90 percent of air commerce worldwide was flying DC-3s.
Commercial planes were drafted for military service, and 10,000 more
DC-3s were specially built as C-47 Skytrains. "Arguably the most
significant aircraft of all time," says the Complete Encyclopedia of
World Aircraft.[92]

C-54: The Douglas DC-4/C-54 Skymaster was a different design
than the DC-3, had larger capacity, was lighter in construction, had a
new high-aspect ratio wing, a conventional tail unit with a single fin
and rudder, retractable tricycle landing gear, and twin wheels on the
main gear. The DC-4s on the drawing board were militarized for
transport of troops, cargo and casualties. The basic civilian version
provided for a crew of four with 44 passengers and plenty of leg
room. Some versions seated up to 86 passengers. It had four 1450-hp
Pratt & Whitney R-2000 Twin Wasp radial piston engines. Length:

---

[92] Complete Encyclopedia of World Aircraft, general editor, David Donald. See
endnotes.

93' 10"; wingspan: 117' 6"; cruising speed: 227 mph. Variants were also built for the Navy with total construction exceeding 1,000 aircraft. The DC-4 had many record-breaking flights and is remembered for its contribution to the Berlin Airlift of 1948-49.

C-87: A transport variant of the Consolidated B-24, the C-87 had nose and tail gun positions deleted, a large cargo door installed in the port side of the fuselage, accommodation for a crew of five and passengers or cargo, and sometimes equipped for VIPs. The USAAF acquired 276 of these.

C-109: The ATC has a special link from its website to C-One-Oh-Boom, their name for the C-109. This was a special logistics variant of the B-24 Liberator, a fuel tanker used to ferry 2900 gal. of aviation fuel per load over the Himalayan hump to supply B-29s operating from forward bases in China.

"If there has ever been an airplane that received outright hatred, fear and loathing from the men who flew it, it would have to be the Consolidated C-109. Flying Coffin, Widow Maker and C-One-Oh-Boom were just three of the major derisive names applied to the tanker version of the famous B-24 Liberator bomber. The C-109 was a killer, there is no doubt about it, and its crews had reason to hate the airplane."[93]

B-29: Boeing's 345 Model, the B-29 Superfortress, made its maiden flight on Sept 21, 1942. Deliveries began almost immediately, with nearly 4,000 total produced. This four-engine, long-range,

---

[93] Quote from http://members.aol.com/BlndBat/C109.html.

strategic bomber and reconnaissance aircraft seated 10 in a pressurized cabin. Length: 99'; wingspan: 141' 3"; cruising speed: 230 mph. Armament: two 12.7-mm machine-guns in each of four remotely-controlled power-operated turrets, and three 12.7-mm or two 12.7-mm guns and one 20-mm cannon in the tail turret. The tail gunner was also in a pressurized compartment but isolated from the rest of the crew. Crawl tunnels went over the fore and aft bomb bays. The B-29 carried the atomic bombs dropped on Japan. They also were used operationally during the Korean War.

B-24: Consolidated's B-24 Liberator was the most extensively produced of the USA's wartime aircraft—more than 19,000. It was powered by four 1200-hp Pratt & Whitney R-1830-65 Twin Wasp turbocharged radial piston engines and designed around the Davis wing, a high-mount, shoulder wing configuration as long range was paramount. First flight: Dec. 29, 1939. Tail unit is the highly recognizable oval-shaped endplate fins and rudders. Length: 67' 2"; wingspan: 110'; cruising speed: 215 mph. Armament: ten 12.7-mm machine-guns in nose; upper, ventral ball and tail turrets; and beam positions. Maximum bomb load: 12,800 lbs.; normal bomb load: 5000 lbs. Called "Maids of all Work" in the Pacific due to long range and versatility.

P-40: The Curtiss P-40 Warhawk, a single-seat fighter-bomber, went through many variations in attempts to improve capabilities. Despite shortcomings, it was the most extensively produced (15,000) fighter next to the P-47 and the P-51. One hundred of the RAF's allocation were diverted to China, 90 of these reaching the American

Volunteer Group operating from Kunming and Mingaladon. Many were fiercely painted with jaw-like teeth under the pointed nose, enhancing the menacing effect. One 1200-hp Allison V-1710-81 inline piston engine; length: 33' 4"; wingspan: 37' 4"; max speed: 343 mph at 15,000 ft. Armament: six 12.7-mm machine-guns plus up to 1500 lbs. of bombs.

Japanese Betty: The Mitsubishi G4M was a Japanese-built roomy mid-wing monoplane powered by two 1530 hp Mitsubishi radial engines. Allocated the Allied code name Betty, these planes were recorded in aviation history for participation in many events: sinking of ships HMS Prince of Wales and Repulse; first air raid on Darwin, Australia; MXY7 missile carriers; and finally carrying the Japanese surrender delegation. The Betty lacked sufficient armor and really needed four engines for necessary range. Length: 63' 11 ¾"; wingspan: 82' ¼'; max speed: 292 mph; max range: 294 mi. Armament: four 20-mm cannon and two 7.7-mm machine-guns plus one 1764-torpedo or 2205 lbs. bombs.

Short Sunderland: The Short S.25 Sunderland bomber was developed in Britain by the Short Brothers and later the Blackburn Aircraft Co. to meet the requirement for a military general reconnaissance flying boat. The prototype was first flown Oct. 16, 1937; the definitive version was the Mk V. Length: 85' 3 ½"; wingspan: 112' 9 ½" max speed: 213 mph; range: 2690 miles; bomb load: 1668 lbs.; four engines. This was the first British flying boat to have power-operated gun turrets. It was armed with two 7.7-mm

Vickers 'K' guns in beam positions, two 7.7-mm Brownings in the nose turret and four similar weapons in the tail turret.

B-36: Convair built the first intercontinental bomber. It was huge—the biggest bomber ever built. First flown on Aug. 8, 1946, in production until 1954, retired in 1959. Length: 162' 1"; span: 230'; engines: six P&W 3800 hp and four GE turbojets; max speed: 411 mph; range: 6800 mi. with 10,000-lb bombload; max take-off weight: 410,000 lb.

Sources for information on aircraft:

<u>100 Planes 100 Years: The First Century of Aviation</u>, by Winkowski and Sullivan, © 1998 by Winkowski and Sullivan, published by SMITHMARK

<u>A Field Guide to Airplanes of North America</u>, second edition, by Montgomery and Foster, © 1984, 1992 by M. R. Montgomery, published by Houghton Mifflin Company.

<u>The Complete Encyclopedia of World Aircraft</u>, edited by David Donald, © 1997 by Orbis Publishing Ltd. and Aerospace Publishing, published by Barnes & Noble, Inc.

<u>The Golden Age of Aviation</u>, by Williamson, © 1996 by Todtri Productions Limited, published by SMITHMARK.

The Internet—especially the following sites:

<u>www.bcbr.com/feb2500/airbrf.htm</u>

<u>www.marchfield.org/rouen02.html</u>

<u>http://members.aol.com/SamBlu82/atc.html</u>

<u>www.workersforjesus.com/dfi/880.htm</u>

(Stories of Eleanor Zabel Willhite)

<u>www.wpafb.af.mil/museum/early_years/ey20.htm</u>

shell4.bayarea.net/~elias/hnoh/HNOHMEMORIES3.html

(The story "Airborne" begins on page 9.)

About the Author

Manhattan, Kansas, has been hometown for several generations of the McCord family. Marilyn's great-grandfather homesteaded there in 1878; her youngest grandson was born there in 2001.

Ms. McCord spent nine years on a farm in Western Kansas, taught school in Wichita and Topeka and has three degrees from Kansas State University. During the 1970s, she served as full-time volunteer staff with the Ecumenical Institute including three years in Taiwan and a year in rural India.

In the 1980s, she was employed by Texas Instruments in Dallas where she programmed software for seismic survey boats then taught artificial intelligence classes.

Currently she teaches programming in industry and lives near Durango, Colorado, with her companion Don Anderson and her Labrador, Nelson Nelson.

Printed in the United States
910500001B